AIDS Doesn't Show Its Face

AIDS Doesn't Show Its Face

Inequality, Morality, and Social Change in Nigeria

DANIEL JORDAN SMITH

The University of Chicago Press
Chicago and London

Daniel Jordan Smith is associate professor in and chair of the Anthropology Department at Brown University. He is the author of *Culture of Corruption: Everyday Deception and Popular Discontent in Nigeria* and the coauthor of *The Secret: Love, Marriage, and HIV.*

The University of Chicago Press, Chicago 60637
The University of Chicago Press, Ltd., London
© 2014 by The University of Chicago
All rights reserved. Published 2014.
Printed in the United States of America

23 22 21 20 19 18 17 16 15 14   1 2 3 4 5

ISBN-13: 978-0-226-10866-7 (cloth)
ISBN-13: 978-0-226-10883-4 (paper)
ISBN-13: 978-0-226-10897-1 (e-book)

DOI: 10.7208/chicago/9780226108971.001.0001

Library of Congress Cataloging-in-Publication Data

Smith, Daniel Jordan, 1961– author.
    AIDS doesn't show its face: inequality, morality, and social change in Nigeria / Daniel Jordan Smith.
        pages; cm
    Includes bibliographical references and index.
    ISBN 978-0-226-10866-7 (cloth: alkaline paper) —
ISBN 978-0-226-10883-4 (paperback: alkaline paper) —
ISBN 978-0-226-10897-1 (e-book)   1. AIDS (Disease)—Moral and ethical aspects—Nigeria. 2. AIDS (Disease)—Social aspects—Nigeria. 3. Nigeria—Social conditions—1960– 4. Social change—Nigeria—21st century.
I. Title.
RA643.86.N6S558 2014
362.19697'92009669—dc23   2013023573

♾ This paper meets the requirements of ANSI/NISO Z39.48-1992 (Permanence of Paper).

This book is dedicated to

Gretchen Jordan McKnew
and
Donald Harrison McKnew Jr.

CONTENTS

INTRODUCTION

As passengers and their belongings were loaded, the bus conductor recruited other travelers, shouting his destination, "Umuahia! Umuahia!" and adding in the local Igbo language: "Leaving *just* now." But the bus would not leave until it was packed tight, with four people squeezed into each row of seats designed to hold three and an improbably large load tied to the roof. The minibuses that run between Aba and Umuahia are crowded and hot, and this particular July afternoon was no exception. As a young man worked to secure the precariously balanced cargo of luggage, live animals, and all manner of goods—many of the passengers were traders from Umuahia who came to refurbish their stocks—there was plenty of time to buy plastic sachets of cold water, boiled groundnuts, fried yams, and scores of other snacks and knickknacks sold by busy hawkers, many of them children, carrying their livelihoods on their heads.

When the bus was finally loaded, the driver appeared for the first time and we set out on the short journey to Umuahia—about an hour, assuming no tire punctures, mechanical troubles, or long searches by the police. As the bus left the park, a young man stood up (to the extent that it was possible to do so in the cramped bus) to ask that we "pray for journey mercies." Southeastern Nigeria is a heavily Christian region. The local Igbo-speaking people are the third largest ethnic group in Nigeria's mosaic of more than 300 tribes and more than 160 million people. They are also increasingly likely to be Pentecostal, evangelical, or, as they commonly say in Nigeria, "born again." So I was not surprised when, after leading the prayer, this young man continued to preach the word of God.

Evangelists commonly proselytize on Nigerian buses. Passengers are, after all, a captive audience. Occasionally, I'd seen travelers rebel and force one of these peripatetic pastors-in-the-making to sit down and cease evangelizing, but usually Igbos listen politely—and even enthusiastically, if the preacher is good. This young man was good, very good. He spoke with passion and charisma, and he connected his biblical stories to examples from everyday life in Nigeria. He had the whole group enthralled, with passengers shouting, "Amen!" "Hallelujah!" "*Eziokwu!*" (Igbo for "you speak truth"), and "Praise the Lord!" at exactly the right moments to punctuate his lively oration.

The young evangelist spoke about bad leaders, corruption, and the ways that ordinary Nigerians suffer in a land of plenty. Like so many of the country's most successful Pentecostal pastors, he tapped into Nigerians' ambivalence about the consequences of social change. On the one hand, he promised prosperity and health to those who follow Christ, acknowledging and drawing on people's aspirations for wealth, consumer commodities, and modern lifestyles. On the other hand, he railed against greed, crime, and wanton sexual behavior—social ills perceived to be sweeping Nigeria's cities and towns and placing in peril not only a new generation of Nigerians, but the future of the country as a whole. I had heard Pentecostal preachers make such critiques many times, and ordinary citizens talked about these issues every day. But this man preached with uncommon passion, a filmmaker's eye for detail, and a social scientist's penchant for encompassing explanation. No wonder his fellow passengers found his message exciting.

At the time, I was conducting research on social aspects of Nigeria's AIDS epidemic, focusing specifically on marriage, masculinity, and men's extramarital sexual behavior. I had become fascinated and concerned by the degree to which many Nigerians conceived of the nation's AIDS problem as a symptom and a product of a collective moral crisis. So when this man began to talk about AIDS, I was even more intrigued. Given his ruminations on other social problems in Nigeria, I expected him to have something noteworthy to say. He did not disappoint.

I'd heard many preachers—and ordinary Nigerians—explain AIDS as the consequence of the failure of modern morality, citing often-repeated platitudes about fornication, adultery, promiscuity, and the demise of Christian values in the face of greed, unbridled desire, and insincerity. Instead, this preacher told a story. He narrated the account of a young woman from his village. She had contracted HIV after migrating to the city in search of work. Although it was parable of sorts, mostly aimed to show the consequences of sin, the man told the story in a way that also evoked sympathy for the girl. She had been lured into a sexual relationship by an older married man—and by the devil—because she needed money to pay her rent and she wanted to be able to dress in nicer clothes like other migrant girls she had met in the city. She also felt pressure to help her parents pay the school fees for her younger siblings back home in the village.

Unlike many of the messages about AIDS in Nigeria that attribute an individual's HIV infection to sin and that blame the national epidemic on a country-wide moral crisis—thereby obfuscating the social, political, and economic underpinnings of the disease—this man's story connected sin to the realities of difficult lives and attributed the failures of societal morality to systematic inequality. I am not sure whether his story was heard in this way by my fellow passengers on the sweaty bus ride from Aba to Umuahia. Perhaps I deduced more sympathy for the girl and more of a political critique than he intended. Indeed, like so much of what I have heard about AIDS in Nigeria, his message emphasized the moral underpinnings of Nigeria's current problems. But his words also nurtured a growing sense I had that examining the relationship between inequality and morality was crucial for understanding people's experiences with the disease and for analyzing its consequences for society. Further, the bus preacher's anecdote about the girl from his village was yet one more example of the way popular responses to AIDS in Nigeria seem to be about more than just health and disease: they provide a window onto people's aspirations, experiences, and ambivalences regarding a host of social changes. These changes range from urbanization and the fitful penetration of capitalism to the spread of desires for modern consumption and new configurations in the social organization of communities and families. All of these transformations are bound up with people's perceptions of rising levels of inequality. Yet among the people in southeastern Nigeria I have studied, the causes and consequences of these changes are most commonly discussed and explained in moral terms.

By "moral" I mean simply the human capacity and propensity to evaluate the world—and most especially human behavior—in terms of "good" and "bad" and "right" and "wrong." As James Ferguson has observed, in Africa, "economic realities are routinely apprehended in fundamentally moral terms" (2006, 71). Building on a wide body of scholarship about Africa, Ferguson further emphasizes that "the production of wealth . . . is understood to be inseparable from the production of social relations" (2006, 72). In contemporary Nigeria, concerns about the moral—and social relational—causes and consequences of growing economic inequalities are widespread, and much of the popular moral discourse about AIDS reflects these same concerns. A growing literature on AIDS in Africa suggests that in many settings the disease is emblematic of perceptions of social crisis, and there is a widely shared belief that moral decay underlies these problematic shifts (Yamba 1997; Guerts 2002; Dilger 2006; Haram 2010).

In a recent book about Kenya, Wenzel Geissler and Ruth Prince suggest that in the era of AIDS, "tropes of loss have become a leitmotif of conversations about sociality and change" (2010, 3). As Hansjörg Dilger has suggested, in Africa, AIDS has become "a disruptive and morally disturbing force in the productive and reproductive orders of kinship networks, community constellations and society at large" (2010, 3). What Rachel Spronk observes about Kenya seems to be common across much of the continent: "The understanding of AIDS as a disease of 'immorality' has become a key concept and has gained a dominant position in public debates, demonstrating how AIDS has come to be seen as a sign of the times by many people" (2012, 98). All these scholarly assessments underscore that, in Africans' popular imaginations, the epidemic is intrinsically connected with seemingly shifting foundations of contemporary morality and social life. Whether Africans see AIDS as primarily a cause or a consequence of broader transformations is arguably impossible to disentangle; my argument is that AIDS and its connections to moral anxieties are fundamentally imbricated.

Without delving into anthropologists' more philosophical musings about morality and ethics (see Lambek 2010 for a cogent treatment of these issues), I take my cue from the Nigerians I have studied, who are certain that the most pressing problems in their society are moral in nature. Rather than ignore or minimize the moral aspects of AIDS, inequality, and social change, I integrate into my analysis an attention to the moralizing discourses that permeate Nigerians' responses to these issues. Although AIDS is central to my story, the debates it inflames connect with much wider processes of transformation. As Geissler and Prince note, "AIDS brings many tensions and conflicts in social relations to a head, but the situation of this sociality cannot be reduced to it or explained by it" (2010, 7). AIDS is a major problem in Nigeria, as elsewhere in Africa, but the moralizing popular discourses it generates in Nigeria also encompass many other aspects of social life that concern people at least as much as the epidemic.

This book focuses on social responses to AIDS in Nigeria—on the ways people have interpreted, discussed, and reacted to the disease. In addition to exploring how AIDS has affected Nigerian society beyond its health consequences, this perspective provides a means to better understand the complex relationship between inequality and morality. The epidemiology of AIDS in Nigeria (as everywhere) is strongly shaped by various dimensions of inequality, and yet it is impossible to understand the impact of AIDS in

Africa's most populous country without tracing the moral interpretations it has generated. The chapters that follow show how the AIDS epidemic has been exacerbated by the moralizing discourses that accompany it across a variety of social arenas. More broadly, my argument is that a wide range of social processes in Nigeria that produce or result from inequality are interpreted in moral terms. These moral interpretations in various ways hide, protect, and even strengthen the social underpinnings of inequality. By unraveling the intertwined relationship between inequality and morality, I demonstrate not only the power of moral discourses as agents in the reproduction of inequality, but also how such moralizing responses to AIDS and to the social context in which it unfolds can prove a source of resilience, and even resistance, for people in the throes of troubling disparities.

The AIDS epidemic in Nigeria has killed more than 2 million people, left 1.7 million children orphaned, and continues to infect more than 300,000 citizens every year (National Agency for the Control of AIDS 2010). But the lesser known story of AIDS in Nigeria is that the moralizing responses to the epidemic—what most people believe about the causes, meanings, and social implications of AIDS—have been in many ways as consequential in Nigerian society as the virus itself. Numerous anthropologists and public health scholars working across Africa have discussed the importance of local moralities for the efficacy of prevention, treatment, and testing campaigns (Fassin 2007; Thornton 2008; Nguyen 2010), but my argument extends further: these moralizing discourses about the epidemic have been so powerful because they express and stand for people's experience of and ambivalence about certain consequences of ongoing social changes and in particular, their discontent about rising levels of social inequality. Nigerians both aspire to and feel great anxiety about the entailments associated with unfolding processes like the penetration of the global capitalist economy, popular preoccupations with consumption, increasing rural-to-urban migration and urbanization, and changes in family and community life that appear to privilege the individual over the group. As I trace in the coming chapters, public health officials, politicians, pastors, elites, and ordinary Nigerians all discuss and express concern over the AIDS epidemic in ways that reflect and perpetuate their moral attitudes toward this array of social changes that the country has been experiencing in the same period as the rise of HIV.

Although attitudes toward AIDS by no means offer the only lens onto broader experiences of societal transformation, the epidemic's prevalence in everyday talk about Nigeria's shifting norms and values make it a valuable and even necessary starting point for comprehending how people understand the relationship among illness, entrenched and exacerbated social inequalities, and perceptions of widespread immorality. Focusing on these relationships, rather than just on the experiences of infected individuals, allows us to better recognize the resonance of the epidemic in the public imagination and its consequences beyond ill health.

My approach builds on a long tradition in medical anthropology, wherein scholars learn about social processes by studying sickness, healing, and the organization of health systems (Turner 1967, 1968; Janzen 1978; Nichter 1992). The idea that sickness is but one manifestation of misfortune has bequeathed a venerable legacy in anthropology. This is perhaps especially so in Africa, where the enterprise of studying healing practices has yielded both pioneering and classical scholarship about ritual, knowledge production, and the fundamental dynamics of social organization (Evans-Pritchard 1937; Horton 1967, 1993; Whyte 1997). Anthropologists have continued to learn about social life by situating health and illness in a broader context and by showing how people's efforts to protect or restore their health are also concerned with larger questions, producing effects on the world that extend well beyond biology and the body (Scheper-Hughes 1992; Whyte, van der Geest and Hardon 2002; Biehl 2007).

Scholars responding to the AIDS epidemic have produced accounts that show how the virus exploits inequalities of class, race, and gender, resulting in a greater burden of disease for some groups (Farmer 1999; Schoepf 1992; Fassin 2007). In the wake of Paul Farmer's seminal work, many anthropologists have compelled us to recognize that AIDS is not just a health crisis but also a political problem and a moral challenge. Further, now-classic accounts like Susan Sontag's *AIDS and Its Metaphors* (1989) and Paula Treichler's *How to Have Theory in an Epidemic* (1999) teach us that the ways people think and talk about AIDS can be as consequential as CD4 counts, seroprevalence, viral loads, and the number of dollars spent by the Global Fund for AIDS, Tuberculosis, and Malaria.

This book builds on the insights of these scholars and many others. So long as the epidemic rages on, there can be no doubt that there is still work to do to understand AIDS in Nigeria—and all of Africa—whether it is because we have not learned enough to contribute to effective prevention and treatment or because the knowledge we have has not been properly communicated or implemented. I applaud anthropologists and other scholars who conduct research and disseminate findings that can help combat the epidemic; however, this book has a different emphasis. I try to reverse the usual dynamic in which Africa is seen as a vehicle to explain AIDS. I focus instead on AIDS as an optic to help understand Nigeria and Nigerians. In so doing, I seek to rethink the ways scholarly and policy literature has represented AIDS and turn the epidemic into a point of entry to explore the complex and changing social worlds of Africa's most populous nation. The moral discontents about AIDS expressed by the bus evangelist and echoed in everyday conversations across Nigeria are, I propose, as much—or more—about anxieties related to growing inequality and the consequences of contemporary social transformations as they are about the illness itself. If we focus too narrowly on the epidemic as an object of study, we risk missing what AIDS can teach us about people and about society.

In many ways, contemporary Western understandings of Africa are filtered through the lens of mainstream Western media's interpretation of the AIDS epidemic. This continues a long trend in which Africa, including Nigeria, has been represented primarily by its crises and dysfunctions (Mudimbe 1994; Ferguson 2006). Policy literature and media alike frequently depict the continent's problems as a product of culture, blaming traditions—and therefore ordinary people—for troubles that have much deeper political and economic origins. In this book, I turn this common and misleading perspective inside out. Rather than allowing the specter of AIDS to distort what we know about Nigeria—and Africa—I try to use what Nigerians believe about AIDS and what they've done in response to the epidemic to learn about them and their country.

The Arrival of AIDS in Nigeria

In 1989, when I first arrived in Owerri, the capital of Imo State, as the project advisor for a US nongovernmental organization working on child survival, AIDS was just barely beginning to penetrate Nigeria's national consciousness. By then, public health specialists had known for several years that Uganda had a serious epidemic. But even though Nigeria's first documented case had occurred three years earlier, in 1986, almost no Nigerians knew this and hardly anyone I met believed that AIDS actually existed in Nigeria.

After several months in Owerri, I settled into a routine of playing tennis after work at a local sports club. Men—mostly elites—gathered there every evening for end-of-the-day recreation and conversation. It was a masculine social environment, something quite common in Nigeria, where men and women tend to socialize in gender-segregated spaces and associations. These male-dominated contexts produced remarkably candid discussions about intimate topics.

One evening at the tennis club someone brought up the subject of AIDS. Donor-supported public health programs were just beginning to disseminate information about the disease, and HIV- and AIDS-related bumper stickers, posters, signboards, radio spots, and television public service announcements had started to appear—accompanied, in the governmental and nongovernmental sectors, by countless workshops, seminars, conferences, training sessions, and a dizzying myriad of project proposals, surveys, statistics, evaluation reports, and policy recommendations. AIDS would eventually spark a full-blown industry (Patton 1989; Altman 1998; Iliffe 2006). On that humid evening in 1990, however, it seemed like more of a problem elsewhere than a reality in Nigeria.

As the discussion unfolded, one of the more senior men warned, with something of a wink, that the current generation of bachelors needed to be more careful in their premarital exploits, lest they "go and carry AIDS" (a common local expression for becoming infected with HIV). There was little understanding then of the distinction between HIV and full-blown AIDS, and even now, in 2013, more than six years after antiretroviral drugs became more widely available in Nigeria, many people conflate the virus and the disease.

Odi Nwaeze, one of the younger men in the sports club and one of the few who was not yet married, had a keen sense of humor.[1] He was quick to retort against his senior's warning, asserting that there was no AIDS in Nigeria. Looking mischievously at me, he said, "AIDS is a problem for whites and homosexuals, not for Africans." The association of AIDS with whites and gays (both groups considered equally "un-Nigerian") signaled the moralistic interpretations of AIDS that would come to dominate Nigerian understandings and responses to the epidemic. The insinuation that AIDS was a gay disease marked it as non-African because few people acknowledge that some Nigerian men have sex with men, and those who do admit to the existence of homosexuality attribute it to the corrupting influence of Western (and white) culture. Homosexuality was but one example—albeit a particularly egregious one in the minds of most Nigerians—of the negative influence of Western culture on African society.

Eventually, stigma would turn against fellow Nigerians, seemingly forced in that direction by the reality that local heterosexual people were getting sick and dying from the disease. As years passed and the epidemic evolved from a mythical threat to a reality—as more and more Nigerians knew or heard about someone in their social worlds who was sick with AIDS—the connections between the epidemic and a perception of social and moral crisis grew. As Julie Livingston points out for Botswana, "Foreign visitors to Botswana often puzzle over the seeming incongruity between the much-publicized high rates of AIDS-related illnesses and the rarity of seeing a person one imagines to be an AIDS patient in a public setting. Yet with

AIDS . . . what remains invisible as a public situation (except through sta-
tistical knowledge and ubiquitous media coverage) is quite visible to many
Batswana as they move within their networks of friends and relatives"
(2005, 11). In Nigeria, as result of lower prevalence, reluctance to test for
the virus, and a disinclination on the part of those who know they are HIV
positive to disclose their status, AIDS as a disease is even less visible than
in a place like Botswana. But I argue that while AIDS the disease remains
remarkably well hidden in everyday life, AIDS as a symbol of social crisis
dominates public discourse beyond its actual health impact.

Understandings of AIDS in Nigeria are connected to broader concerns
about the situation in the country. Capitalism and urbanization—the major engines of contemporary change in Nigeria—and attendant promises of
democracy and development have not only failed to produce better lives
for most people; they also appear to increase inequality and put sacred values and traditional forms of social organization at risk. When Nigerians
talk about their discontents, they frequently focus on morally questionable
social changes brought about by rural–urban migration, the influence of
Western media, rising aspirations for material consumption, and the monetization of social life more generally—the very same factors people associate with the rise of the AIDS epidemic. The narratives that accompanied the
arrival of AIDS epitomized Nigerians' perceptions that problems of illness
were related to the problems of inequality, which were in turn related to
failures of morality.

A few years after that discussion at the tennis club, it was clear to those
men, as to any observer, that Nigeria was experiencing a full-blown epidemic. But the reality of an HIV epidemic in Nigeria did not displace the
power of the moralizing discourses that accompanied the virus's arrival; if
anything, it fueled them. Even now, these moral narratives and the AIDS
industry created to address the epidemic continue to shape social life in
Nigeria as much or more than the demographic and medical repercussions
of the virus itself.

The moral narratives about AIDS unfold in a setting where accurate information about the epidemic is difficult to obtain, even for experts, much
less for ordinary citizens. The statistics publicized by government, international agencies, and the Nigerian media often created more misunderstandings and confusion than clarity. For example, according to the most recent
report to the United Nations by Nigeria's AIDS control agency, the country's
adult prevalence increased from 1.8 percent when first estimated in 1991
to a peak of 5.8 percent in 2001 and declined to 4.6 percent in 2008 (National Agency for the Control of AIDS 2010). These estimates were based

on a sentinel surveillance system set up at about 80 antenatal clinics across the country. Positive tests from a sample of pregnant women who come to clinics for prenatal care serve as a proxy for country-wide adult infection. Although sentinel surveillance is a common method for estimating prevalence in resource-constrained contexts, it is not as reliable as a population-based survey in which individuals are tested randomly from a wider population, assuring a more representative sample.[2] Nigeria's first (and to my knowledge only) national seroprevalence survey was undertaken in 2007 and returned an adult prevalence of 3.6 percent (Federal Ministry of Health 2009). This figure, now the most frequently used prevalence estimate in UN and other international documentation about AIDS in Nigeria, has been widely touted by federal government officials as evidence of the success of the country's AIDS control programs. Some of the Nigerian media also reported it this way, though other accounts suggested that it proved a fairly common belief that the seriousness of the epidemic had been overblown. The latter was certainly a view that I sometimes heard from ordinary Nigerians.

Most AIDS experts I've spoken with in Nigeria—foreign and local—say that they do not think the 3.6 percent figure from 2007 represents a true decline in prevalence. Rather, the conventional wisdom is that the scientifically rigorous population-based survey simply provided a more accurate picture than the cruder sentinel surveillance surveys. Indeed, the revised, lower estimate for prevalence in Nigeria reflects a wider trend, where UNAIDS and other organizations monitoring the global epidemic have mostly shifted estimates downward in light of data from more rigorous methodologies (WHO 2007).

Despite what may seem like relatively low prevalence compared to nations in southern Africa where population prevalence is in the double digits, it is important not to understate the human costs of AIDS in Nigeria. Even at the lower prevalence calculation of 3.6 percent, this translates into three million people living with the virus, 300,000 new infections annually, and 200,000 deaths each year (National Agency for the Control of AIDS 2010). These figures make Nigeria's epidemic, in absolute numbers, the third largest in the world, following only South Africa and India.

In my research I have met scores of Nigerians who are HIV positive, and some have become my friends. I have seen them sick and suffering. Some have died. It feels almost irresponsible to claim that moralizing discourses and the stigma of AIDS in Nigeria have been as consequential as the disease itself. And yet that is what many—indeed, most—of the Nigerians I know who are infected with HIV have told me. HIV-positive people in Nigeria talk about fears and experiences of prejudice, discrimination, and ostracism as being even more difficult to cope with than their health problems. Reluctance to test, failure to disclose one's status, inconsistent adherence to treatment, and low rates of condom use are all exacerbated by fears of stigma.

For all the talk about stigma, however, it is not always immediately apparent what Nigerians or public health practitioners mean by the concept. From the early stages of the epidemic, the issue of stigma was intimately tied to virtually all discussions of the social epidemiology of HIV and AIDS (Sontag 1989). Scholarship today continues to blame stigma for Africans' low rates of compliance with prevention measures and for failures of adherence to drug regimens (Campbell, Skovdal, and Gibbs 2011; Parker and Aggleton 2003; Link and Phelan 2001, 2006; Kalichman and Simbayi 2003). Efforts to trace the "source" or cause of stigma have provided answers ranging from the association of AIDS with death (Niehaus 2007; Castro and Farmer 2005) to the connection between HIV and promiscuity or aberrant sexuality (Brown, Macintyre, and Trujillo 2003) to conspiracy theories about AIDS as an instrument of Western nations' suppression of African sovereignty (Fassin 2007; Rödlach 2006) to "spiritual insecurity" and fears of pollution or contagion (Ashforth 2005, 2011)—all of which are often attributed in the international public health community to a simple lack of knowledge or education about the etiology of the disease. That said, it is remarkable how many scholarly publications about HIV-related stigma lack any discussion of the root causes of stigma, instead focusing solely on its manifestation in terms of people's avoidance behaviors associated with a refusal to engage in protection, prevention, testing, and treatment.

In this book, I argue that to understand the etiology and full weight of the moral stigma associated with AIDS in Nigeria, it is necessary to observe and unravel the connections between people's anxieties about AIDS and their much broader ambivalence and unease about the consequences of wider social changes that are associated with the epidemic. Nigerians have come to perceive a host of transformations—from urbanization and the fitful penetration of capitalism to changes in kinship and family relationships (wherein traditional gender and generational hierarchies are threatened) to ever-increasing access to Western education, modern commodities, and global media—as offering attractions that undermine values and practices that they value. According to many, duties and obligations to family are giving way to rampant individualism. Desires for money and modern consumption are judged as eclipsing honorable behavior and commitment to community. Criminal pursuits are regarded as the new norm, creating a sense that from the highest echelons of government to the ordinary man on the street, people not only survive but often thrive through activities that are illegal and unethical. New freedoms and desires are viewed as cheapening sex and marriage, and young unmarried women's sexual behavior in particular is deemed improper and indicative of moral decay. Worst of all in the eyes of many Nigerians, in these selfish pursuits, people have turned away from God. Of course, ironically, as Nigerians will be the first to say, many people actively pursue the same modern lifestyles they find so problematic.

In the coming chapters, I show that interpretations and social responses to AIDS must be understood in this context. The stigma associated with AIDS builds on a much wider sense of social and moral crisis in Nigeria, all connected, I argue, to people's discontents about rising inequality. A sexually transmitted disease that afflicts and kills young people, seemingly especially urban people with modern lifestyles, has become an emblem for all that Nigerians see wrong with their society, and the disease has taken on a symbolic significance even beyond its horrific health consequences.

Moral Stigma and "Iatrogenic" Interventions

The reasons for AIDS stigma in Nigeria are deeply rooted. Unfortunately, however, Western-funded or -inspired interpretations and interventions have often contributed to rather than ameliorated the negative moral narratives associated with the epidemic. Specifically, the first 15 years of AIDS prevention interventions in Nigeria exacerbated the widespread belief that AIDS is the consequence of a moral crisis. Stigma around AIDS has been nourished in part because internationally led prevention programs have addressed the disease in terms that encourage its association with many preexisting social anxieties—particularly issues like extramarital sex, the breakdown of kinship as a social control mechanism, youth independence, and an increasing obsession with materialism and popular consumption. These are, of course, fundamentally moral concerns. The "iatrogenic" effects of AIDS programs—a term borrowed from biomedicine that refers to medicine that itself makes the patient sick, sometimes even sicker than the original illness—are mostly the product of good intentions, all the more reason why these programs must be closely scrutinized (Morrell et al. 2001; Watkins 2004; Parikh 2007). Three examples below illustrate good intentions gone awry.

The first example stretches back to the early 1990s, when few Nigerians knew anyone with HIV and the global scientific debates about the origin of AIDS had just begun to make their way into Nigerian national discourse. The emerging scientific consensus was that AIDS had an African origin and that HIV originated from monkeys—a simian virus somehow transferred to humans. In Nigeria, this stirred anger, resentment, and conspiracy theories. The nuances of the Western scientific debates about the jump from primates to humans did not register among people I knew. Although most scientific accounts posited hunting, food preparation, or dietary intake as the mode of original transmission to humans, many Nigerians heard these accounts as blaming Africans for AIDS and implying that some Africans must have had sex with apes. To Nigerians, these accounts of an African origin of HIV smacked of racism and fit easily into a trajectory of long-held Western prejudices that assumed blacks were closer to nonhuman ancestors in appearance, intelligence, and level of civilization. Nigerians knew full well that such racist ideas were the moral rationalization for slavery and colonialism and that these beliefs still undergird some of the structures of contemporary global inequality.

Not surprisingly, Nigerians had different theories about the origin of HIV and AIDS—theories that blamed the West rather than Africa. Among the most common was the story that HIV was created by the CIA to reduce African population growth, a rumor that found support in the legacy of decades of international efforts to get Africans to have fewer children. A growing African population was a threat to the West, the thinking went, and AIDS was a way to curtail that threat. Nigerians are brilliant at inventing playfully critical new meanings for common acronyms, and one clever reinterpretation of "AIDS" was "American Initiative to Discourage Sex." Certainly not all Nigerians believed such stories. But these narratives had consequences. For example, in 2003, the global polio eradication campaign ground to a halt in northern Nigeria, just short of success, largely because of the influence of a rumor that the vaccination campaign was an American plot to infect Muslims with HIV or, in another version of the rumor, to make young girls infertile (Obadare 2005; Renne 2010).

Such conspiracy theories are a common expression of an awareness of, and arguably a resistance to, perceived inequalities. The AIDS literature is replete with examples from many settings (Farmer 1992; Rödlach 2006; Epstein 2007; Steinberg 2008). In most cases, these "untrue" stories do possess a kind of veracity and authority, in that they provide both an idiom and a means for the marginalized to speak truth to power. But they do not always serve popular interests overall. For example, Didier Fassin's compelling account *When Bodies Remember* (2007) helps explain "AIDS denialism" and its consequences in South Africa. South African President Thabo Mbeki's view that AIDS was caused by poverty rather than a virus—a perspective he insisted on for years and to which some people still subscribe today—spoke to the political and economic underpinnings of sickness and suffering. But Mbeki's view, shaped by historical and contemporary inequalities, undermined public health interventions and delayed the availability of treatment to hundreds of thousands of people, further exacerbating those inequalities.

A second example of the role of the international community's complicity in intensifying the moral narratives associated with HIV that led to counterproductive misunderstandings about Nigeria's epidemic is the accumulation of dire projections that suggested Nigeria's AIDS problem would quickly reach apocalyptic proportions. As experts looked at the numbers of infected people generated by Uganda's mostly heterosexually transmitted epidemic in the late 1980s and early 1990s, and at southern Africa's even worse situation a decade later, they concluded that without drastic and successful prevention interventions, Nigeria was headed for a similar scenario. The most widely publicized example of such alarming predictions was the 2002 US National Intelligence Council (NIC) report *The Next Wave of AIDS*, which focused on five heavily populated and politically strategic countries—Nigeria, Ethiopia, Russia, India, and China. In that report, NIC predicted that by 2010 Nigeria would have between 10 and 15 million people infected with HIV. As mentioned above, the current scientific consensus is that Nigeria has approximately 3 million people living with HIV, meaning that NIC's most conservative prediction was more than three times too high.

Most Nigerians did not read the NIC report, but it was widely publicized in Nigeria, and it contributed to a larger discourse promulgated by international donors, multilateral agencies, and nongovernmental organizations (NGOs) that AIDS was a crisis of monumental proportions for the country. That these projections were made at a time when most Nigerians did not know someone sick with AIDS and that ultimately they did not come true only added to the distance between what people imagined about the disease and its epidemiological reality. These exaggerated and dire predictions had two intertwining and seemingly contradictory effects: they contributed to the collective belief that AIDS was a consequence and also harbinger of social and moral crisis, and they made it easier for people to dismiss the possibility that they themselves might be at risk for contracting HIV. This paradoxical dynamic—that AIDS is seen as part and parcel of a broad societal crisis and that the actual personal risk of HIV is typically minimized in the minds of individuals—has played out throughout Nigeria's unfolding epidemic. In a tragic way, exaggerated and overly moralistic understandings of the disease contribute to underestimating personal risk, enabling the spread of the epidemic. When popular understandings of AIDS are so

1. Abstinence messages have dominated Nigeria's "ABC" approach to AIDS prevention.

bound up with moral stigma, people adopt behaviors that minimize their exposure to accusations of immorality, but ironically these behaviors also sometimes increase the risk of infection. The problem of condom use in particular, introduced below, is indicative of this dynamic.

A final example of the iatrogenic effects of international public interventions is the impact on condom use that resulted from the "ABC" (Abstinence, Be Faithful, Use Condoms) approach to AIDS prevention, which has dominated programmatic efforts in Nigeria since about 2000. The President's Emergency Plan for AIDS Relief (PEPFAR), created under US President George W. Bush's administration, promoted a conservative approach to AIDS prevention through its ABC messages, which were (1) abstinence is the only true prevention; (2) if one is in a sexual relationship, stay faithful to one partner; and (3) if one can't do either, use condoms. As I will explain further below, it is too simplistic to pin either the specific shape of Nigeria's ABC approach or the larger moralistic understanding of AIDS in Nigeria solely on foreign donors in general, or the Bush administration in particular. Nonetheless, the donor-influenced ABC approach ended up turning condoms into symbols of AIDS, signaling sexual immorality and sin rather than a sensible strategy for safe sex.

In interviews beginning in 2001, young people told me repeatedly that they only used condoms early in a relationship and that when they had sex with people they trusted, they did not use them. But what I heard was about more than just a diminution of condom use that comes with intimacy and relationship longevity, something that happens in many cultural settings, even outside the context of serious HIV risk. Instead, people said that condom use signaled promiscuity and even the possibility that the person who advocated using them might already be infected. The reputation of condoms was by that time so bad that it was not uncommon to hear people say that condoms themselves might be vehicles for HIV transmission, another version of the kinds of conspiracy theories described above. It became clear to me that, in response to the perception that proper (moral) sexual behavior was the best prevention for AIDS, many Nigerians were eschewing condoms in order to convince themselves, their partners, and their various publics that the sex they were having was not immoral (Smith 2003a, 2004a).

The public health literature—as well as a considerable body of scholarship in medical anthropology—has criticized the ABC approach and pointed out its limitations (Barnett and Parkhurst 2005; Gray et al. 2006; Cohen and Tate 2006). The model for ABC prevention programs, as appropriated by PEPFAR and other donors, is usually presented as having been derived from Uganda's successful homegrown prevention effort, known as "zero grazing" (Green 2003). But as Shanti Parikh (2007), Robert Thornton (2008), and others have shown, Uganda's program employed a much less moralizing style in its early iterations than was characteristic of either the Bush administration's PEPFAR policies or the messages about the relative moral hierarchy of abstinence, faithfulness, and condom use in the pantheon of prevention behaviors as they have been promoted in Nigeria.

Each of the above three examples suggests the ease with which messages about AIDS—whether promulgated by the global scientific community, international organizations, or the Nigerian government—became enmeshed in popular Nigerian discourses about social and moral crisis. They also illustrate the predominant role of global (and local) inequalities in engendering vitriolic reactions to policy and research on how AIDS should be prevented and treated. The moral stigma associated with AIDS in Nigeria is directly connected to the way the disease has become associated with a wider sense of social crisis.

AIDS Doesn't Show Its Face

As I suggest above, the moralistic tone of AIDS prevention messages in Nigeria is not simply a consequence of donor influence or pressure. The relationship between PEPFAR's focus on the importance of individual behaviors for prevention and Nigerians' notions of AIDS as a consequence of immoral sexual behavior is one of elective affinity. As I show in the ensuing chapters, the propensity to interpret AIDS in moral terms is reflective of a broader pattern in which the Nigerian public responds to the anxiety-provoking consequences of modern economic, social, and domestic transformations—and to the realities of growing inequality more generally—through an idiom of moral crisis. PEPFAR, ABC, and other internationally supported interventions simply supplied Nigerians with more reasons—and a large package of financial incentives in the form of donor dollars—to keep seeing things this way.

My argument in this book is that Nigerian interpretations of and responses to AIDS must be seen in the context of wider discontents about social changes that reconfigure and exacerbate inequality; in other words, the ways Nigerians grapple with the epidemic are a fruitful and important entry point into understanding their broader anxieties about their culture, their values, and an increasingly unequal society. People are experiencing ongoing transformations with tremendous ambivalence. Desires for money, consumption, modern conveniences, global fashions, Western education, urban lifestyles, and the appeal of individual choices liberated from the collective pressures and obligations of kin and community motivate and explain a huge spectrum of aspirations and behaviors in contemporary Nigeria. And yet these same desires are producing novel forms of conduct, unfamiliar social realities, and new inequalities related to individualism, greed, urban anonymity, neglect of kin, and the like, which people see as threatening to proper sociality and notions of long-cherished cultural values (see Geissler and Prince 2010 and Spronk 2012 on similar issues in Kenya).

In their views on these things most Nigerians do not fall unequivocally on one end or the other of this spectrum; instead, in the course of daily life ordinary Nigerians constantly counterbalance their aspirations for modern lifestyles and their distaste for the associated inequalities and perceived immoralities. This book will explain how and why AIDS is at the nexus of these ambivalences, connecting people's concerns about sexuality, religion, economic changes, gender, kinship, and political corruption. As I will show in the coming chapters, much of the discourse about morality is a means to express and to criticize (but also in various ways, ironically, to protect) the changing face of deep and growing inequities.

The AIDS epidemic is truly emblematic of these troubles. One of the country's the most common billboard, radio, and TV prevention messages is the Nigerian Pidgin English phrase, "AIDS no dey show for face" (AIDS does not show on the face)—that is, you cannot tell if someone has the HIV

2. The Nigerian Pidgin English warning "AIDS no dey show for face" is meant to warn that the virus can be spread by people who do not look sick, but it also unwittingly confirms the reality that many of the epidemic's effects in Nigeria extend beyond ill health.

virus just by looking at him or her. Although the message was designed to encourage all Nigerians to recognize their risk and not assume that the virus can be detected by a person's outward appearance, it has largely failed to serve its purpose because people now rely less on physical signs to decide whether someone might be a risky partner and more on moral judgments about character and reputation. The result is another interpretation of the ubiquitous prevention message: AIDS doesn't show its face because people resolutely avoid confronting the disease, eschewing effective prevention behaviors to protect themselves from the stigma associated with the virus, such that even condom use is a moral tarnish.

If we focus only on the disease, its social implications are hidden. If we understand AIDS in Nigeria only as a public health crisis, we miss how deeply it is intertwined with other aspects of life and how much it can tell us about society. Seeing the complete face of AIDS requires looking not just at the disease but also at the wider relationship between inequality and morality as it plays out in contemporary society. Further, an overly biomedical perspective has contributed to the missteps and misrecognitions that have characterized much of the public health response. Recognizing that AIDS can serve as a lens to illuminate Nigeria—and Africa—will, I contend, help us better understand and address the epidemic, too.

The Consequences of Social Change

In the ensuing chapters, I focus on domains of everyday life in Nigeria where the changes I have observed over the past 23 years seemed most profound, and where people's beliefs about and responses to HIV and AIDS offer significant insight into broader social processes that produce and reproduce social inequalities and their consequences for people.

Before proceeding to the chapters, however, I briefly introduce here each area of focus. They include (1) Nigeria's growing urban economy, especially the informal economy, where people not only pursue their hopes, values, and aspirations, but also confront the realities of surviving in a setting of deep and growing disparities; (2) gender inequalities as they are mediated by the intertwined and sometimes competing arenas of sex, money, and morality; (3) religion—specifically the popularity and social effects of Pentecostal Christianity and its "prosperity gospel"; (4) civil society, with a focus on AIDS NGOs and the intersections of corruption, norms about proper sociality, and changing expectations about the relationship between public institutions and citizens; (5) kinship, which continues to be the foundation for sociality in southeastern Nigeria, providing people's most cherished relationships, even as kin are increasingly likely to be seen as burdensome and kinship itself is perceived as threatened by social changes such as urbanization, the monetization of prestige, and the rise of individualism; and (6) reproduction, a domain where interpersonal intimacy and broader processes of social reproduction intersect powerfully, perhaps especially for people living with HIV and AIDS.

Urbanization

More Nigerians are moving to and living in cities than ever before. It is estimated that 44 percent of Nigerians now live in cities and that Nigeria will become a majority-urban society within a decade (Population Reference Bureau 2006). With rural–urban migration and urbanization come numerous opportunities and challenges, not least the necessity of finding a livelihood in an urban economy. Further, as they navigate these new urban economies, Nigerians face a host of changes in social life, which they both welcome and lament.

Ordinary Nigerians, especially younger people, continue to move to cities because cities offer hope and opportunities for education, employment, better infrastructure, and more accessible social services, as well as greater engagement with the wider world through access to media, consumer products, and a faster and more cosmopolitan circulation of people and ideas. Nevertheless, for many Nigerians urban life is also widely associated with the perceived growth of social problems such as inequality, greed, crime, and unfettered individualism. Even as cities are seen as both oases of hope and citadels of social ills, they also generate powerful moral discourses that help people understand these changing worlds and shape their behaviors. Nigerians blame AIDS, and many other social problems, at least in part on the immorality spawned by city life.

Gender Relations

Urbanization is but one of several factors that affect the dynamics of gender relations in Nigeria. Migration to the city, expanding (albeit still difficult) employment prospects, increasing access to formal education, and the penetration and circulation of globally produced ideas about gender equality all create new opportunities for women that sometimes conflict with entrenched gender hierarchies. For both men and women, new ideas and practices around sexuality, marriage, and reproduction offer some of the most appealing—and problematic—examples of changes associated with contemporary social life.

As men and women in southeastern Nigeria navigate the intersection of wider societal transformations and the changing configuration of the domestic sphere—with a rise in "love" marriages, lower levels of fertility, and more nuclear family organization—the structure, meaning, and dynamics of gender inequality are being simultaneously challenged, reinforced, and renegotiated (Smith 2010). As has been the case in many other cultural contexts (see, e.g., Wardlow 2006; Johnson-Hanks 2006; Merry 2006), patriarchal gender relations in contemporary Nigeria have been and continue to be justified and protected through moralistic discourses about women's bodies, sexuality, and reproductive capacities. The AIDS epidemic has been a powerful generator of normative narratives about women's behavior. Certainly, women bear a disproportionate share of the global burden of HIV and AIDS for both biological and social reasons (Hirsch et al. 2009), yet it is also true that across Africa women share a disproportionate burden of the stigma of HIV (Bond, Chase, and Aggleton 2002). Connections between love and money and sex and sin saturate popular understandings of the epidemiology of HIV (Smith 2004a). And yet, as I show, moral discourses about women's sexuality also reflect and even open up spaces in which patterns of gender inequality can be criticized and transformed.

Religion

Perhaps not surprisingly, the tremendous social changes unfolding in Nigeria have been associated with a kind of religious revolution as well. Across southern Nigeria, Pentecostal Christianity has burgeoned to become the region's most popular faith. Its popularity and its social impact appear to be directly related to its capacity to speak to both people's desires for and concerns about the consequences of ongoing social transformations as well as to social problems such as the AIDS epidemic.

Many Pentecostal churches have been purveyors of stigma about HIV and AIDS, propagating moralistic messages that associate individual infection with sin and the national epidemic with a collective moral crisis. It is therefore at first blush rather surprising that individuals who discover they are HIV positive have been flocking to these churches in large numbers, seeking hope, social support, and miracle cures. Just as the relationship of Pentecostal Christianity to AIDS is complex—perpetuating stigma but also offering hope to the suffering—so too have these churches been contradictory in their moral messages about social inequality. On the one hand, pastors like the bus preacher in the opening anecdote rail against greed, corruption, and the selfish pursuit of money. On the other hand, the most popular pastors preach the "prosperity gospel," promising material wealth and success to those who become "born again" and follow God's ways. Nigerian Christians' seemingly insatiable appetite for Pentecostal and charismatic pastors and churches reveals just how effectively these preachers and institutions have tapped into people's simultaneous desires for and discontents regarding many of the transformations associated with a modernizing society.

AIDS NGOs and Civil Society

Both the international community and Nigeria's political leaders have promised people that the troubles associated with modern changes will be mitigated and ultimately made worthwhile by the twin pillars of democracy and development. Even as the Nigerian state and international donors have mostly failed to deliver on these promises, a whole world of NGOs has evolved. Although these organizations ostensibly further enable the aims of democracy and development, they just as often seem to perpetuate the same corruption that has long frustrated ordinary people. The AIDS epidemic has produced its own industry of NGOs and an attendant discourse about corruption, inequality, and morality.

AIDS NGOs exemplify some of the key dynamics that characterize the reproduction of inequality in Nigeria, both vis-à-vis Nigeria's position in the global economy and with regard to the shifting landscape of inequality within the country. At the global level, AIDS NGOs, including "local" NGOs (those founded and staffed by Nigerians rather than foreigners), are intimately tied to the international aid/AIDS industry, which commonly justifies its work on the basis that NGOs are agents of humanitarianism and development, making the world a better place for poor people in places like Nigeria. And yet to ordinary Nigerians these NGOs often look like financial bonanzas for those who run them. NGOs are regularly perceived to be producers of inequality rather than remedies for it, as they frequently seem to concentrate resources in the hands of the already-privileged individuals who run them, all under the veneer of charity. Local NGOs are positioned precariously in relation to the moral discourses about inequality within Nigeria. Ideally, they are imagined to be modern institutions that can contribute to addressing social problems and make the state more accountable to the people. In practice, the performance of these institutions and the people who run them is often judged in relation to principles of patronage; that is, based more on whether people connected by kinship, friendship, and patron-clientism are benefiting from them than by whether the NGOs are achieving their official objectives. Even as the reciprocal obligations of patron-clientism appear to be eroding in the face of a more individualistic orientation, many NGOs are perceived merely as vehicles for the enrichment of their founders.

Kinship

No arena of social life epitomizes Nigerians' aspirations and apprehensions about the consequences of contemporary social changes more than kinship. People remain deeply committed to their extended families and the values associated with kinship but at the same time are highly disgruntled about the burdens that these obligations impose as life becomes more urban and individualistic. This is true across Africa; as Jennifer Cole and Deborah Durham write, "Kin work, caring, and domestic labor have always been integral to the organization of capital and the regulation and management of populations, but they are being stretched and used in new ways" (2007, 13).

AIDS has added to the perceived threats to kinship but has also reminded people of its profound importance.

Kinship remains a vital arena of human relationship and social connection as Nigerians navigate the challenges of urbanization and a changing economy. Yet these same changes threaten traditional extended family systems. They are accompanied by shifts in domestic and family life that increasingly privilege nuclear household relationships above extended families. Further, the inequalities that accompany contemporary changes sometimes increase the strains within families, as tensions emerge around processes of accumulation and redistribution. Moral narratives about the problems with modern families abound, often directly focusing on the failures of kin who achieve disproportionate wealth to adequately help their relatives. These moral stories signal the seminal importance of kinship in people's reckoning with the consequences of social change and the implications of new and growing inequalities. Not surprisingly, moralizing accounts that seek to explain who gets infected by HIV similarly draw on this perception that bad behavior is a result of the undermining of kinship and its associated values.

Reproduction

Directly related to kinship are the imperatives of reproduction, both social and biological. Interestingly, as broader processes of social reproduction are perceived by Nigerians to be increasingly threatened and uncertain in the contexts of capitalism, urbanization, and growing individualism, the social significance of biological reproduction appears all the more charged. People in contemporary Nigeria are obsessed with problems of marriage and childbearing, and this is perhaps most true among people who know they are living with HIV or AIDS. The epidemic has become a symbol for larger anxieties about social reproduction, making the need to participate in normal biological reproduction seem all the more acute.

Like most of Africa, Nigeria is experiencing a gradual fertility decline. But the perceived value of having at least three or four children remains high, even as an urbanizing economy, growing expectations about educating children, and the rise of nuclear family household organization put pressures on people to limit their fertility. As Nigerians experience rapid economic, social, and demographic changes, the importance of family-making—of marrying and having children—remains a core collectively shared value. Sometimes people talk about it as a bulwark against unwanted (or at least ambivalently perceived) aspects of social transformation associated with capitalism, urbanization, and Western cultural influences. In people's fears about HIV infection, the prospect of a social death sentence—not only the idea that one would be shunned if others found out one's positive status but also the belief that marriage and childbearing would be impossible—stand out as much or more than the possibility of sickness and death. As I show later, once antiretroviral treatment removed the certainty of biological death, HIV-positive people in treatment became preoccupied with reproduction. Marriage and childbearing are the ultimate assertions of a meaningful life. For ordinary Nigerians experiencing the uncertain consequences of contemporary social changes, and especially for HIV-positive people attempting to restore normality and futures, reproduction becomes a paramount aspiration.

Of course in real people's lives the domains of economics, gender, civil society, religion, kinship, and reproduction are more or less inseparable. Young migrants move to the city, leaving kin in village communities with which they nonetheless maintain ties; they join Pentecostal churches; and they are the target populations for NGOs' AIDS interventions, affected in one way or another by both AIDS and the moral discourses it has spawned. But in order to gain some analytical leverage, I examine each sphere separately, providing ethnographic examples from the lives of ordinary Nigerians. In the following chapters, each focusing on a different domain of social life, I use social responses to the AIDS epidemic as a vehicle for understanding people's experiences of the consequences of contemporary social transformations. Central in each instance is the intersection of inequality and morality, where people interpret the troubling processes of social differentiation that are unfolding in their lives and respond to them in moral terms. Exploring the intersection of inequality and morality offers a chance not only to illuminate and explain Nigerians' experiences of social change but also to understand the broader social consequences of AIDS.

Studying AIDS in Nigeria

I accumulated the material for this book over 23 years of work in southeastern Nigeria. In the 1990s, AIDS was not a topic that I was actively researching. When I wrote my dissertation (Smith 1999), I was focused more on the consequences of "modernity" in people's family lives. But even then, it was apparent to me that certain aspects of social changes impinging on families produced considerable ambivalence among the people I knew. This ambivalence commonly manifested itself in moral discourses about problems related to the perpetuation, exacerbation, and changing character of inequality. When I began to study AIDS explicitly just after 2000, I undertook several projects with the aim of contributing to medical anthropology and advancing more effective, ethnographically informed public health interventions. It was only with time that I realized that studying AIDS was also a revealing way to understand the intersection of inequality and morality more broadly.

My AIDS-related research has involved three principal foci: youth, married couples, and people receiving antiretroviral therapy. My research with young people, particularly adolescents and unmarried young adults, focused primarily on rural–urban migration and the effects of migration and adjustment to city life on young Nigerians' sexual identities, beliefs, and behaviors. In these studies, the ways that economic and gender inequality shaped young migrants' sexual behavior and the degree to which young people conceptualized AIDS in moral terms first became apparent (Smith 2003b, 2004a, 2004b). Nigerian youths appeared not to see HIV risk as driven mainly by social inequality but rather attributed AIDS to immorality. Ironically, these interpretations created new risks, as—for example—condoms became associated with the virus and condom use was stigmatized.

I undertook the project on young rural–urban migrants over two summers (2001–2002) spent mostly in Kano in northern Nigeria and Aba in southeastern Nigeria, the cities of migrant destination in the study. The research involved a survey of approximately 400 young Igbo-speaking migrants in each city, 40 in-depth interviews with a subset of the survey respondents, and continuous participant observation during the research period. I also hired a research assistant, Chidozie Amuzie, to continue interviewing and observations during the entire final year of the project. Although I relied on the survey to provide a broad portrait of the beliefs and behaviors of young migrants related to sexuality and AIDS, the in-depth interviews and informal conversations that unfolded during participant observation, as well as Amuzie's astute interviews and observations, provided what I think were the most important insights into young migrants' experiences, understandings, and behaviors.

The project on marriage and HIV transmission was spurred by the growing recognition that for many women the greatest risk of becoming infected was through having sex with their husbands—perhaps the ultimate indicator of the limitations of the ABC approach. In this study, carried out as part of a multicountry research effort, the prevalence of men's extramarital sexual relations and married women's relative tolerance of men's infidelity was situated in the context of changes in marriage and persistent economic and gender inequalities (Smith 2007b, 2008, 2009, 2010; Hirsch et al. 2009). I conducted the Nigeria-based fieldwork for this project, which we called "Love, Marriage, and HIV," during a sabbatical year in 2004–5, when I spent six months in the Southeast. The research included in-depth interviews with 20 married couples, with every husband and wife interviewed three times separately, for a total of almost four hours with each respondent. I also conducted numerous key informant interviews with religious and community leaders, health professionals, NGO personnel, government officials, and others with relevant interests in or knowledge about marriage, masculinity, or HIV and AIDS. Throughout the fieldwork I undertook participant observation in households, in a range of everyday community settings, and in venues where men socialize with each other or with their extramarital partners. I worked with three female research assistants who interviewed most of the women and one male research assistant who helped me extend the study to two venues: the semi-rural community of Ubakala and the city of Owerri, both in Igbo-speaking southeastern Nigeria.

The findings from this research reinforced my understanding of the interconnections between inequality and morality in the social landscape of the AIDS epidemic. Men's extramarital sexual behavior had to be situated not only in a context of persistent gender disparities but also in a setting of striking and growing class inequalities. Men's motivations for extramarital sex were bound up with economic status. Aspirations related to masculinity and to social class were tied together. Further, married women's relative tolerance of their husbands' infidelity made sense only in relation to the intersection of gender inequality and moral values about marriage, child rearing, and family that are given even greater force in an era when people feel they are in peril.

Finally, I also did research with Nigerians who are HIV positive and receiving antiretroviral therapy. In this work it became clear that for people living with HIV and AIDS, other priorities besides health shaped their behavior, most especially their desire to construct normal lives that included marriage and childbearing (Smith and Mbakwem 2007, 2010). Many of their stories evince difficult struggles around disclosure, adherence to medication, and choices about exposing themselves and others to significant health risks in the pursuit of broader life projects. Over time, I came to realize that the seeming obsession of HIV-positive people to construct normal reproductive lives was also connected to larger society-wide apprehensions about social reproduction. For people who are living with HIV or AIDS, the fact that they symbolize for others the moral (and health) consequences of a wider perceived social crisis made the possibility of reproduction and the importance of the appearance of normalcy all the more acute. Findings from each of these projects are woven into the chapters of this book.

Although I conducted and tape-recorded many interviews for each of these projects, I believe nonetheless that it is through participant observation that I learned most of what I know. It is only through observing people's real lives, listening to multiple unscripted conversations, and seeing people's behavior situated across a wide spectrum of diverse and sometimes contradictory contexts that one can create a reasonably accurate portrayal of what is happening. While acknowledging the partiality and bias that may result from relying so much on participant observation, it is my hope that the ethnographic material in this book offers sufficient evidence for readers to judge for themselves the validity of my interpretations and analysis.

Certainly what I know about AIDS in Nigeria is skewed by where I work in the Igbo-speaking Southeast. The southeastern region was the part of the country that tried unsuccessfully to secede from Nigeria during the Biafran War, Nigeria's civil war lasting from 1967 to 1970. The Igbo people who populate the region have a reputation among other Nigerians (and among themselves) as migratory entrepreneurs who dominate particular sectors of the economy in Nigeria. Like any people or region, they have a history and a culture that makes them different from others. Nevertheless, they are very much integrated into Nigerian society, and they share many experiences with AIDS and with the consequences of various aspects of social change that are common across the country. It is my contention that much of what I observed in the Southeast applies in other parts of the country—perhaps most especially in other parts of southern Nigeria, where Christianity is also widely prevalent and many cultural traditions are similar to the Southeast. In some respects, at least, there will surely be many more differences in people's experiences between the Southeast and the mostly Muslim and Hausa-speaking northern half of the country. Indeed, I have often been struck that my scholarship rooted in southeastern Nigeria regularly resonates more for people working in other countries—and other regions—of sub-Saharan Africa than among people who study or know the north of Nigeria. I wouldn't be surprised if the same were true of this book. But I do think that much of what I present here has implications outside the Southeast, across other parts of Nigeria and in other parts of Africa. By stating from the beginning that I aspire for wider generalizability *and* acknowledge limitations in this regard, I hope to dispense with the need for constant (and I think distracting) qualification every time I use the words Nigeria or Nigerians. The

Nigeria and the Nigerians I refer to and know best are in the Southeast. In some ways, this story is theirs, but in other ways I suggest that it stands for wider realities in Nigeria, and perhaps beyond.

AIDS, Inequality, and Morality

Much of what is written and said about AIDS in Africa exacerbates misunderstandings of the continent and its people. By using Nigerians' social responses to AIDS as a window onto the complex intersection between inequality and morality as people interpret and respond to the consequences of social change, this book attempts to counter misguided renderings that portray African societies only through images of exotic and dysfunctional sexualities, overly simplified cultural explanations, and tragic problems of poverty, war, and corruption.

AIDS and Africa are indelibly linked in popular consciousness throughout most of the world. Despite widespread awareness of the epidemic, much of the story of AIDS remains hidden, even in anthropology. The prevalent focus on issues like condoms, commercial sex workers, and antiretroviral drugs has crowded out attention to even larger implications of the disease. In Nigeria—and I think in other places as well—popular responses to the epidemic reveal anxieties about the future and about the consequences of ongoing transformations, as AIDS is viewed as both a product and a harbinger of moral crisis. Whereas Western images of Africa's AIDS disaster tend to blame traditional culture and sexuality for the continent's disproportionate suffering, many Nigerians link AIDS to modern life—to inequalities associated with urbanization, formal education, and economic development. Education, jobs, and money are things to which people aspire but about which they are also uneasy because they come at tremendous cost.

Home to more than 160 million people, Nigeria is a telling case not only because of its size but also because it exemplifies the social—not just the health—consequences of the AIDS epidemic. One might imagine that with a relatively low prevalence the impact of HIV in Nigeria would be modest. This book argues, however, that the epidemic—whether through infection with the virus or through the moral narratives circulating about the disease—has touched the lives of almost everyone in Nigeria. I examine the ways that AIDS has reverberated in popular imagination and contemporary life, becoming a flashpoint for transformations in multiple spheres of Nigerian society. Each chapter foregrounds popular responses to AIDS as a revealing lens onto different domains of the intersection of inequality and morality—in the urban economy, gender relations, religion, civil society, kinship, and reproduction.

This book suggests that understanding Nigerians' moral anxieties about their changing world can offer a revealing perspective on the shifting contours of inequality and the problems that Nigeria's new and growing disparities create for its people. I show that much of the moralizing Nigerians do about AIDS is connected to larger concerns about the changing dynamics of social relations that come with modern urban life, including the increasing, if fitful, penetration of a capitalist economy and its associated aspirations and constraints. Although the book is more about these wider social trends than about medical issues, ultimately many of the dynamics that drive Nigeria's epidemic have their roots in this broader context. As I will discuss in the conclusion, successful efforts to address the disease must better understand the intersection of morality and inequality as well as the power of moral narratives to protect and propel inequalities that drive the spread of the disease.

ONE

Okada Men, Money, and the Moral Hazards of Urban Inequality

July 21, 2004. As the day broke and the city came to life, dozens of men on motorcycles gathered at the gate of Imo State University, as they did every morning at scores of other locations around town. Each student who approached—perhaps on his or her way to the market, an Internet café, or a distant part of campus—was met with a chorus of *"I na ga?"* (Igbo for "Are you going?"). It was a call so common that throughout southeastern Nigeria the phrase itself was one of the popular monikers for these once ubiquitous motorcycle taxis. At the dawn of the new millennium in Owerri, the bustling capital of Imo State, perhaps the two most striking features of the city's human landscape were the tens of thousands of students attending five fast-growing local universities and the many hundreds of motorcycle taxis——also known as *okada*. Eventually, for reasons I will explain below, *okada* were banned from the cities of southeastern Nigeria, but in their heyday they were a vital part of the expanding urban landscape.

Owerri's university students represent a growing group of young Nigerians whose aspirations for employment, urban amenities, and middle-class lifestyles are brought closer to reality by admission into a tertiary institution. *Okada* drivers were comparatively uneducated, most never having completed secondary school. Driving a motorcycle taxi for a living was considered a rough job. The men——*okada* drivers were all male——who ferried Owerri's residents to and from work, school, church, the market, and every other conceivable destination endured blazing hot sun, torrential rains, horrendous traffic, inconsiderate drivers of much larger vehicles, choking pollution, police extortion, and an occasionally abusive clientele. University students and the men who drive *okada* for a living represent divergent trajectories in Nigeria's economic future, examples of rising levels of inequality in Africa's most populous country.

Yet in the midst of Nigeria's AIDS epidemic, in which Owerri is believed to be a hub of HIV infection, stories connecting *okada* men and university girls were legion. These narratives emphasized the moral hazards of the intersections among growing and frustrated economic aspirations, the perceived societal preoccupation with money, liberalizing sexual mores, and AIDS. Over the last 20 years, as Owerri's university student population has grown from just a few thousand to well over 100,000, the city has developed a reputation as a sexual marketplace. Scores of hotels have been built in the past decade, and most of their business comes from letting rooms to men (many, if not most, of them married) who rendezvous with female lovers, believed by most Owerri residents to be university women. The popular presumption is that these students reserve their sexual favors for men of relative means. So I was at first surprised, and even incredulous, when I was told in 2004——and many times since——that *okada* men quite regularly succeeded in having sex with the university girls who were frequently their passengers.

When I asked why university students, who are widely perceived to be concerned with improving their social status, would deign to have sexual intercourse with *okada* drivers, who are symbolic of the struggle to survive in urban Nigeria, the ubiquitous answer was "cash." A friend who worked for the Imo State government in a midlevel position as a civil servant and who, like most of Owerri's residents, had come to depend on *okada* for everyday transportation, put it this way: "Those guys have cash, physical cash. Many of them make 2,000 naira [about 20 dollars at the time] a day. When they approach a girl, they offer them cash, straight up. It's not like the rich guy in a Mercedes-Benz, who may pick a girl up, take her for dinner, buy her drinks, and even stay in a five-star hotel, but in the end will give her no cash. It's about money, here and now. Money solves problems."

Although university girls having sex both with *okada* drivers and with wealthy older men may provoke labels such as "prostitution" or "transactional sex," the intertwining of intimacy and material exchange in Nigeria, as in much of Africa (Cole and Thomas 2009), is such that the commonly espoused Western opposition between love and money (i.e., "money can't buy love") does not hold. Of course, one might argue that even in Western societies the dichotomy is more imagined than real (Zelizer 2005). Nonetheless, Nigerians seem quite comfortable with the idea that economic support is a crucial way to demonstrate affection. Still, in most sexual relationships in Nigeria, the monetary dimension of the relationship is embedded, euphemized, and carefully negotiated. While economic support is considered part and parcel of a man's responsibility in a sexual relationship (whether it is short-term sex, a romance, or a marriage), usually only in relationships that are most obviously brief and transactional would a woman negotiate compensation as a specific amount of cash. Most Nigerians would identify a university student having sex with an *okada* driver for 2,000 naira as transactional sex of the starkest kind, tantamount to prostitution.

Rather than accepting as fact the rumored cash-driven sexual access of *okada* drivers to university girls, I tried to find out to what extent this was true or whether it was a kind of urban legend. Further, regardless of their truth, why did such stories have great purchase in contemporary Nigeria? I asked a lot of people about the phenomenon, including at least a dozen young women who attended Imo State University or Alvin Ikoku College of Education, two of the tertiary institutions in Owerri. As I explained in the introduction, I have talked with scores of young people in southeastern Nigeria in recent years about intimate issues such as romantic love, sexuality, and AIDS. But despite my best efforts to build trust and rapport, I do not believe that young women attending university in Owerri would actually tell me if they had had sex with an *okada* driver for cash. Indeed, not a single woman I asked said she had done so. The most common response was "Tofiokwa!" which is usually translated as "God forbid such an abomination!"

But interestingly, although no one owned up to engaging in such behavior, many young women said that other female students did so. The university girls' explanations were the same as those I'd heard from others——it was about cash. The women were as judgmental as the rest of Owerri society about the moral stigma of such behavior. Someone who would have sex with an *okada* man for cash was seen as cheap, dirty, and immoral. Particular young women who I knew were involved with married men and receiving money and gifts as an expected part of the relationship were as quick as anyone else to condemn the notion of sex for money with an *okada* driver. Tellingly, the risk of contracting HIV was frequently voiced as part of the moral branding. As one third-year student at Imo State University put it: "Such girls don't respect themselves. For the sake of money a person will go and carry AIDS," meaning that a woman having sex with an *okada* driver for cash ran the risk of HIV infection.

In this context——as is so commonly the case in Nigeria——AIDS was understood as a consequence of immorality and employed in discourse to assert moral claims about people, society, and the consequences of the pursuit of money unmoored from traditional values. Although it is impossible to know how frequently university girls in Owerri had sex with *okada* men for cash, my sense is that it was more urban legend than fact. But even as myth it is a revealing example of the way that AIDS is bound up with Nigerians' aspirations for economic advancement, their apprehensions about the monetization of desire, and the moral anxieties associated with these transformations. To understand why stories that circulated about *okada* men's sexual access to university girls were so resonant, it is necessary to know more about these men and their highly marked profession. In what follows I try to make clear how *okada* men occupied an economic, political, and cultural position that made them an emblem of social inequalities, urban insecurity, and the moral hazards associated with the struggle to survive in contemporary Nigeria.

Okada men were totemic figures whose experiences encapsulated many of the realities of a changing Nigeria. They sought to better their lives by making more money, yet they were competing for their income in an occupation associated with patterns of behavior viewed as inimical to widely shared ideas about sociality. Indeed, one of the primary reasons that contemporary forms of inequality generate so much critical moral discourse in Nigeria is that people perceive these new disparities to be impersonal, monetary, and unchecked by norms of reciprocity. Social inequality is by no means unique to modern times, but the common view among Nigerians I know is that as money and consumption become the measures of success, social disparities have become starker and the possibility of mitigating the worst human effects of inequality through social relationships such as kinship and patron-clientism has eroded. Nigerians consider driving *okada* as a job that someone would do only because of a desperate need for money, which itself suggests the breakdown of kin-based support and the failures of one's wealthier relatives to provide financial safety nets that might otherwise have permitted *okada* drivers to pursue more palatable vocations.

In conversations with me, many *okada* men expressed a sense that the problems of contemporary Nigeria were inscribed on their bodies through the work they did. Although many other occupations in urban Nigeria could justifiably be described as similarly difficult, or even worse, *okada* drivers were constantly the focus of popular discourse. With the exception of the elite, everyone in urban Nigeria used *okada*, and everyone talked about them. They were the vehicles with which Nigerians literally traversed stressful urban arteries, but they were also a central symbolic means by which ordinary citizens imagined, debated, criticized, and made sense of the challenges of new economic realities, the aspirations and hardships associated with urban life, and the perception that in today's Nigeria people will (and maybe even must) do anything possible in order to get money. The idea that university girls would engage in fleeting sex-for-pay encounters with such low-class citizens only further encapsulated the very same moral anxieties about the greed and materialism associated with frustrated economic aspirations.

The Rise of *Okada*

When I first lived in Owerri, while working as the expatriate advisor for a US-based NGO from 1989 to 1992, *okada* did not exist there or anywhere else in southeastern Nigeria. Owerri had less than half of its current population and probably only a tenth of the present number of university students. The streets were far less congested. The city's public transportation consisted of jam-packed minibuses (known in Nigeria as *danfo*) that ferried people along established routes, particularly from the central market areas to the outskirts of town, where most residents lived. These buses were cheap, but they only stopped on main roads and passengers frequently had to walk considerable distances to and from the regular stops.

Owerri also had a large number of automobile taxis, typically very old vehicles that had been imported into Nigeria in various states of disrepair. These used automobiles (and, indeed, any product imported from overseas that was already well used) are known in Nigeria as *tukunbo*. *Tukunbo* taxis in Owerri generally ran prescribed routes and carried multiple passengers at one time. They functioned more like buses than what would be conventionally understood as taxis in the United States or Europe, though one could arrange to use the taxi all for oneself or to be dropped at a specific location. This arrangement, known as a "drop," was three or four times as expensive as simply joining a taxi along its regular route (and taxis——even shared along their prescribed routes——were roughly 50 percent more expensive, and more comfortable, than the *danfo* minibuses). In the late 1980s and early 1990s, transportation in Owerri was a struggle for the common person. The buses and taxis never seemed to be plentiful enough, and people often waited half an hour or more to catch a ride.

By 1995, when I returned to Nigeria for dissertation research, *okada* motorcycle taxis had emerged as the main form of transportation in the urban centers of southeastern Nigeria. They became popular in rural areas, too, where they would cluster in places where buses dropped passengers returning from town, providing transportation all the way to their passengers' village houses. *Okada* (also known as *achaba* in Hausa-speaking northern Nigeria) became the most common form of public transportation in just about every city in Nigeria, with the exceptions of the capital, Abuja, where things are so far apart that motorcycle travel is impractical, and Lagos, the commercial capital, where there are so many fast-moving buses and cars that ordinary Nigerians found motorcycle taxis to be too dangerous. But even in Abuja and Lagos, *okada* were adopted for shorter journeys, functioning much as they do in rural areas, ferrying customers between bus stops and their residences.

The origin of the name *okada* is itself perhaps the first tip that these motorcycle taxis were not only practical solutions to the transportation problems in Nigeria's ever-growing cities but also significant symbols that Nigerians would find appealing to "think with." A few years before *okada* motorcycles arrived on the scene, Nigeria's domestic airlines experienced significant growth, with the emergence of a number of private airlines serving many of the country's biggest cities. Okada Air was the largest of these new fleets during this time and was owned by a wealthy businessman from Benin City named Chief B. O. Igbinedion. Behind each of Nigeria's newly founded airlines was a single rich man. Igbinedion and his rivals flaunted their private airlines as symbols of their extreme wealth. Passengers on these commercial flights were also a rarefied (albeit quickly multiplying) elite, as flying from Port Harcourt in the Southeast to Lagos in the Southwest, for example, was more than 10 times costlier (but also literally 10 times faster) than taking a bus. I don't know how long it took before someone humorously attached the name *okada* to the new motorcycle taxis, but by the time I returned for fieldwork in 1995, the name was ubiquitous in the Southeast and common throughout much of the country.

Calling motorcycle taxis *okada* was a playful means of recognizing and criticizing inequality. While Nigeria's super-elite were busy buying fleets of jets to set up private airlines, ordinary citizens were condemned to ride on the backs of motorcycles to get where they had to go in order to survive. "The elite have their *okada*; we have ours," one friend told me when I first asked why motorcycle taxis shared the same name as the country's biggest private airline.

Although most Nigerians recognized and appreciated the irony inherent in calling motorcycle taxis *okada*, these motorcycles taxis were much more than the nickname that became attached to them. As a sector of Nigeria's urban economy, as an arena of political ferment, and as an object of constant popular discourse, *okada* offer a revealing window onto the aspirations and discontents associated with urbanization, a more monetized economy, and new patterns of social inequality that accompanied these changes. In other words, *okada* became emblematic of people's anxieties about the nature and future of social reproduction. Like the AIDS epidemic, popular understandings of *okada* reflect Nigerians' sense of social and moral crisis.

Like other trappings of modernity, *okada* were both a welcomed innovation and a symbol of decline.

The Economics of *Okada*

The first *okada* driver I knew was Nwabuko Osundu. Nwabuko worked as a night watchman at the compound in Owerri where I lived when I worked for the NGO. In those years, as I mentioned, there was no such thing as a motorcycle taxi in Owerri. But Nwabuko owned a motorcycle that he used for personal transportation. Nwabuko did not earn much as a night watch-man——I knew that in order to survive, he and his wife also had a small business in the local market, where he spent much of the day before arriving for his night job. Nwabuko had 11 children and was barely making ends meet.

When I returned to Nigeria in 1995, Nwabuko was still working as a night watchman at the NGO compound, but by then *okada* had emerged as a new and popular form of public transportation. Nwabuko had capitalized on this development and was using his motorcycle for the *okada* business during the day. He left his wife to oversee their market stall. He told me that driving *okada* had made a big difference in his ability to feed his family.

In 1995 Nwabuko was probably in his mid- to late fifties. His hair was al-most fully gray. Many Nigerians have advised me that, when given a choice, it is better to select an older *okada* driver——one who obviously has a fam-ily. The popular perception is that *okada* drivers drive too fast and too care-lessly, even recklessly. Older men are presumed to be "more likely to value human life because they have responsibilities to others," as one friend told me, than are single young men, who are not tethered to wives and children. Older men like Nwabuko were certainly not rare in the *okada* business, nor was it uncommon for men to combine *okada* with other efforts to earn an income. But it was much more typical for these motorcycle taxi drivers to be young, and for their motorcycles to be their main, and usually exclusive, form of income.

Nwabuko explained to me the hardships of driving *okada*. In addition to describing the unforgiving sun, the heavy rains, and the dangers of driving on crowded roads amid cars, trucks, and buses, whose drivers who often exhibited little regard for the safety of motorcyclists, he recounted numer-ous instances of harassment and exploitation by the police. Although the motorcycle taxi business started and remained more or less informal, at various junctures state and local governments tried to impose regulations. These included requiring *okada* drivers to register their motorcycles and receive official numbers as well as a brief attempt to mandate the use of helmets. Drivers like Nwabuko perceived these regulations as opportunism by bureaucrats who wanted to capture a portion of the *okada* drivers' small profits, and above all as avenues for police to extort bribes when motorcyclists could not provide appropriate paperwork, a helmet, or whatever else the officers requested based on a changing (and often only partly verifiable) legal code. In Nwabuko's opinion, the bottom line in all this regulation and police harassment was money: "In Nigeria there is no space for a poor man to earn a living. And even when we find something meager, like driving *okada*, police and the big men who run government will find ways to chop [eat] the little we gain. All these checkpoints and rules they impose, it is just because they know we are carrying cash. They just want a share of the money. Nigeria na war-o! [Nigeria is a war]." The notion that *okada* drivers both desperately need and frequently have cash, the ultimate symbol of aspirations as well as discontents in contemporary Nigeria, reverberates through popular discourse about them.

Another *okada* driver I got to know well was Chidi Aguyi. Chidi drove a motorcycle taxi in the southeastern city of Umuahia for several years. I met him because he was from a household just near where I lived in Ubakala. He attended primary school close to his modest village home, where he lived with his parents and his six brothers and sisters in a compound that included two uncles and their wives and many cousins. He attended Ubakala Secondary School for three years before he was forced to drop out because his parents could no longer pay his school fees. A third son, Chidi had not performed particularly well in school. His parents chose to invest more in their other children's education. This practice of selective investment is common in southeastern Nigeria: although education has become an increasingly valued credential for success, it by no means guarantees a job in Nigeria's weak economy, and the cost of school fees and the high levels of unemployment for graduates mean that more parents are careful in how they spend their limited financial resources for their children's education.

One of the surprises associated with the proliferation of secondary and university education in southeastern Nigeria is that girls now attend and graduate from secondary school in higher numbers than boys (Federal Ministry of Education 2006). In popular discourse, this is explained by the fact that boys are dropping out of school to pursue business (often encouraged by their parents' struggles to pay school fees), while parents continue to pay for their daughters' education because educated daughters fare better in the marriage market. An educated young woman is seen as more likely to find a good husband. Even for young men, the marriage market looms as a factor in the decision to pursue business rather than education. Most young men in southeastern Nigeria anticipate the costs of marrying with dread because of the escalating expense of bridewealth, the expectation to perform both a traditional wedding ceremony and a Christian ceremony, and the reality of the exorbitant costs of "befitting" traditional and church ceremonies. Formal education and a job in the civil service (historically, a common path for graduates) won't, by themselves, generate the amounts of money required.

In this context, when Chidi's parents explained to him in 2001 that they could no longer afford his school fees, his first thoughts were that he would pursue business. But of course business requires capital, which he and his family didn't have. A common strategy among Igbos for entering business is to become an apprentice to a person with an established trade (Silverstein 1984; Meagher 2010). Typically, an apprentice will work for his master for a number of years learning the business, usually with little or no formal pay but often with a provision of room and board. At the end of the apprenticeship period, when the trade has been well learned, the master is expected to provide the apprentice with the capital to start his own business. The apprenticeship system spans skilled occupations like carpentry, masonry, plumbing, and shoe-making to more commercial enterprises like small businesses that specialize in selling pharmaceuticals, textiles, electronics, or motor vehicle spare parts, all of which are sectors that Igbos are renowned for dominating in Nigeria (Silverstein 1984; Chukwuezi 2001; Meagher 2006, 2009, 2010). Although many apprenticeships go well, disputes commonly arise——for example, accusations that the apprentice is stealing money, perceptions that the master is keeping the apprentice too long and with too little compensation, and, especially, disagreements over the amount of capital provided upon "graduation."

When Chidi was forced to drop out of secondary school at age 16, his father arranged for him to become an apprentice to a relative who ran a business selling electronics in Aba, the bustling commercial city about 30 miles from Ubakala. Chidi worked for this "uncle" for about a year but complained bitterly to his parents that he was not well treated. He slept uncomfortably on a mat in the "boys' quarters" behind his uncle's house in Aba. He reported that the food he was given was not sufficient. The long hours at his uncle's shop and the poor treatment made him——and eventually his parents——skeptical that his apprenticeship would result in the expected capital from his master. Eventually, he left Aba and returned to the village. By this time he was nearly 18 years old. He hoped his parents would consider helping him resume secondary school, but they were finding it increasingly difficult to pay his elder brother's university tuition and the fees of Chidi's younger siblings who were still in school. They could not afford it. Chidi approached a number of his uncles in the village in the hope that they might be willing to pay his fees, but no one was able to do so. He spent almost two years in Ubakala living in the family compound, helping his parents with some farming and doing occasional odd jobs. But mostly he was idle and anxious for an opportunity to earn money.

The desire to make money was a regular refrain among young men and women in southeastern Nigeria. The completion (or early termination) of schooling produced an intense focus on finding ways to make money—whether it was through employment, business, or occasionally more nefarious means. The need for money was motivated by many factors. Of course, the need to survive—to pay for food, clothing, and shelter—was a paramount reason why people, especially the poor, needed money. But the importance of money was also driven by loftier goals than survival. Increasingly, young Nigerians—and many older people, too—measure status in relation to consumption. The desire for money was not just to pay for necessities but also to enable the purchase of fashionable clothes, cell phones, and, ultimately, automobiles and fine houses. Certainly the vast majority of Nigerians still cannot afford cars or fancy houses, but the aspirations for them are widespread—arguably almost ubiquitous. Money was considered by almost all the young people I knew as the key to fulfilling their dreams.

But it would be inaccurate to attribute Nigerians' desire for money to pure materialism. In many respects, people's perception that money is imperative for a good life is tied to prosocial values. Young Nigerians commonly mention the cost of marriage, child rearing, and funerals—three of the most significant arenas of sociality and social reproduction in Nigeria—as the reasons they are so anxious to make money, along with obligations to assist to parents, siblings, and extended family. When Chidi was languishing in Ubakala after his failed apprenticeship and we talked about his prospects for employment, he said, "I need to make money. Everything in Nigeria is costly now. Without enough money I cannot marry and have children. Without money I am nothing. I am nobody."

It is important to note that the monetization of social reproduction—the fact that marriage, child rearing, care for kin, funerals, and just about every other significant element in the creation and maintenance of families and communities seems to cost more and more money—generates at least as much anxiety as the perception that individualism, greed, and the readiness to act immorally to get rich are on the rise. In other words, Nigerians consider the monetization of everyday life associated with urbanization and the ever-wider expansion of a capitalist economy to be problematic not only because so-called traditional values and institutions are threatened or eroded, but also because even highly valued prosocial behaviors like marrying, raising children, and caring for kin are now seen as dependent on having money. Ironically, that the pursuit of money is believed to be necessary for prosocial goals and not just for individual accumulation or aggrandizement means that the desire for cash is even more intense, and the monetization of everyday life feels, to many, intractable, even as it is often lamented.

Nigerians' seeming obsession with money——both the desire for it and the concerns about its social consequences——animates popular culture. For example, stories about "money magic" have circulated at least since the rise of the oil economy in the 1970s, when the amounts of wealth people amassed seemed magical indeed (Barber 1982; Apter 1999, 2005; Smith 2001a, 2007a). These narratives about magical wealth reflect the hopes and discontents engendered by new possibilities for wealth associated with the rise of a money economy as well as the frustrations of Nigeria's tremendous economic inequalities. When Chidi and I talked about his experience as an apprentice in Aba, he related a story about a magical process called "washing money" that was similar to others I'd heard many times before:

> One of the businessmen selling near my uncle lost plenty trying to wash money. A Yoruba man [among Igbos, Yorubas from southwestern Nigeria are renowned for their prowess in magic] came to our area boasting that he had a portmanteau full of 500-naira notes that had been coated black by the Central Bank for security purposes. Only a special formula would enable the money to be cleaned and usable, and the Yoruba man said he'd cracked the formula. To prove it, he brought several notes from the stacks of blackened notes and rubbed them with a liquid which removed the black coat. I saw it myself. He said the police were tracking him and he had to offload the money, but that he would give the portmanteau and the formula to a buyer for 500,000 naira. The bag contained notes worth 5 million [the equivalent of about $40,000 at the time]. My uncle didn't have enough cash on hand, but his neighbor was able to raise the money the same day. Upon being paid, the Yoruba man assisted the buyer to wash the first several bills and then departed. When the man and his apprentice continued to wash the money, several more notes came clean and then the formula stopped working. The man was duped out of 500,000 naira.

As with so many of these narratives I've heard over the years, many elements intersect to tell a complex story about aspirations for wealth, the possibilities for seemingly magical enrichment, and the realities of frustrated ambitions in Nigeria. The scam Chidi recounted includes an unscrupulous conman who gets rich at the expense of others but also a victim who falls for the scam because of his own greed. Much of the popular discourse about scams and fast wealth involves some notion of the culpability of the victims. Further, there is often a sense that the magical achievement of wealth really is possible. Chidi was unsure about whether the Yoruba conman never had the power to wash money or whether he simply failed to actually share it as promised. Despite (and perhaps partly because of) the prevalence of scam stories, many people do believe that money magic is real. As Andrew Apter (1999, 2005) and others (Barber 1982) have noted, in Nigeria's oil economy, the methods and speed by which people actually become fabulously rich do indeed appear magical. But for the vast majority of ordinary Nigerians——and certainly for the vast majority of unemployed young men who became *okada* drivers——there are no magical ways to accumulate the money they so desperately want and need. The road to survival is much more arduous. Like many thousands of young men before him, to pursue his ambitions, Chidi eventually became an *okada* driver.

In 2004, someone advised Chidi that an Ubakala man——a distant kinsman——with a successful business in Umuahia had acquired a number of new motorcycles and was looking for riders to use them as *okada*. Chidi's father approached the kinsman to see if Chidi might be able to drive for the man. Such personal connections are crucial to finding employment in Nigeria, whether in the formal or the informal sector. The businessman agreed to let Chidi be an *okada* driver. The arrangement was a common one. The businessman handed over the motorcycle to Chidi with the expectation that Chidi was fully responsible for fueling and maintenance. Based on local knowledge about the amount of money a motorcycle taxi can generate in a single day, the two parties agreed on an amount that Chidi would pay to his patron each month, with whatever profit made above that amount being Chidi's. Further, it was agreed that if Chidi was able to pay this monthly amount for two years, the motorcycle would become his. If he defaulted, the vehicle would revert to the businessman who, in effect, leased it to him.

Although there were some months when Chidi was not able to pay the full amount that was agreed——either because he was sick, because he had family problems that required him to contribute money, or because he simply overspent his earnings, by and large the arrangement worked out well. The businessman was tolerant of Chidi's few lapses, and at the end of two years he transferred ownership of the motorcycle to Chidi. At this point Chidi began to think about saving to purchase a new motorcycle, as two years is actually a long life for the Chinese-made motorcycles used by *okada* drivers.

Okada Men, Inequality, and the Moralization of AIDS

Personal, political, and economic insecurity marked the lives of *okada* drivers like Chidi. What is more, *okada* drivers themselves became such pronounced sources and symbols for urban insecurity that it ultimately led to their demise. The insecurities *okada* men experienced, represented, and to some extent created in urban Nigeria speak to the complex connections between money and morality throughout contemporary Nigeria. The anxieties provoked by *okada* drivers' behavior are similar to the angst associated with AIDS in that both focus on the moral hazards of behaviors tied to desires for money. Nigerian interpretations of and responses to HIV and AIDS are ultimately grounded in discontents about how society is changing in ways that ordinary people perceive as exacerbating inequality and undermining morality. The phenomenon of *okada* crystallized many complex and entangled elements of this unease, including the recognition that people are complicit participants in the monetization of everyday life even as they commonly and simultaneously lament these trends.

That *okada* drivers became the objects of popular rumors purporting that they had easy access to sex with university girls because they had cash is indicative of these connections. Such stories signaled collective apprehension about a demise of morality associated with monetary greed, excessive consumption, and commodified sex. However, these stories also represented misgivings about the effects of formal education, long periods of adulthood before marriage, and the difficulties of maintaining collective, kin-based control over behavior, since urban living allows and even cultivates greater individualism.

When Chidi was driving *okada*, it was evident that his parents developed concerns about the effects of the job on his behavior. Although he generally lived in Ubakala, driving his motorcycle to Umuahia each morning to find passengers, many nights he did not come home. His parents worried (and, as I observed, not without cause) that he sometimes failed to come home because he had spent the night drinking with fellow *okada* drivers or cavorting with prostitutes. Further, although Chidi did contribute to family expenses like siblings' school fees, a bill for medical services for his mother, and financial obligations to the church and the village development union, he frequently told his parents he was without cash. His father found this annoying when Chidi was also sometimes sporting new clothes, carrying a cell phone, and meeting friends in the evening at local joints in Ubakala. Although his parents were happy Chidi was earning money, they worried that being an *okada* driver was corrupting him morally.

To fully understand how Nigerian responses to AIDS are tied to entangled concerns about inequality and immorality that also frame the experiences of *okada* drivers and the popular mythology that arose about them, I now turn to a further exploration of the position of these drivers in popular interpretations of the local moral economy. The pervasive collective sense of crisis in Nigeria must be understood along economic, political, and moral dimensions. *Okada* drivers were positioned at the nexus of these intersecting forces, the same intertwining dynamics that drive both Nigeria's AIDS epidemic and the moralizing discourses it has engendered.

I have already highlighted the economic insecurity that underlies the *okada* occupation, both in the social structural factors that created space for this commercial niche and in the daily struggle to survive that these men and their clientele experienced. Equally illuminating are the ways that *okada* men responded to this insecurity, a story that connects economics to politics and shows how *okada* men were both active agents and unwitting pawns in the larger saga of growing inequality associated with social change in contemporary Nigeria.

Insecurity, Injustice, and *Okada* Politics

The pervasive presence of *okada* in the urban Nigerian landscape was accentuated by the fact that *okada* drivers frequently assembled in very large numbers. When scores of *okada* congregated, it was often in response to their own feelings of insecurity, their numbers creating a sense of collective solidarity and power. But when they gathered en masse, they also often generated a sense of insecurity among the individuals who could be the target of their ire, whether customers, car or bus drivers with whom an *okada* driver had an accident, or even the police, with whom they frequently had disputes. As is the case for anyone who has spent time in southeastern cities in Nigeria, on many occasions I witnessed *okada* drivers swarming together for some reason. These throngs of *okada* men evoked the sense of a mob. More than once, I saw these gatherings erupt with violent consequences. To understand these (albeit not widespread) instances of *okada* drivers participating in collective violence——and the symbolic effects of these occur-

3. In Nigeria, *okada* motorcyclists have come to symbolize the many
struggles, aspirations, and insecurities of urban life.

rences on the wider public——it is necessary to examine the *okada* business
in the context of a sense of insecurity in Nigeria more broadly.

In addition to the pickup points around town where *okada* congregated
because business was best——for example, outside the main market, in
front of schools and offices at the close of the day, and by bus stations——
the most common venues where *okada* assembled in large numbers were
those connected to issues of political and economic tension. For example,
in southeastern cities like Umuahia, Owerri, and Aba, one could always find
a score or more of *okada* gathered by newspaper vendors' stands or sidewalk
spreads. Here the drivers read the papers (or listened to a comrade read a
story aloud); interpreted local, national, and international news; discussed
politics; and embellished the journalism with their own stories and rumors.
These were sites of highly charged political debate. It was common to hear
loud arguments and heated discussion. Yet although *okada* drivers were
known for their lively and contentious discourse, politicians also targeted
them as a potentially potent collective block of political support.

The governor of Abia State from 1999–2007, Orji Uzo Kalu, actively
cultivated the support of *okada* men in the lead-up to the 1999 and 2003

elections, particularly in Aba, the state's commercial hub and most populous city. He provided hundreds of motorcycles, either free or through generous "hire-purchase" arrangements, and he made improving Aba's deteriorating roads one of his most publicized campaign promises. *Okada* drivers were staunchly behind Kalu, and they proved effective in mobilizing support among the much larger populations of young people in the city, including the tens of thousands working in the informal economy. Given that Nigerian elections are notorious for vote-rigging, intimidation, and outright violence, it is not surprising that many citizens saw Kalu's cultivation of *okada* drivers as tantamount to recruiting an extensive band of thugs whom he could mobilize for nefarious purposes. Although most *okada* men certainly did not participate in election violence, many stories circulated of fraud and intimidation in both the 1999 and 2003 elections in Abia State, including accusations that *okada* drivers were among Kalu's thugs.

Another venue where *okada* commonly amassed was at petrol filling stations. Despite the fact that Nigeria is the world's eighth largest petroleum producer, supplies of domestic petroleum products are regularly scarce because of corruption, poor maintenance of the country's refineries, and constant hoarding by marketers in anticipation of deregulation of the highly subsidized domestic market. Indeed, in the long queues that frequently frustrate motorists' efforts to refill their vehicles, *okada* drivers and other customers routinely discussed the country's fuel shortages as emblematic of the larger problems of inequality and injustice associated with a state-dominated oil economy (Smith 2007a). Tensions frequently arose in fuel queues as motorcycle taxis, buses, and private motorists vied for access to the pumps after longs hours waiting under a scorching sun (or in driving rains). During Nigeria's epidemic fuel shortages, hardly a day passes without news reports of violence at the pumps, sometimes resulting in deaths. *Okada* drivers were often in the middle of these conflicts. They could be mafia-like in protecting what they saw as their right to access (at their insistence, it was accepted practice that several motorcycles could fuel for every car or bus that reached the pump) and vigilante-like in enforcing proper conduct, including among their own ranks. My own experience watching *okada* enforcement of "the rules" in Nigeria's fuel queues was also an ambivalent combination of gratefulness that they were there to impose some order in a highly charged atmosphere and unease because the nature of this order always felt like a tinderbox on the verge of explosion.

It is worth noting that in contemporary Nigeria, where people are justifiably highly distrustful of government, and where suspicions about the motives of others have filtered into everyday life, fear of deception and fraud permeate many arenas of life (Gore and Pratten 2003; Smith 2007a). Such distrust is what gave rise to the kinds of anxieties that underlay the early HIV conspiracy theory stories I discussed in the introduction, as well as the tensions around *okada* men. At the same time, in the world of informal businesses, stringent moral codes that require high levels of trust operate quite effectively and are absolutely necessary for these enterprises to succeed (Meagher 2006, 2009, 2010). The rules that *okada* drivers enforce in queues at filling stations are an example of this, and the solidarity that *okada* drivers exhibit when one of their own is in an accident is evidence of a moral community they have created in the face of inequalities and injustices they confront every day in their work. The consequences of this moral solidarity can be positive or negative, offering protection but sometimes producing violence.

The mafia/vigilante dichotomy characteristic of the *okada* drivers' role in policing filling station queues also aptly captures my final example of frequent *okada* mass assembly in southeastern Nigeria: their response to a traffic accident involving one of their own. Every car and bus driver in southeastern Nigeria realized that a crash with an *okada* meant potential trouble. Drivers of larger vehicles commonly cursed *okada* for their aggressive and often reckless tactics in traffic, and indeed many car and bus drivers used their size advantage to try to intimidate motorcyclists, but an accident with one of them inevitably brought a swarm of their two-wheeled compatriots within seconds.

There are two main ways to read the mass response by *okada* men to an accident, and, in my view, each of them contains some truth. First, the rapid arrival of fellow riders was a way of insuring *okada* drivers' security——both in terms of prevention, because auto and bus drivers came to know that hitting a motorcycle taxi was considered an offense against a whole army of *okada* men, and in terms of treatment, as the huge gathering of riders would pressure auto and bus drivers to pay for hospital or repair bills and also prevent police from mistreating or extorting bribes from a motorcyclist. In this view, *okada* drivers were responding to their own sense of insecurity——as drivers of vulnerable vehicles and as poor workers in an informal economy who might be exploited by wealthier and more powerful elites who own cars, or by the police who carried guns and were notorious for turning motor vehicle accidents into personal paydays.

Second, the swarming response of *okada* can be read as a means by which these men contributed to the prevailing sense of insecurity in urban Nigeria and used their numbers and their reputation as ruffians to exploit a situation for their own gain. I heard countless stories from automobile drivers, and witnessed several instances myself (though, fortunately, I never had an accident with a motorcycle taxi), where the *okada* "mob" extorted a large payment from an automobile, bus, or lorry driver, ostensibly for medical treatment or motorcycle repair, in exchange for dispersing the crowd and relieving the fear of collective violence. Sometimes the motorcyclists forced auto drivers to pay even when it seemed obvious that the fault for the accident lay with the *okada* driver. If the police arrived before negotiations were concluded, one could see on full display the complex dynamics of inequality and injustice as they unfolded at the intersection of the informal economy, the state, and the citizenry, because the police must be "settled" (paid off) as well.

The Demise of *Okada*

The anxieties linked to *okada* drivers——the popular concerns about the political and economic insecurity they indexed——ultimately gained more weight than their use-value could offset. In January 2010, when I returned to Nigeria after more than two years' absence, perhaps the most remarkable change was the absolute and sudden disappearance of *okada* from all the cities in the Southeast. They had been banned in the middle of 2009 by the governments of the Igbo-speaking states (Abia, Anambra, Ebonyi, Enugu, and Imo) because of their perceived connection to and facilitation of crime, especially the spate of kidnappings for ransom that appeared to be the latest enterprise of criminal gangs in Nigeria. In late 2008 and early 2009, a number of high-profile kidnappings resulted in murder, and stories circulated that the kidnappers routinely used *okada* to perpetrate their crimes and facilitate their getaways.

In May 2009 my friends in Nigeria were so worried about the epidemic of kidnappings that they convinced me to postpone a trip I had planned for June and July because they believed I would not be safe. I kept tabs on the stories of kidnappings in the Nigerian media and followed up on them when I did return to Nigeria the following January. I think it is fair to say that the popular fear exceeded what was warranted by the actual prevalence of these crimes. But during my trip that January, I found myself looking over my shoulder more than I used to, and I changed my behavior to accommodate my friends' concern about my safety and my own fears, mainly by heading home before dark and telling fewer people about my planned journeys between Ubakala, Umuahia, and Owerri. Numerous people remarked that these kidnappings commonly involved "insiders," evoking a sense of mistrust that is common in a society where concerns about deception and betrayal in the pursuit of wealth and power are widespread.

The kidnapping-for-ransom "epidemic" evolved from years of such practices in the Niger Delta, where militants have kidnapped oil workers in an enterprise that often blurs the boundaries between the political and the criminal (Watts 2007). In the Southeast, it seemed to be purely a criminal pursuit, though obviously the fact that the targets were elites and the belief that the perpetrators were disaffected youths (including *okada* drivers) together suggest a political-economic dimension. But my sense is that these crimes were not actually very common, and that the collective panic they instilled reflected a larger sense of insecurity in Nigeria, in which the poor feel exploited by inequality and elites feel threatened by the instability of their position in a tremendously unequal society. Arguably, the underlying criminalization of *okada* drivers——banning all of them because of suspicions that some of them were involved in kidnapping and other crimes—— projects blame onto one segment of the urban poor, thereby avoiding a more politically oriented critique that would be threatening to the elite.

Whether intentional or not, this deflection of culpability away from the political elites seems to have been the result of the ban. Although the prohibition of *okada* was undertaken by the state governments and could be seen as an effort by the state to protect elite interests, it has proved widely popular, even among ordinary people. *Okada* motorcyclists have been replaced on the streets of southeastern cities, to some extent, by three-wheeled vehicles common in India and known there as auto-rickshaws. In southeastern Nigeria they are known as *keke-na-pep*. Each one can comfortably carry three passengers. Almost without exception, everyone I asked viewed them as an improvement, in part because they feel much safer to ride in but also because, as one friend put it, "they have restored some semblance of order to our streets." Even though the alleged involvement of *okada* in the kidnapping spree was the foremost justification for their ban, popular support for the demise of *okada* was connected to the general sense of insecurity and disorder associated with this sector of Nigeria's urban economy. The perception that the causes and consequences of inequality are rooted in moral problems——such as *okada* drivers' behavior in domains ranging from their domination of public space to their suspected sexual practices——leads to morally focused solutions, like banning these "bad" men from the streets. As with moralistic responses to the AIDS epidemic, addressing social inequality as a moral problem neglects, and arguably protects, the underlying social and political structures.

I wondered how *okada* men were now making a living. I was told that some managed to become *keke* drivers. Others moved their *okada* business to the periphery——they were still permitted on the outskirts of town, ferrying passengers from bus stops to more rural suburbs and villages. But clearly, many motorcyclists simply lost their livelihood.

Conclusion

In this account of motorcycle taxis in southeastern Nigeria, I have made the argument that the moral discourses that circulated about *okada*, like those about AIDS, were rooted in Nigerians' anxieties about and ambivalent experiences regarding urbanization, the increasing monetization of social and economic life, and the sense that new and disquieting inequalities are both caused by and exacerbating the demise of collective morality. AIDS and *okada* were directly connected in the stories of university girls willing to exchange sex for cash. But what is more, both AIDS and *okada* are simultaneously seen as products of the precarious struggle to survive in Nigeria——symbols for the things that Nigerians see going wrong in their society. Whether it is people sacrificing their bodies to earn their living, individuals eschewing long-accepted notions of civility and propriety in pursuit of money, men and women choosing to have anonymous and risky sex, or taking another person hostage for ransom, such examples all reflect a sense of the impossibility of proper social relations in a world where the economic promises of education are not available to all and can disappoint even those who attain schooling, where the traditional system of patronage cannot satisfy people's needs, and where violence exacted both structurally and personally is widespread. Beyond the number of people infected, sick, and dead from AIDS, beyond the hardships of *okada* drivers, the havoc they wrought, or any actual role they played in urban crime, both AIDS and *okada* are evocative icons of concerns about greed, individualism, political and economic insecurity, and widespread perceptions of moral crisis. Although AIDS and *okada* are both popularly seen as consequences of and contributors to these problematic forms of social change, they are also evocative symbols through which Nigerians grapple with much wider perceived threats to morality, sociality, and social reproduction.

TWO

Gender Inequality, Sexual Morality, and AIDS

In 1996, while I was conducting dissertation fieldwork, riots erupted in Owerri. They were spurred by a case of child kidnapping and murder, which had led to allegations that the city's new elite were using cannibalistic rituals to enable them to accumulate fabulous wealth so quickly that only witch-craft could explain it. Sociologically, the riots and the rumors of magical "fast wealth" appeared to be expressions of discontent about the changing face of inequality in Nigeria, where "big men" were no longer honoring their obligations to ordinary people, and patron-clientism was devolving into unbridled greed, naked exploitation, and unchecked power on the part of elites (Smith 2001a, 2007a). During the riots, the houses and businesses of the so-called new elite were burned, as were a few Pentecostal churches that were believed to be helping these people in their nefarious activities (Smith 2001d).

Receiving less attention in the media, and in the government report about the riots published later, was the fact that the rioters had stripped naked many young women, sometimes beating them as well (Imo State Government 1997). In interviews I conducted around Owerri in the days af-ter the riots, I was told that some of these women were stripped and beaten for their "indecent dressing." The offenders had blamed the women's cloth-ing choices——variously described as tight jeans, midriff-baring halter tops, short skirts, or any outfit perceived as sexually provocative——for an array social ills, including men's extramarital sex, male students' poor grades in secondary school and university, the failure of a younger generation of men to marry (because young women they might have married were instead sell-ing themselves as mistresses to "sugar daddies"——older married men with money), and, most disturbingly, the plague of AIDS in Nigeria.

Over the years the "problem" of women's indecent dressing has been a recurrent theme in Nigeria, both in the Muslim North and the Christian South. Numerous evils like those listed by rioters in Owerri are commonly attributed to this sartorial expression of women's perceived wayward sexual morality. Many Nigerian universities have adopted rules against indecent dressing. Secondary schools require all students to wear uniforms, and many mandate girls to cut their hair nearly down to the scalp so as to temper the sexual allure of styled long hair. Pentecostal pastors regularly preach against the temptations to sin created by indecent dressing. Nigerian parliamentarians have on more than one occasion proposed legislation to ban provocative attire to protect the nation. The focus on women's dress and the attribution of the cause of AIDS to women's material and sexual desires are overt manifestations not only of gender inequality but also of the centrality of concerns about sexual morality in how Nigerians think about problems associated with many contemporary social changes more generally. In an insightful edited volume, Adeline Masquelier reminds us that "the scholarly literature on dress, bodies, and personhood suggests . . . that, far from being rooted in discrete sets of unambiguous and unchanging contrasts, understandings of nudity, propriety, and modesty are produced and reproduced in historically specific contexts" (2005a, 3). By extension, dichotomies between appropriate and inappropriate dress are never simple binaries but rather fruitful spaces for contestation over social morality.

These tensions are not exclusively about the nature of clothing. A broad range of things have come to be seen as indices of sexual morality. Public discourse about gender, sexuality, and AIDS is animated by concerns about the dynamic between interpersonal intimacy and material exchange——or, more crudely, between sex and money. Certainly the intertwining of love and money in sexual relationships predates AIDS and the broader social changes I address in this book. As mentioned in chapter 1, in many African societies the very expression of love involves gifts, economic support, and a range of material exchanges that both solidify and build upon the sexual and emotional dimensions of intimate relationships (Cole 2004; Cole and Thomas 2009; Hunter 2002).[1] But in contemporary Nigeria the blurry boundary between economics and emotion has been sharpened by the material aspirations and growing inequalities brought about by social transformations associated with interrelated phenomena such as the expansion of capitalism, modern consumerism, urbanization, and the monetization of social and economic life.

In Nigeria, people's sense that the intertwining of sexual intimacy and exchange has become more baldly materialistic is colloquially captured in

4. Bars, restaurants, and hotels are common places of employment for young
female rural–urban migrants, and such occupations frequently
entangle them in gender-unequal sexual economies.

the widely recognized saying that there is "no romance without finance."
The phrase can be employed differently by men and women to advance
individual or gendered agendas, but it is also used as a discourse of com-
plaint. Among women, the phrase can signal the importance of making sure
men back up their desire for sexual intimacy with tangible care and support.
Among men, it usually alludes to what is perceived as women's growing
demands for money and material things as part of any romantic or sexual
relationship.

The AIDS epidemic has heightened the stakes of normative gendered
practice and sexual intimacy. As the spread of the disease has magnified the
risk of infection, sickness, and death, the moral discourses that AIDS has
generated have made behaviors related to sexuality——whether it is how
people dress, whom they have sex with, or how they negotiate relationships with their partners——the object of increased social scrutiny. Even as
changes associated with modern, urban social life in Nigeria have provided
people——perhaps especially women——with new liberties and opportunities, gender inequality is reproduced in novel and powerful ways. In this

chapter, I examine how unmarried young Igbo women navigate the complicated landscape of work, sex, and social relationships in the era of AIDS, where their strategies to survive and to improve their lives are often judged through moral lenses shaped by the epidemic. I then examine the reverse side of the gendered dynamic, focusing specifically on married men and their extramarital sexual behavior. The analysis links economic and gender inequality to powerful moral economies that undergird gendered disparities and also influence Nigerians' understandings of and responses to AIDS and the social changes associated with the epidemic.

"Survival Sex": Gender, Economics, and Sexuality

The literature on sexuality in Africa has multiplied seemingly exponentially in the wake of the AIDS epidemic, with researchers working to understand the political-economic, social, and cultural underpinnings of patterns of risk and infection. Given that Africa's epidemic is overwhelmingly driven by heterosexual transmission, most scholarship has focused on heterosexual cultures and behaviors. Sometimes unwittingly, scholarship about African sexualities and AIDS has fed into pernicious stereotypes about promiscuous African sexual traditions (Caldwell, Caldwell, and Quiggen 1989). As I will show in this chapter, it is more accurate to explain risky sexual behavior in the context of the contradictions created by conservative sexual moralities combined with situations of profound material deprivation and growing economic aspirations than to attribute behavior to some sort of "African" cultural promiscuity. I argue that understanding morally driven interpretations and responses to social inequality are central to making sense of patterns of risky behavior and infection.

Further, a disproportionate amount of research and scholarship about AIDS and sexuality focuses on women's sexual behavior, though there have been many important exceptions that address heterosexual men's sexuality (Setel 1996, 1999; Campbell 1995; Hunter 2005; Parikh 2007; Simpson 2009; Skovdal et al. 2011; Spronk 2012). A good deal of the literature on Africa has focused on understanding the degree of women's agency in sexual decision making, and particularly the relationship between gender inequality, economic deprivation, and women's sexual behavior. By focusing on both women and men, in this chapter I try to address not only the contexts and motives of women who are involved in what is variously described as survival sex (Preston-Whyte et al. 2000), transactional sex (Leclerc-Madlala 2003), and informal sex work (Wojcicki 2002a), but also the sociological reasons why men participate in these kinds of sexual unions (i.e., moving beyond the notion that somehow men just "need" multiple partners or extramarital sex) (Swidler and Watkins 2007; Hirsch et al. 2009; Spronk 2012).

In African studies, the recognition that women's sexuality can be an economic resource, that the meaning and deployment of women's sexuality is deeply connected to entrenched systems of gender inequality, and that sexual relationships between men and women that have an economic dimension are nonetheless not necessarily easily or accurately characterized as "prostitution" precedes the AIDS epidemic (Bleek 1976; Dinan 1983; White 1990). But in recent years scholarship aimed at understanding patterns of heterosexual transmission in Africa has focused particularly on the complex relationship between women's vulnerability and women's agency, as their sexual behavior can put them and others at risk of HIV infection. Scholars have rightly pointed out that for many African women the combination of poverty and gender inequality is often deadly, as women have been put in positions where risky sexual relations are one of the only means of survival (Schoepf 1992; Ulin 1992). The idea that circumstances of gender and economic inequality put women at risk of HIV infection remains pertinent, and the concept of "survival sex" as articulated by Preston-Whyte et al. (2000) and others (e.g., Wojcicki 2002b) emphasizes the extent to which women are structurally constrained and therefore often forced to rely on risky sexual liaisons to support themselves and their families.

Without discounting the extent to which many women rely on prostitution and other forms of transactional sex simply to survive, a considerable body of literature has shown that women use sexual relationships with men not simply to survive but also to advance their aspirations for consumption, to achieve educational and employment goals well beyond mere survival, and to enable them to help fulfill obligations to family (Hunter 2002; Leclerc-Madlala 2003; Johnson-Hanks 2006; Cole 2010). Acknowledging women's agency and the aspirations beyond survival that motivate various kinds of transactional relationships need not contradict the fundamental point that economic hardships and gender inequalities create contexts that put women in vulnerable positions, increasing the likelihood that they will become infected with HIV and infect others. But attention to women's agency and to the panoply of socially mediated expectations and desires that frame and motivate sexual behaviors offers a more nuanced perspective on the relationship between economics, gender, sexuality, and HIV risk. In this chapter I build on this approach and also emphasize the importance of people's moral understandings of these contexts. I explore the behavioral consequences of the desire to perceive (and have others perceive) one's sexual behavior as morally appropriate. Even in its breach (for example, among women who work openly as prostitutes), the importance of morality in explaining people's understandings and behaviors related to AIDS is manifested.

As I try to illustrate in the second part of the chapter on men's extramarital sexual behavior, the contexts and motives that explain men's conduct also require unraveling the complex intertwining of materiality and morality. While African men's heterosexual behavior has received increasing attention, and many important studies have deepened our understanding of men's positions and their role in perpetuating the epidemic (Setel 1999; Luke 2005; Simpson 2009), relatively little work has explored the relationship between material and moral aspirations as they shape male sexuality (though for a recent example, see Spronk 2012). Ann Swidler and Susan Watkins (2007) offer a major contribution by pointing to the ways that men with multiple partners are building on and reflecting much wider societal patterns and traditions in which acting like a good patron is a culturally rewarded and socially productive aspect of competent masculinity. They argue persuasively that it is just as important to understand the social logic of men's choices in so-called transactional sexual relationships as it is to situate women's behavior. Below I argue that men in extramarital sexual relationships are highly attuned to social expectations related to masculinity, social class, and the fulfillment of duties to kin and community. As with women, men's sexual behavior——including behavior that appears to be conducive to spreading HIV——must be understood as taking place in a context where men care deeply about the perceived morality of their conduct. Seeing men who cheat on their wives as moral actors——even as they engage in seemingly immoral behavior——offers a more nuanced and accurate perspective on their motivations and conduct. Before turning to married men, however, I focus on the young, unmarried women who are the object of so much critical moral discourse in Nigeria.

Young Women's Economic Aspirations and Migration

In recent decades, demographers and other social scientists have drawn attention to the growing proportion of rural–urban migrants in sub-Saharan Africa who are female, young, and unmarried (Brockerhoff and Eu 1993; Gugler and Ludwar-Ene 1995; Makinwa-Adebusoye, 1990). This trend represents a relatively new pattern, as previous rural–urban migration streams had been predominantly male, and women tended to move as the married partners of male migrants rather than as single and independent agents. In

Nigeria, as in much of the continent, the factors that propel this migration are numerous and reflect the multifaceted and tangled ways in which this pattern of mobility is indicative of both persistent gender inequality and significant transformations that can be seen as positive for women.

In southeastern Nigeria, it is a relatively recent idea that socially acceptable trajectories for success for women include education, employment, and other means of income generation beyond traditional occupations of farming and local rural trade. In most circumstances, a decision to migrate is viewed in economic terms, whether the goal is more immediate, as when looking for a job, or longer term, as when seeking higher education as a gateway to future economic success. Women's personal aspirations are reinforced by changing norms. More often than not, young unmarried women undertake migration with the consent of their parents and extended family.

Although most young women make migration decisions in consultation with kin, the spectrum of experiences is broad. Regardless of the relative level and tenor of family support or coercion, nearly all young female migrants are expected to try to help their extended families through whatever success they achieve as migrants. Indeed, for the vast majority of young rural–urban migrants in Nigeria——both men and women——the continued ties and obligations to parents, siblings, and wider networks of kin in their rural places of origin are paramount in how they navigate the opportunities and challenges of city life (Gugler 2002; Chukwuezi, 2001). Most young female migrants leave for the city with loftier hopes than working in hotels, restaurants, or bars, but many are compelled to find work in these sectors in order to survive and to help their families back home.

The first sections of this chapter focus on understanding how single young women from southeastern Nigeria traverse and survive urban life in Kano, the largest city in northern Nigeria and a major destination for Igbo rural–urban migrants. Although scholars have typically identified the ways young female migrants participate in urban sexual economies as evidence of gender-unequal economic and cultural systems and processes, the ethnographic data presented below suggest that the situation is more nuanced. As Cole has observed in Madagascar, "not all anxiety about women's behavior is generated for the same reasons, nor does it always lead to the greater control of women" (2010, 18). In Nigeria, the scope and diversity of the local sexual economy, the spectrum of young women's experiences, and the moral discourses about migration, gender, and sexuality that are produced in response to this situation reveal the complexity and contradictions inherent in the country's changing structure of gender inequality.

Although many forms of young female migrants' participation in Kano's sexual economy can be viewed as exploitive, in other circumstances women employ their sexuality productively, benefiting from their relationships with men. This suggests that the ultimate effects and meanings of these practices vis-à-vis gender inequality may be multidimensional and not simply negative for women (Susser and Stein 2000; Leclerc-Madlala 2003). Further, the experiences of young female migrants in Nigeria suggest that the moral dimensions of this sexual economy can have equal or greater consequences for the reproduction of gender inequality than do the more material aspects—a reality exacerbated by the AIDS epidemic.

Brothels, Bar Girls, and Nigeria's Urban Sexual Economy

In 2001 I began a two-year study of unmarried Igbo rural–urban migrants from southeastern Nigeria who were between 15 and 24 years old and residing in Kano (Smith 2003a, 2004a). At the time, the Igbo community in Kano was large. Tens of thousands of migrants from the Southeast lived in the city. Many of them resided in an area called Sabon Gari, often translated as "Strangers' Quarter" (Paden 1973). Because of their outsider status as Christian Igbos in the predominantly Hausa-speaking Muslim North, the migrant community was cohesive and in some ways insular (Anthony 2002). My study included a survey of 431 male and female migrants (roughly half men and half women), intensive interviews with 20 young people from the larger sample, and several months of participant observation. Most of the participant observation entailed spending time with migrants in the places where they lived and socialized, but especially where they worked. To get access to young women, this meant spending a lot of hours at restaurants, taverns, and hotels because these locations offered among the few available occupations for female migrants from the Southeast.

In analyzing the strategies that enabled young women to adapt to city life, it became clear that female migrants inevitably navigated the local sexual economy in one of several ways. For most of these women, sexual relationships with men proved to be a major means for garnering economic support, albeit through practices that spanned a wide range of forms with regard to the explicitness of the economic basis for the relationships, the intimacy and duration of ties, and the moral valence for the women, their partners, and the larger community.

For analytical purposes, I differentiate three positions available to young Igbo women on the spectrum of relationships in Kano's sexual economy: (1) commercial sex work, mostly associated with brothels; (2) sexual relationships, often transactional, that usually originate from connections established in the plethora of local bars, taverns, eateries, and hotels that serve alcohol in Kano's migrant quarter; and (3) longer-term relationships that are less explicitly economic and often include a notion of romance and commitment. Of course, as the above discussion of the literature suggests, many kinds of relationships do not fit neatly in one category. Some relationships evolve over time from one type to another, and many women experience more than one type of relationship, either over time or concurrently. In this chapter, I focus on the first two categories. Chapter 3—which focuses on the influence of religion, especially Pentecostal Christianity, on Nigerians' interpretations of and behavioral responses to AIDS—deals more directly with the third category of sexual relationship.

"My Daughter Is Working in Kano": Commercial Sex Workers, Economic Dependence, and Moral Independence

When my survey team, made up mostly of young Igbos who were students and faculty at Bayero University in Kano, fanned out across the city to interview migrants, one of the supervisors, a middle-aged university lecturer from the Southeast, expressed considerable surprise at the number of young migrant women working as commercial sex workers in brothels. He characterized his palpable dismay in a phrase that was repeated frequently by members of the research team over the study period. He lamented that he would never again react the same when, back home in the Southeast, the parent of a young female migrant announced proudly: "My daughter is working in Kano." Little did their parents suspect, he suggested, what sort of work their daughters were doing.

By coincidence, one of the elders among the Ubakala migrants in Kano to whom I had been directed when I started my research was the owner of a brothel. Through this connection I was able to gain entry to his hotel and other similar establishments with greater ease than if I had simply tried to observe brothels and interview sex workers on my own.

Interviews with young women working in brothels indicated that most of them resorted to sex work in response to economic circumstances in which they felt they had few other viable options. Data from the larger survey sample confirmed that women who were sex workers commonly had no kin in Kano who could help them. In the Igbo migrant population generally, more than half of the young female migrants had kin in the city, and many of them boarded with a relative. The lack of local kinship ties increased young women's economic insecurity, but it also freed them somewhat from the moral gaze of extended family who would have considered sex work extremely stigmatizing.

Ogadimma, one of the sex workers I interviewed, migrated to Kano from the Southeast when she was 18 years old, after dropping out of secondary school when her mother could no longer afford the school fees. Her father had died several years earlier. She came north because one of her father's relatives (she called him her "uncle," as is the custom) had a business selling cosmetics in Kano, and he agreed to employ her and provide her room and board. Within weeks of arriving, Ogadimma knew that she would not be happy with the arrangement. Her uncle made her work long hours in the shop, and her uncle's wife expected her to do heavy domestic chores like cooking, cleaning, and washing clothes. "She treated me like her maid," Ogadimma said, "only I had to do the maid's job after spending all day minding the shop." Further, Ogadimma complained, her uncle rarely paid her anything beyond room and board.

She wanted to go home to her village and sent messages to her mother to that effect. But Ogadimma had three junior siblings, and her mother begged her to keep working. Ogadimma knew the extent of her mother's burdens, but eventually she could not bear her mistreatment and she left her uncle's house and shop. She took a room in a cheap local hotel that doubles as a brothel. She said she did not intend to embark on sex work, but when her meager savings were exhausted, she began commercial sex work in order to provide for herself. She later moved to another hotel, where she negotiated a firmer arrangement with the proprietor.

Ogadimma's working conditions were fairly typical of the social organization of prostitution in Kano, at least of the sex work that occurs in Sabon Gari's brothels. She maintained a permanent room in the hotel, which had perhaps 20 to 25 rooms. About half were occupied by sex workers; the other half were let as hotel rooms just like in any hotel. Ogadimma's arrangement with the proprietor was that she paid a weekly "rent." Factored into that rent was the proprietor's knowledge that Ogadimma was using the room for prostitution, which gave him leverage to negotiate the price upward. But also factored in was her knowledge that she was a permanent tenant in a hotel business that otherwise can suffer from fluctuating occupancy, enabling her to negotiate the price downward. Not all the women in the hotel paid exactly the same amount, but the rates fell within a reasonably close range——as did the price that customers paid for having sex with Ogadimma or another sex worker.

The arrangement between the proprietor and Ogadimma also included an informal code of conduct vis-à-vis regular hotel customers. On the one hand, both the proprietor and the sex workers knew that many hotel customers were potential clients for the sex workers, and the sex workers were expected and encouraged to make their services available and enticing to hotel guests. On the other hand, not every hotel guest was seeking commercial sex, so Ogadimma and her fellow tenants were expected to know when to draw back and not push their trade too hard, so as not to alienate this segment of the hotel's clientele. Further, because many clients (and many sex workers) liked to drink alcohol as part of their experience, the sex workers had to strike the right balance between being good hosts and not raising such a ruckus that everyone in the hotel was kept awake. During the time I spent conducting research in brothels in Kano and interviewing migrant sex workers like Ogadimma, I witnessed several instances where these boundaries were contested and reestablished as proprietors argued with sex workers about noise or about complaints from hotel guests over aggressive behavior. The sex workers held their own in these arguments because the proprietors were well aware of how much of their profits were generated by keeping these women in residence.

The living conditions for Ogadimma and her peers were poor. By and large, these brothels were cheap, dirty, and dangerous places. Ogadimma's room, which I asked to see during the daytime, had a simple bed, a bedside table, a larger table, a ceiling fan, a black-and-white TV, a sink, and a large suitcase that contained most of her possessions. The floors and walls were concrete, and the paint was peeling. The kitchen, toilet, and shower were communal, and water often did not run. Electricity was sporadic, although the proprietor usually ran a generator until about one in the morning while the hotel bar was open. All of the sex workers I interviewed said they always used condoms with clients. When I asked to see them everyone showed me supplies, but several admitted that others would sell sex without condoms if the price was high enough. Many of the sex workers had a more stable relationship with an individual man, which they defined differently than their commercial relationships with clients. Most admitted that they didn't always use condoms with their boyfriends.

In addition to the risks of STIs and HIV, the specter of violence loomed large. Ogadimma and others told me of stories of drunken clients who hit——even beat——them in negotiations over money. More recently, as Islamic sharia became the de facto law in Kano, as in much of northern Nigeria, brothels in Sabon Gari have become targets of vigilante groups purporting to promote Muslim values. Numerous brothels were raided and vandalized by these groups (often as part of wider ethnic/religious conflicts in the city), and many of the sex workers had been beaten in these raids. On top of the economic insecurity, gender inequality, and health risks associated with this niche in Nigeria's informal economy, Kano's commercial sex workers experienced insecurity associated with the moral stigma attached to their way of making a living.

But as much as young migrant women like Ogadimma live precarious lives on the edge of survival in an occupation that stigmatizes them, it is important to acknowledge the degree to which their aspirations, decisions, and lives are still very much embedded in the networks of kinship and community that motivate most Nigerians. Although Ogadimma's life in Kano was in many ways marginal——she did not participate in the meetings of her hometown association, and those Igbos who knew she was a prostitute shunned her in various ways——back home in the Southeast she maintained her family ties. She visited once every year or two, and she regularly sent remittances home to her mother to help with food and schooling for her junior siblings. "I do this work because I have to," she said. "When I can save enough money and my juniors are trained, I will leave Kano and go home. I want to marry and have children like anyone else."

Ogadimma, like many other Igbo sex workers in Kano, maintained ties and had aspirations connected to her family, community of origin, and cultural traditions, but it is also true that being a sex worker offered certain freedoms that most Igbo women don't have. Young migrant women who engaged in professional sex work seemed to escape many of the moral boundaries that constrain the behavior of typical women. They drank alcohol and smoked much more commonly and openly than other women. More significantly, they talked to men with much greater liberty, arguing with them, laughing at them, and cursing them in ways that most women would find difficult and dangerous. They also had more autonomy in spending their savings and more latitude with regard to mobility than single young women living with kin.

I do not mean to suggest by any means that female sex work is a path to gender equality. In addition to the physical dangers, commercial sex work is highly stigmatized both in the larger Igbo migrant community in Kano and in Nigeria generally. But because sex work puts women "beyond the pale" morally, their source of economic livelihood offers them considerable liberties that are unavailable to women who are more observant of social and moral norms. My point is not to put forth some misguided celebration of sex work but rather to compare and contrast it with other ways that young migrant women navigate Kano's urban sexual economy. For many young migrant women who work in other sectors in Kano, shared notions of morality and perceptions that city life is undermining traditional norms intersect with their livelihoods and their sexual behavior. Morality reinforces gender inequality as much as economics does. This occurs in ways that also indicate how social responses to AIDS must be interpreted in the context of people's aspirations and anxieties about the future. Women who work in bars, restaurants, and hotels who do not see themselves (and are generally not seen by others) as sex workers nonetheless find themselves caught up in economic and moral economies in which AIDS looms large.

"Is She or Isn't She?"

Full-fledged commercial sex work is undertaken by a relatively small fraction of unmarried Igbo migrant women; many more work in jobs at bars, taverns, eateries, and hotels that do not double as brothels. Sabon Gari is renowned for its booming nightlife. Cities in the Southeast——like Umuahia and Owerri, where I normally conduct fieldwork——close down quickly after dark, partly out of fear of crime. By 9 P.M. in Igboland, few businesses are open aside from vendors selling cooked food and small provisions. By midnight the streets are virtually empty and the danger increases because the police assume that anyone out and about at that hour might be a criminal. By contrast, in Sabon Gari in 2001 (long before fears created by the recently emergent violent Islamist group, Boko Haram), nightlife was just beginning by 10 or 11 P.M. The quarter's many restaurants and taverns set up chairs and tables outdoors, and the smell of grilled meat, boiling pepper soup, and fried yams filled the air.

The reasons for Sabon Gari's once vibrant nightlife are many. First, northern Nigeria is extremely hot during the day, thus the night brings a welcome respite that makes socializing outdoors appealing. Second, as the city's migrants' quarter, populated mostly by southerners who are Christians, Sabon Gari is a haven of vices (especially the sale of alcohol and commercial sex) that are strictly prohibited in the Muslim areas of the city. As a result, many local Hausa men come to Sabon Gari at night to partake in activities that they would not want to be seen doing in their own neighborhoods and that are not available there. Indeed, this is a source of much criticism among the southern migrants, who complain that Hausa Muslims are hypocrites——sending young vigilantes to burn brothels, break beer bottles, and beat prostitutes, even as men of means from the same communities come to Sabon Gari to partake in these very vices. No doubt there are Hausa Muslims who are hypocrites——just as there are Igbo Christians who are hypocrites——but the local Hausa clientele in Sabon Gari was a much different segment of the population than the vigilantes. During my fieldwork in Kano, it seemed obvious that most Muslims did not drink alcohol or visit prostitutes. Nevertheless, many of my Igbo interlocutors reveled in painting Hausa Muslims with a broad brush, especially when they could point out contradictions between their professed beliefs and their behaviors.

A third reason for the animated nightlife in Sabon Gari comes from within the migrant population itself. Igbos (who make up the majority of southerners in Kano) and other migrants work hard to earn their livings, and the active nightlife offers an opportunity to enjoy the few hours they have to themselves. Additionally, most migrants lived in extremely cramped quarters, and therefore used their accommodations only for sleeping and storing their belongings; there was no space to do anything social at home. Kano's energetic nightlife provided business opportunities for some migrants and much-needed leisure for others.

The women who work at the scores of nightspots in Sabon Gari tend to be single and in their twenties. At taverns and restaurants these young women cook food, wash dishes, serve drinks, and wait tables. Their arrangements with their employers (who are often older migrant women) vary, spanning from simple wage-labor contracts (so many nights of work for a fixed amount of pay) to apprenticeship-like agreements, where the employee receives room and board from her "madam." Where these young women sit on the spectrum of Kano's informal sexual economy is also highly variable, and it is this landscape that I will now illustrate and explain.

Ngozi worked at a late-night tavern that served beer and an assortment of food, including grilled fish, pepper soup, and *ishi ewu*, or goat's head soup, a nationally renowned Igbo delicacy. At 22 years old when I first interviewed her, Ngozi had been in Kano for two years. She completed secondary school in her village but had been unable to secure admission to a university. After a couple of years living in her parents' house without a job, it was agreed that she would migrate to the city in search of work. She came to Kano because an "auntie" related to her mother had a business selling drinks (beer and soft drinks) wholesale, and she had agreed to let Ngozi board with her in exchange for working there.

The arrangement with her auntie lasted several months, but it was never intended to be enduring. Ngozi was eager to find something better. Good jobs are scarce in Kano, as they are throughout Nigeria, and although Ngozi would have preferred something like a job in a bank or in the civil service, the opportunity did not materialize. She was able to secure the job at the tavern because the "madam" proprietor was a customer of her auntie. The madam assured Ngozi that she would make more money at the tavern—— not only would her salary be slightly higher; she could also make money in tips from patrons. In addition, the madam could offer Ngozi a room in the quarters she kept near her business. The independence appealed to Ngozi. Her auntie was skeptical about the job, openly airing her worry that such jobs were for "harlots" (which is a stereotypical view). But she was not prepared to continue supporting Ngozi, so she didn't try to prevent the move by reporting and complaining to Ngozi's parents back in the Southeast.

Many of the young women I talked to who worked in this sector spoke of how the work "hardened" them. Their explanations of what they meant by this referred to the long and late hours and the drudgery of the work, which meant carrying out domestic-like chores, but in the service of a paying public. Cooking, serving, and washing dishes are very much women's——or children's——work in Nigeria. This gendered division of labor is in many ways naturalized. Questioning it can be difficult and even taboo. But the dynamics are a bit different when clients, who are mostly men, are paying for this service. It produces more conscious resentment among the women who work in these sectors, in part because the clientele also frequently allude to sex or openly harass female workers.

The sometimes abusive treatment by customers—who commonly speak to the young women working in these jobs with a tone of superiority and even derision, and also with frequent allusions to sex—magnifies women's feelings of being "hardened." Although the gendered division of labor in the domestic sphere in communities where these young migrants come from is highly unequal and quite clearly benefits men, the inequality is tempered by norms of kinship and the fact that those relationships are regular and enduring. Even men who order their wives and daughters around the house quite dictatorially must be sure to maintain socially sanctioned norms of respect for their women. In commercial settings like taverns and restaurants, this is not necessarily the case. Further, inequality is exacerbated by the fact that male patrons feel doubly entitled to their sense of superiority because they are paying. It is important to note that female customers can also be condescending to male service providers, but the added element of gender inequality means that young women in the service sector are particularly subject to maltreatment.

All of this is heightened by the added element of sexual tension that pervades these venues. It is a complicated milieu. The young women often feel harassed by male clients, but there is no doubt that many young women who work in taverns and restaurants also actively take advantage of the gender-unequal sexual dynamics that characterize interactions with customers. They do so for several, often interrelated reasons.

First, both their employers and their customers expect it of them. Even relatively polite customers generally want to be able to banter and flirt with the staff. Second, the young women themselves are highly motivated to perform this gendered sexual dynamic because this is how they are most likely to receive a tip (or "dash"). When a customer does give a dash, it is usually the result of a rapport that the service provider has successfully cultivated. Third, and not insignificantly, such flirtation leaves open the possibility that a nice man might become a supportive sexual partner or even a steady boyfriend.

In addition to the instrumental incentives for such banter, it is important not to underestimate the shared pleasure of such sociality. Although the gender-unequal dynamics of these interactions and the fairly blatant sexual allusions that pepper such talk would be politically incorrect in most Western contexts (and, indeed, might constitute prosecutable sexual harassment), these behaviors are not typically judged as negatively in Nigeria. There is no doubt that gender inequality and a fundamental double standard characterize men's and women's positions in these interactions in Nigeria, but to see them only in these terms would be to overlook the pleasures that both men and women take in these dynamics in this setting. It may seem like a contradiction to say that circumstances that reproduce gender inequality and put women in positions where they must endure sexual harassment can also be contexts of enjoyment that sometimes create opportunities to advance their goals. But this is the reality.

An example from one evening when I sat with members of my research team at the tavern where Ngozi worked will convey some of the nuances of these situations. By midnight the place was busy, with the 25 or so tables outside each occupied by one to four customers. Ngozi and one other waitress were responsible for serving all these customers, with one other worker at the bar to give them beers and soft drinks and two women overseeing the cooking and dishing of food. The proprietor supervised it all and also engaged in her own banter with customers, many of whom were regulars. As Ngozi did her work, she engaged in playful conversation with customers, much of which had sexual undertones, but other elements that personalize the relationship between service provider and customer were also evident, especially in the idiom of kinship, as I will elaborate below.

At the table next to ours were three men, all Igbo and all probably in their late thirties or early forties. One was obviously a regular——he knew Ngozi's name, and Ngozi knew his brand of beer. The other two men were his guests visiting Kano on business, as I learned overhearing some of the conversation. Over the course of the evening, both visitors engaged in openly flirtatious conversation with Ngozi. Much of the interaction centered on the fact that Ngozi was from the same area in the Southeast as one man's mother. He made much of the idea that "his people" and "her people" commonly married and suggested that she might make a good wife. There was every possibility that this man was already married and little possibility that he actually intended to court Ngozi. But the playful talk about marriage served at once to personalize the customer–service provider interaction and to suggest the possibility that the conversation could transform into something more——the "something more" being tacitly understood as a sexual relationship.

It would have been unusual for Ngozi to end up sleeping with one of these men. Each night she engages in playful flirtation with many customers, and she certainly could not have sex with all of them, even if she wanted to——and she most definitely did not want to. But I know from building rapport over several months of periodic conversations that she did on occasion end up in sexual relationships with men she met at the tavern. In comparison with the number of men who propositioned her, these were rare liaisons, and she insisted that it was only with men she got to know well over time. She told me more than once, "I am not a harlot," contrasting herself with other women working in her tavern and in nearby joints who, she said, "go about here and there."

The spectrum of entertainment establishments, the intentions and behaviors of young women, and the kinds of relationships that unfold are highly diverse. In some cases, the line between sex work and tavern work is blurry; in others, young women only sleep with a man when the relationship could be understood as a romantically inclined or emotionally committed. Ngozi portrayed herself as closer to the latter, though she did not say that she had to be "in love" in order to have sex. But in almost all instances neither partner views what they are doing as commercial sex, although it is true that a man is almost always expected to provide some form of economic support.

Young women working in these sectors must be careful not to behave too much like sex workers, as their physical attraction, emotional appeal, and reputation depend on obscuring or euphemizing the economic aspect of a sexual relationship. In the evenings when my Igbo research team sometimes assembled at a tavern for a meal or a drink, male members of the team openly speculated about whether some of the bar girls were "really" commercial sex workers. Most illuminating was the fact that these male researchers——like many men——seemed to find most alluring those young women who appeared least obviously interested in their money. Perhaps ironically, in-depth interviews and informal discussions with many men and women revealed that the actual level of economic support that men provided in any sexual relationship was similar, even when the encounter was perceived in less overtly economic terms. Indeed, I found considerable evidence to suggest that young women actually accrued greater financial rewards the more able they were to shroud any economic motivations. The importance of sexual relationships appearing moral——and, implicitly, not purely economic——did not undermine the reality that sexual relationships typically include male economic support for female lovers.

Perhaps not surprisingly, women who behaved more conservatively—— exhibiting shyness, a degree of submissiveness to male authority, and a naïveté (whether genuine or feigned) about the sexual undertones of men's overtures——were both less likely to be judged as sex workers and more likely to be pursued by men who sought a less-stigmatized sexual union than commercial sex. In certain respects, the decorum necessary for a young female migrant to distinguish herself from a prostitute required behavior that reinforced gendered stereotypes that keep women subservient to men. Perhaps the most significant and potentially deleterious example of this was attitudes toward the use of condoms. Many young women reported that it was difficult and awkward for them to suggest using condoms with their lovers, partly because such a suggestion made them appear, as several men and women put it, "too professional." This contrasted starkly with the accounts of women working in the brothels, who reported the most regular use of condoms of any women in the sample, and who commonly asserted that they demanded their clients use them. The contrast between sex workers and other women with regard to the capacity to negotiate condom use with men is but one example of how morality can be as powerful as economics in reproducing gender inequality.

"No Finance without Romance": Gender Inequality, Economic Struggle, and Morality

Young unmarried women in cities in Nigeria must steer their way through entrenched forms of gender inequality, traversing a complex sexual economy as they try to survive and succeed in urban environments. My findings in Kano, which emphasize the moral as well as the material dimensions of social systems, do not suggest that the economic foundations and consequences of gender inequality are any less significant than has been emphasized in the literature (Presto-Whyte et al. 2000; Wojcicki 2002a). But by examining the complex terrain of the Kano migrant community's sexual economy, we see the multifaceted and sometimes contradictory circumstances, strategies, and consequences that are entailed in negotiations between sexual mores and economic aspirations. While an ideal scenario would move women toward both economic and moral equality, the realities of the sexual economy in Kano suggest that young migrant women frequently must navigate uneven moral and material terrains, trading currencies across domains, risking failure in one realm for success in the other, trying to keep their reputations intact even as they secure their livelihoods, and reinforcing some aspects of gender inequality even as they challenge others.

Relatively few women end up as commercial sex workers like Ogadimma, yet most must find their way through the complex intersection of monetary, moral, and sexual economies as they both struggle to pursue their aspirations and work to preserve their reputations. The pressures that bar girls and others in the service and entertainment sectors faced in concealing any economic motives also affected those young women who were neither commercial sex workers nor service industry employees. While my research suggested that sex workers and service workers tended to be more economically and socially vulnerable than many other migrant women (as they generally had less income, poorer housing, and fewer Kano-based kin), many young migrant women who fit neither category also had precarious livelihoods and relied on men with whom they had sexual relationships for economic support. For such women, the importance of assuring the perceived morality of the relationship was paramount, as men were much more likely to spend significantly on women who they believed were sexually exclusive and emotionally bound to them——even in cases where the men were already married to someone else.

As I explained at the beginning of the chapter, throughout Nigeria, young women commonly express self-awareness about the economic motivations for sexual relationships with men by the phrase "there is no romance without finance." While this expression suggests women's strategic economic use of their sexuality, it is equally revealing to invert the phrase and note that for women to succeed in securing the most valuable male support——that which is not only the most financially lucrative but also the most socially acceptable——they must behave in ways that privilege other aspects of the relationship above blatant material exchange. In this sense, for women seeking to avoid the stigma of prostitution, "there is no finance without romance."

Most young women interviewed in Kano wholeheartedly preferred relationships where they received financial support in the context of emotionally supportive and socially and morally sanctioned relationships. But it was clear that in this gender-unequal society, in order to please men, women had to behave in ways that reinforced their dependence on them (see also Swidler and Watkins 2007). Men expected significant degrees of acquiescence to male needs and priorities before conveying economic support and moral approval.

Over the past two decades, these challenging circumstances have been complicated by Nigeria's AIDS epidemic. For women like Ogadimma, who sell sex in order to survive and whose ability to adopt protective behaviors is directly affected by what clients are willing to pay for as well as by the threat of violence that accompanies their trade, the threat of HIV infection looms large. Yet, ironically, because commercial sex work is so ubiquitously associated with immorality and AIDS, sex workers appear to have an easier time negotiating condom use and protecting themselves from infection than other women do.

I do not mean to minimize the risks to sex workers. Over the past 10 years, I have interviewed about two dozen of them, not only in Kano but also in the southeastern towns of Owerri and Umuahia. Although all of these women were among the most forthcoming I have encountered in Nigeria when it comes to talking about AIDS and condom use, there is no doubt that they face many risks——from violence, from clients who are willing to pay extra for sex without condoms, and from their own boyfriends, with whom they are much less likely to use protection. Indeed, it is in this latter instance that sex workers are much like the majority of young migrant women I have studied, who must navigate not only economic hardships, frustrated aspirations, and the biological risk of HIV infection, but also the moral hazards associated with women's sexual behavior in the era of AIDS.

For women like Ngozi, and dozens of others I have interviewed and gotten to know over the past 20 years, it is a continuous challenge to balance economic exigencies, their social reputations, and their own emotional and physical desires. As Nigeria changes so rapidly——with increases in rural–urban migration, higher levels of formal education, ever-growing exposure to globally circulating ideas, practices, and commodities, and a huge young population that is increasingly likely to stay unmarried for up to a decade after reaching sexual maturity——the sexual and moral lives of young women and the country's AIDS epidemic are interconnected in a collective imagination that is deeply ambivalent about all these transformations. Both AIDS and young women's freer sexuality are emblematic in many people's minds of the social and moral crises that are understood as accompanying wider social changes.

Nigerians' collective ambivalence about inequalities generated by contemporary social changes in general, and about the AIDS epidemic in particular, has focused significantly on the lives of young people. The younger generations are viewed as personifying new aspirations and lifestyles that reflect transformations in the country's political economy that many Nigerians find both appealing and troubling. The popular concern with young people, and especially their sexual practices, is also a product of the fact that the social lives and cultural mores of the next generations embody the outcome of current processes of social reproduction (Cole and Durham 2007). As the stories about young people's lives suggest, many Nigerians are anxious about how changes in the political economy and in social relationships affect shared morality. These worries are most tangibly voiced with regard to young people's sexual behavior and the widely shared understanding of AIDS as the consequence of these collective moral failings. Condemnation of youthful sexual morality is focused especially on young women because of gendered double standards but also because their virtue and their failures stand symbolically for the moral state of society more generally.

Men's Extramarital Sex: Masculinity, Money, and Morality

Concerns over rising inequality and degenerating morality are directed not only at the youth, nor are they exclusively targeted at women. In Nigeria, a perceived epidemic of men's extramarital sex is also a topic of intense public discourse. While some of the blame for men's infidelity is projected onto their younger female partners, who are portrayed as trading sexual favors too easily in order to satisfy their increasingly materialistic ambitions, unfaithful married men are also sometimes the objects of derision. As with so many aspects of people's discontents about contemporary sexuality, modern immorality, and processes of social change, though, men's extramarital sexual behavior occurs in a context where widely shared aspirations and social rewards accompany the same social practices about which Nigerians are uneasy. Further, men's extramarital sex in contemporary Nigeria cannot be understood independently of tremendous transformations in marriage that have occurred over the past several decades, changes about which Nigerians are also highly ambivalent. While many people celebrate and embrace the emergence of the idea that selection of a marriage partner should be based, at least in part, on individual choice and the ideal of romantic love, there is a sense that marriage is becoming unmoored from ties to kin and community, which creates considerable apprehension.

The transmission of HIV within marriage is a significant contributor to Nigeria's AIDS epidemic. Over the past decade, studies have suggested that for many women around the world, a primary path to infection is having sex with their husbands (Hirsch et al. 2002; Hirsch et al. 2007; Parikh 2007; Wardlow 2007). In light of the emphasis on abstinence and being faithful (the "A" and "B" in the ABC approach to AIDS prevention) in public health campaigns to combat AIDS in Nigeria, the fact of marital infection is obviously deeply problematic for women, and for the assumptions that underlie the entire ABC enterprise——which only works if both partners are HIV negative and if both partners remain faithful. The problem with messages of abstinence and faithfulness is that moral understandings of HIV risk interfere with efforts to understand and address the ways various forms of inequality underpin actual patterns of infection. In the remainder of this chapter, I focus on the relationship between the changing institution of marriage, shifting but persistent gender inequality, and men's extramarital sexual behavior.

Modern Marriage in Southeastern Nigeria

Scholars of West African society have long recognized the pronounced social importance of marriage and fertility in the region (Fortes 1978; Bledsoe and Pison 1994; Smith 2001b). Over the past several decades, African societies have changed dramatically, and with these changes the institution of marriage has also been transformed. Modern marriages were becoming increasingly common in urban centers in West Africa more than 50 years ago, and in some places these changes have even earlier roots (Little and Price 1973; Harrell-Bond 1975; Mann 1985). In Igbo-speaking southeastern Nigeria, urban elites have practiced what might be called modern marriage since the 1950s, but only in the past two or three decades have new forms of marriage become common among ordinary people, including in rural areas (Obiechina 1973; Okonjo 1992).

Perhaps the most concise way to contrast modern Igbo marriages with those of the past is to note that modern couples see their marriages as life projects in which they are the primary actors, whereas marriages in the past were more obviously embedded in the structures of the extended family. The differences are most pronounced in narratives about courtship, in the way husbands and wives describe how they resolve marital quarrels, and in the way they make decisions about and contribute to their children's upbringing and education. In each of these arenas people in more modern marriages tend to emphasize the primacy of the individual couple, often in conscious opposition to the constraints imposed by ties to kinship and community.

But it is important not to exaggerate these trends. Even in the most modern marriages, ties to kin and community remain strong, and the reality of marriage and child rearing continues to be a social project, strongly embedded in the relationships and values of the extended family system. Indeed, the continued importance of ties to family and community and ongoing concerns about the collective expectations of wider social networks permeate people's stories of modern courtship, the resolution of marital disputes, and decisions about child rearing. The choice of a future spouse based on love is, in almost all cases, still subjected to the advice and consent of families. The fact that modern marriage in southeastern Nigeria remains a resolutely social endeavor creates contradictions for younger couples, who must navigate not only their individual relationships but also the outward representation of their marriages to kin and community. Most couples seek to portray their marriages to themselves and to others as being modern and moral. This is crucial to explaining the dynamics of men's extramarital sexual relationships, married women's responses to men's infidelity, and the risk of HIV infection in marriage.

Modern Marriage and Men's Infidelity

The prevalence of married men's participation in extramarital sex in Nigeria is well documented (Karanja 1987; Orubuloye, Caldwell and Caldwell 1991; Lawoyin and Larsen 2002; Mitsunaga et al. 2005). Conventional scholarly understandings and explanations for the phenomenon are problematic, however, because they tend to reproduce common stereotypes; they often ignore the diversity and complexity of these relationships; and they usually overlook the ambivalence that sometimes accompanies this behavior. As in many societies, people in southeastern Nigeria commonly attribute married men's frequent participation in extramarital sexual relationships to some sort of innate male predisposition, and this perspective is well represented in the literature (Isiugo-Abanihe 1994; Orubuloye, Caldwell, and Caldwell 1997). Many Igbo men and women I interviewed as part of the multicountry study on "Love, Marriage, and HIV" articulated this view.[2] In response to a question about why married men seek extramarital lovers, a 54-year-old civil engineer in Owerri repeated a Pidgin English phrase heard frequently among Nigerian men: "Man no be wood. It's something men need, especially

African men. You know we have a polygamous culture. This practice of marrying only one wife is the influence of Christianity. But men still have that desire for more than one woman." Only a piece of wood, he implies, lacks an outward-looking sexual appetite.

The notion that men naturally want or need multiple sexual partners is reinforced by gendered norms that produce and perpetuate a double standard about extramarital sex. Over the past two decades, I have spent scores of evenings in settings in southeastern Nigeria where married men entertain their unmarried girlfriends or talk with their male peers about their extramarital sexual experiences and partners. I remember asking a particularly colorful older Igbo man who was quite blatant in his philandering about the consequences of extramarital affairs for men and women. He replied, quite boastfully, "If I catch my wife, she is gone; if she catches me, she is gone too." In other words, not only was it unacceptable for her to have extramarital sex; it was also unacceptable for her to object to his having extramarital sex. However, as I show below, although this man's claim of male privilege in the realm of extramarital sex is generally reflective of a prevailing double standard, it reveals little about the real contexts of how men and women navigate marriage and infidelity.

Men's extramarital sexual behavior is socially produced and organized. From interviews with men about their extramarital relationships, from listening to men's conversations among themselves pertaining to these relationships, and from observations of men interacting with their extramarital partners in various public or semi-public settings, a number of patterns in the social organization of extramarital sex become apparent. Three sociological factors are particularly important for explaining the opportunity structures that facilitate men's participation in extramarital sexual relationships: work-related migration, the intertwining of masculinity and socioeconomic status, and involvement in predominately male peer-groups that encourage or reward extramarital sexual relations. Each of these factors is integrally connected to the social changes about which Nigerians are so uneasy. Expectations that married men demonstrate both masculinity and economic capability by keeping extramarital lovers also produces worries that men's traditional obligations to their families are being undermined. But in reality, and similar to what Swidler and Watkins (2007) have argued based on ethnographic data from Malawi, married men's behavior vis-à-vis both their lovers and their wives and families tends to observe and reinforce notions of masculinity in which men support dependents. As I will show below, the discretion with which most men conduct their extramarital affairs is driven in part by their own desires to uphold values associated with marriage and kinship, even as they behave in ways that can appear to threaten those same relationships and institutions.

Mobility and Men's Extramarital Sex

Of the 20 married men interviewed in depth in southeastern Nigeria as part of the "Love, Marriage, and HIV" study, 14 reported having extramarital sex at some point during their marriages, and of the six who said they had not engaged in extramarital sex, four had been married less than five years. Approximately half of all the cases of extramarital relationships described in the interviews occurred in situations where work-related mobility was a factor. Men whose work takes them away from their wives and families are more likely to have extramarital relationships, and they frequently attribute their behavior to the opportunities and emotional hardships produced by these absences. A 47-year-old civil servant whose postings frequently took him away from his family explained a relatively long-term relationship with a woman in one of the places he was transferred: "I stayed a long time without my wife. But eventually this woman befriended me. She was a widow and a very nice woman. She cooked for me and provided companionship. Later, I was transferred back home, and it was over. It was like that." While men's representations of hardship as a justification for extramarital sex contradict the realities of male privilege in Nigeria's social order, they nevertheless reflect many Nigerians' experience that labor-related migration creates not only opportunities but also pressures to become involved in extramarital relationships.

Further, extramarital relationships in the context of work-related migration can be more easily hidden from wives, family, and neighbors. Every man in the sample who admitted to having extramarital sex expressed the importance of keeping such relationships secret not only from their wives but also from their extended families. Men's motivations for keeping extramarital relationships hidden included a desire to maintain peace and uphold the appearance of fidelity for their wives and a clear concern to protect their own social reputations. The same man quoted above explained: "I am a mature man with responsibilities in my community——in the church, in various associations. I hold offices in these organizations. I can't be seen to be running here and there chasing after women. My own son is almost a man now. How can I advise him if I am known for doing this and that?" To the degree that male infidelity is socially acceptable, it is even more strongly expected that outside affairs should not threaten a marriage, and this mandates some discretion.

Masculinity and Money

In the vast majority of cases described in the interviews, issues of socio-economic status, specifically the intersection of economic and gender inequality, featured prominently in men's accounts of their extramarital relationships. Most often, a man's relationship to his female lover included an expectation that the man provide certain kinds of economic support. Men frequently view extramarital relationships as arenas for the expression of economic and masculine status. Indeed, it is necessary to understand the relationships between masculinity and wealth, and gender and economics more generally, to make sense of the most common forms of extramarital sexual activity in southeastern Nigeria.

According to popular discourse, the most common form of economically driven extramarital relationship is the "sugar daddy" relationship, wherein a married man of means engages in a sexual relationship with a much younger and much poorer woman with the expectation that the man will provide various forms of economic support in exchange for sex. Many Nigerians, including many of the participants in these relationships, view sugar daddy relationships in fairly stark economic terms, but a closer look at these relationships suggests that they are much more complicated than stereotypically portrayed (for nuanced accounts focusing on other African settings, see Cole 2004; Cornwall 2002; Hunter 2002, 2005; and Luke 2005). Young women frequently have motives other than the alleviation of poverty. Indeed, typical female participants in these sugar daddy relationships are not the truly poor but rather young women who are in urban secondary schools or universities who seek and represent a kind of modern femininity (Leclerc-Madlala 2003). They are frequently relatively educated, almost always highly fashionable, and while their motivations for having a sugar daddy may be largely economic, they are usually looking for more than money to feed themselves.

For married men, the pretty, urban, educated young women who are the most desirable girlfriends provide not only sex but also the opportunity, or at least the fantasy, of having more exciting, stylish, and modern sex than what they have with their wives. At a sports club in Owerri where I spent many evenings during fieldwork, and where men frequently discuss their extramarital experiences, a 52-year-old business man described a recent encounter with a young university student to the delight of his mates: "Sometimes you think you are going to teach these girls something, but, hey, this girl was teaching me." Married men who have younger girlfriends assert a brand of masculinity wherein sexual prowess, economic capability, and modern sensibility are intertwined.

Cheating Husbands and Rewarding Peers

Masculinity is created and expressed both in men's relationships to women and in their relationships with other men (Connell 1995). In male-dominated social settings such as social clubs, sports clubs, sections of the marketplace, and particular bars and eateries, Igbo men commonly talk about their girlfriends and sometimes show them off. Male peer groups are a significant factor in many men's motivations for and behaviors in extra-marital relationships. While some of these male friends may also overlap with the social circles in which men seek to maintain reputations as faithful husbands and family men (like church communities and kin groups), within these male-inscribed social spaces, different and more lax rules govern talk about extramarital sex.

Although it is not uncommon to hear men boast about their sexual exploits to their peers——frequently alluding to styles and practices that are considered simultaneously exciting and modern, another strand of discourse emerges when men explain their motivations. Supporting Swidler and Watkins's (2007) view that the motives and rewards for men's extra-marital sexual relationships need to be understood within a larger context of patronage, wealth in people, and men's roles as providers, many men reported that they enjoyed the feeling of taking care of another woman, of being able to provide her with material and social comforts and luxuries. In a candid discussion I shared with several men over beers about men's motives for extramarital lovers, a 46-year-old man known among his peers as "One-Man Show" for his penchant for keeping multiple young women, explained: "It's not only about the sex. I like to buy them things, take them nice places, give them good meals, and make them feel they are being taken care of. I like the feeling of satisfaction that comes from taking care of women, providing for them." Masculinity proven by lavishing attention and goods upon a girlfriend parallels the way men talk about taking care of their wives and families. It foregrounds the connections between masculinity and money, sex and financial support, and gender and economics more generally.

Many men were ambivalent about their extramarital sexual behavior, but in most cases men viewed it as acceptable given an appropriate degree of prudence so as not to disgrace one's spouse, one's self, and one's family.

In a few cases men seemed genuinely unhappy in their marriages, and in rare instances men fell in love with their extramarital partners. But by and large, men tended to see their extramarital relationships as independent of the quality of their marriages, and in their minds these relationships posed no threat to their marriages so long as they were kept secret from their wives, and so long as men did not waste so many resources on girlfriends that they neglected their obligations to their families.

The primacy of marriage and the ways in which Igbo men collectively enforce this primacy on each other is illustrated by the case of Chibuike, a man in the tennis club who was heavily sanctioned by his male peers for his behavior in an extramarital relationship. At the time, Chibuike was a 36-year-old married father of four. He was involved in an intense relationship with a student at a local university, and he brought her to the club almost daily. Chibuike conducted himself in ways that other men found highly inappropriate. Although it is acceptable to "show off" girlfriends in male-dominated social spaces like the club, Chibuike paraded around with his girlfriend in fully public and sex-integrated settings, such that his wife and in-laws became aware of his affair. He openly touched and kissed his girlfriend in these public environments (whereas most men restrict physical contact with girlfriends to private venues), and he would sometimes spend several nights away from his home, sleeping with his lover. Worst of all from his peers' point of view, he squandered his money on his girlfriend to the extent that he was no longer adequately supporting his family.

To make a long story short, the club members organized themselves and intervened. A group counseled Chibuike to stop the affair, threatened him with suspension from the club, and even visited the wife in solidarity with her predicament, urging her to endure while they acted to rein in her husband. From an Igbo male point of view, competent masculinity allows and even encourages extramarital sex, but not at the expense of neglecting responsibility for one's family. The boundaries that men enforced among themselves were, I think, partly a response to their anxieties that these extramarital relationships represented threats to values associated with marriage and family. While they engaged in these relationships in part to demonstrate their modern masculinity, they also worried about what these new expectations entailed.

Marriage, Infidelity, and the Context of HIV Risk

Although it is impossible to cast the variety of men's extramarital sexual relationships in southeastern Nigeria into one mold, several related issues link an otherwise diverse set of behaviors. Specifically, understanding the social organization of men's extramarital sex requires connecting gender inequality, economic inequality, and moral norms and values. For most Nigerian men, masculinity is closely tied to economic capacity. In the context of contemporary southeastern Nigeria, the paramount test of masculinity for adult men is getting married and having children. With the high cost of bridewealth and the growing expenses of educating children, these tasks alone are a financial challenge for the majority of men.[3] For men who eschew extramarital sexual relationships, it is often the moral imperative of providing for their families that most guides their conduct. Wealthier men are more likely to have extramarital sex not only because their economic status makes them more attractive to potential partners, and not only because they can display both masculinity and social status through their girlfriends, but also because they can have affairs and provide for their girlfriends without the risk of failing to support their families. Indeed, although it is widely known that many men cheat on their wives, those who do so at the expense of providing for their wives and children are most likely to face opprobrium from their peers, as Chibuike's case illustrates. Very few men leave their wives for their lovers, and men are under strong social pressure to take care of their families.

With the changes in marriage in southeastern Nigeria that have occurred over the past few decades, it is important to understand how women in modern marriages deal with their husbands' infidelities, and, more specifically, why they appear to be so tolerant.[4] From observations and anecdotes collected during the "Love, Marriage, and HIV" study, it is apparent that some women do try to challenge and control their husbands' extramarital behavior through a variety of strategies, including drawing on ideals of trust and fidelity implicit in some conceptions of modern marriage. But while almost all women wish for and try to encourage their husbands' fidelity, many choose to ignore their suspicions. Further, among those women who cannot ignore a spouse's infidelity, very few think a man's extramarital affair is in itself grounds for ending a marriage. The reasons for this include not only intense social pressure to stay married, reinforced to varying degrees by women's economic and social dependence on men (including, for example, Igbos' patrilineal system of kinship, which assigns "ownership" of children to the father), but also the knowledge that men's extramarital affairs do not, in fact, threaten marriage——at least not in formal terms. In other words, women as well as men recognize the primacy of marriage, and they know that their husbands will not likely leave them for other women.[5]

Although one might imagine that the AIDS epidemic in Nigeria would create a new urgency for addressing the possible health consequences of prevailing patterns of extramarital sexuality, the popular association of the disease with sexual immorality has, if anything, contributed to the complex web of silences and secrets that surround extramarital sex. I heard some men talk about the necessity of condom use during extramarital sex because of the fear of HIV, but many other men denied or ignored these risks. That a significant proportion of extramarital sex in southeastern Nigeria involves relationships with emotional and moral dimensions——they are not just about sex——means that men imagine these relationships, their partners, and themselves in ways that are quite distanced from the prevailing local model that the greatest risk for HIV infection comes from "immoral" sex. Further, most married women clearly have good reasons to remain silent about and keep secret their husbands' extramarital affairs. The moralistic interpretations of HIV and AIDS only add to the secrets and silences.

Conclusion

For married men who cheat on their wives and for the young women who are their partners——often young women like Ngozi and many thousands of other rural–urban migrants aspiring to better lives——the dynamics of inequality and morality are central to how they navigate gender relations, sexuality, and the AIDS epidemic. There is no doubt that the intersection of gender and economic inequality puts people, especially women, at risk of contracting HIV, but in order to understand people's sexual behavior, one must recognize and account for the potent influence of morality on their decisions. The voluminous literature on sexuality and AIDS in Africa has persuasively shown that explaining people's behavior (not to mention changing it) requires a recognition of not only the powerful structural forces that shape and constrain behavior but also the degrees of agency that individuals can exert even in contexts of great hardship and deprivation. The choices people make are molded not only by their material needs and desires but also by the social imperative to behave and to be perceived as moral actors.

The AIDS epidemic in Nigeria has spread in an era when people are already deeply concerned about the moral consequences of social changes such as the expansion of a capitalist economy, urbanization, rising individualism, and the perceived monetization of everyday life. Anxious moral discourses about sexual behavior are not only responses to the AIDS epidemic. They also give voice to people's discontents about the inequalities and moral hazards associated with contemporary social transformations more generally. Further, as I have tried to show in this chapter, these moralizing discourses can contribute to heightened risk of HIV infection, as sexual partners worry that talking to each other about the risk of AIDS can be tantamount to admitting that one or another has behaved immorally, and as condoms have come to be symbols of sin rather than a means to protect a partner one cares for. In confronting Nigeria's AIDS epidemic, navigating morality can be as challenging as traversing the risks posed by poverty, inequality, and frustrated economic aspirations. For moral guidance, most Nigerians turn to religion. As I show in chapter 3, the popularity of Pentecostal Christianity in southeastern Nigeria is related to its deftness in addressing——and furthering——people's perceptions that Nigeria's current problems, including HIV and AIDS, are the result of a collective moral crisis.

THREE

"Come and Receive Your Miracle": Pentecostal Christianity and AIDS

Several years after the bus ride from Aba to Umuahia that I described in the introduction, during which the young man stood up and captivated all of the passengers—including me—with his passionate preaching, I was on my way to an Internet café in Umuahia when I noticed a wall plastered with posters announcing an upcoming "miracle crusade." After a double take I realized that one of the two faces on the poster was that same bus preacher. In the photograph, Pastor Emmanuel, as I learned he was called, wore a coat and tie; on the bus he'd looked like an ordinary person, even somewhat poor, in a faded, threadbare shirt. But it was him. I was sure. He appeared in the photograph with a middle-aged white man, under whose name was printed "international evangelist." The colorful poster announced the time and location of the crusade, and across the top, large type invited the reader to "COME AND RECEIVE YOUR MIRACLE!"

After I saw the poster, I resolved to attend the event and track down the young evangelist whose bus preaching had been so inspiring. Accompanied by a couple of friends from Ubakala, I attended the all-night observance. It resembled other Pentecostal revivals I had witnessed in Nigeria. A huge generator powered lights, loudspeakers, an electric band, and large video screens. It was a spectacle of modernity that contrasted sharply with the dark, electricity-free night of the surrounding town. Music, singing, and dancing carried people through until morning. The energy was palpable and the mood, ecstatic. Emmanuel and the white American evangelist preached about the deliverance of Nigeria—and Nigerians—from the clutches of Satan. They called dozens of people to the stage to receive their miracles. The crowd whooped as the infertile were promised children, the poor were promised wealth, and the sick were healed. Teams of acolytes moved through the huge crowd during several collections, filling baskets with money from inspired Christians.

Early in the morning, before dawn, after Emmanuel had left the stage, I made my way to the front of the crowd. Behind the stage there was heavy security, and I got through only because the guards assumed that I was an expatriate pastor. I met Emmanuel briefly. His face was familiar, of course, but he looked different. He wore an expensive suit, imported leather shoes, and a Rolex watch. I explained that I had heard him preach on that bus from Aba to Umuahia several years ago and that was why I wanted to meet him. He demurred and said something about how that had been a long time ago and that God had been merciful to him since then. He was polite but clearly didn't want to talk about the past. He seemed to be getting ready to leave, so I thanked him and said good-bye. He handed a bag to his assistant, instructed his driver to bring the car, and drove off in a white Mercedes-Benz.

That night, none of the healed included people with HIV, or at least no one said that was why he or she was sick. But Emmanuel, the white evangelist, and other speakers mentioned AIDS among the scourges plaguing Nigeria as a consequence of individual sin and society-wide immorality. Although they did not promise they could cure AIDS, I knew of many Pentecostal preachers who did. Some even put it on their banners and signboards. Promising to cure AIDS and preaching that it was punishment for sin and social decay symbolize Pentecostalism's complex relationship to the social realities of contemporary Nigeria—simultaneously castigating and offering salvation.

The popularity and social impact of Pentecostal Christianity in southeastern Nigeria have expanded dramatically during the same two decades in which AIDS has emerged as a serious epidemic. AIDS and Pentecostalism are linked in Nigerian public discourse, in popular imagination, and in the lives of individuals who are affected by the virus. These links are moral—whether they are promises of healing through prayer or accusatory Christian critiques that attribute AIDS to God's punishment for individual and societal immorality. They are also social, as Pentecostalism and AIDS are both products of and major contributing factors in Nigeria's changing religious, social, economic, and political landscape.

In this chapter, I try to show how AIDS and Pentecostalism are connected and how they lay bare problems of development, urbanization, inequality, and the changing nature of relationships between individuals, their families, and the larger society. As I have shown, AIDS is widely understood in Nigeria as a consequence of these modern problems, while Pentecostalism is so popular, in part, because it is seen as providing a solution to them.

5. The religious landscape of southeastern Nigeria is increasingly dominated by Pentecostal churches such as Mountain of Fire and Miracles Ministries.

The intersections between Pentecostalism and AIDS speak to the aspirations, contradictions, and ambivalence that many Nigerians experience as their society transforms rapidly. A focus on Pentecostalism cannot and is not meant to stand for all aspects of the relationship between religion and AIDS, but exploring Pentecostalism in Nigeria offers a chance to understand these issues in one of the most powerful—and certainly the fastest growing—religious movements in contemporary Africa.

Pentecostal Christianity in Nigeria

Since the initial conversions to Christianity during colonialism by foreign missionaries, the vast majority of Igbos have belonged to either the Catholic Church or mainline Protestant churches such as Anglican, Presbyterian, Methodist, and Lutheran. In the 1970s and 1980s, Pentecostal churches that emphasized ascetic "holiness" lifestyles and preached reward in the afterlife began to make inroads, particularly among the poor and dispossessed, in the competition for membership with the more established denominations. Members of these holiness churches, such as Deeper Life, dressed conservatively. Women were forbidden from wearing jewelry. Moral codes were puritanical. Relatively few people in the middle and upper classes participated.

But over the past 25 years, and especially during the last decade, a new brand of Pentecostalism has swept Nigeria and other parts of Africa, preaching a gospel of prosperity (Dilger 2007; Gifford 1990, 2004; Meyer 2004). This "prosperity gospel" promises health, wealth, and success in this world. These "new-breed" churches, as Nigerians call them, and their "born-again" members now dominate the religious landscape in southeastern Nigeria. Precise membership figures are hard to come by. The Nigerian government does not ask questions about religion or ethnicity in the national census, viewing these issues as too politically combustible given the tensions between the Muslim North and Christian South. By most accounts, however, in southeastern Nigeria, all the Pentecostal and charismatic churches combined have more members than either the Catholic Church by itself or the mainline Protestant denominations put together.

It is impossible to move around southeastern Nigeria without being struck by the ubiquity of Pentecostal Christianity. The visual landscape is peppered—one might even argue dominated—by signboards for Pentecostal churches, banners announcing a myriad of upcoming revivals, deliverances, and prayer retreats, and bumper stickers and painted signage on trucks attesting to the power of Jesus. Music on buses and in taxis, in markets and lorry parks, and on local radio stations—not to mention in church—is not only likely to be Christian; it is usually a style that is modern, African, and distinctly born-again. At daybreak in people's homes, at workplaces, in schools, and before virtually any kind of public event or ceremony—everything begins with prayer. Igbos were strongly Christian before the Pentecostal revolution, but born-again Christianity has increased the intensity of their belief and practice.

Social science scholarship on Pentecostalism in Africa generally, and in Nigeria specifically, has focused on the way these churches provide people with the religious means to address the challenges of contemporary life (Meyer 1999; Marshall 1991, 1993, 1995, 2009). Pentecostalism is able to incorporate its adherents into a global religion that not only makes followers feel a part of something much bigger than their local world but that also integrates local cultural traditions (Marshall-Fratani 1998). This feature has been hypothesized to be one of "born-again" Christianity's great appeals (Casanova 2001; Robbins 2004). Among other explanations for the popularity of Pentecostal Christianity are (1) that it offers a new and ritually dense system of social organization and cultural meaning for growing ur-

6. Pentecostal Christianity epitomizes a widespread belief in Nigeria that the country's social, economic, and political problems are moral and spiritual in origin and can be corrected only by proper religious practice.

ban populations—as well as for other people who feel frustrated by the failures of the state or alienated by the demands and obligations of traditional kin and community groups; (2) that it promises hope and eternal rewards for people whose lives are marked by inequality and injustice; and (3) that the richness of its rituals and the social life it fosters blur the line between religious worship and leisure (Corten and Marshall-Fratani 2001; Maxwell 1998; Meyer 1998a). In addition, scholars have suggested that Pentecostal Christianity's globalizing pull is part of a larger process in which people in non-Western societies are socialized to become more modern subjects, ritually recruited into the capitalist global economy or, in more optimistic versions, prepared for modernity and democratization.

The most compelling accounts in the literature—the ones that resonate with what I was observing—connect the popularity of born-again Christianity with the problems of modern life (Meyer 1998a, 1998b, 2004; Gifford 1990, 2004; Maxwell 1998). These scholars argue that Pentecostal messages, practices, and new social networks have helped Africans in various ways to interpret, adapt to, and succeed in the rapidly changing circumstances of contemporary Africa. In southeastern Nigeria, Pentecostalism is appealing because it both reflects and addresses Nigerians' ambivalence about the consequences of many aspects of contemporary social change. It endorses—and even promises fulfillment of—people's aspirations for wealth, consumption, and middle-class lifestyles, and at the same time condemns the greed, corruption, and immorality that seem to accompany ongoing transformations.

Pentecostal Christianity in southeastern Nigeria propagates powerful, but sometimes seemingly contradictory, moral messages about inequality. At the same time that Pentecostal pastors promise prosperity to their followers, the leaders of Pentecostal churches, especially the most popular ones—the so-called megachurches—have emerged as some of the richest people in Nigeria. Although these multimillionaire pastors are relatively few, the prosperity gospel seems to validate inequality, explaining it as God's will. In some instances the prosperity gospel appears to be more of a Ponzi scheme than a true religious revolution, but none of the countless Pentecostal Christians I know in Nigeria see it that way. People who have not achieved the promised prosperity say that Christ will deliver them; their own miracles will come. Indeed, many believers, including people who would not, by most reckonings, be considered prosperous, already see their lives as transformed by their faith. Despite some scandals about pastors accused of fraud or theft, none of this has dampened the larger appetite for salvation.

Ruth Marshall's recent book, *Political Spiritualities* (2009), provides the most complete and compelling account of Pentecostal Christianity in Nigeria, including a trenchant critique of the dominant literature. In Marshall's insightful analysis, religiosity is not explained simply by politics or economics. She shows how Pentecostal faith intertwines with political and social life, revealing the paradoxes that characterize contemporary Nigeria. Rather than reducing Pentecostal spirituality to a psychosocial means of "domesticating modernity," as Marshall suggests much of the current literature in anthropology does (e.g., Comaroff and Comaroff 1997, 2002), she shows how Pentecostal beliefs and practices are politically productive as well as religiously powerful. Marshall argues that the subjectivities engendered through Pentecostalism create possibilities for redemption and radical change, having what she calls "insurrectional force" (48). I agree with Marshall that Pentecostal Christianity in southern Nigeria has social and political consequences that extend beyond the halls of these popular churches. But, in my view, the relationship between this popular form of Christianity and the politics of inequality in Nigeria results in forms of political consciousness that ultimately reinforce the entrenched divisions of power between ordinary people and elites, diminishing any potential impetus for revolutionary social change. Certainly with regard to Nigeria's AIDS epidemic, Pentecostal Christianity has been at least as harmful as it has been helpful, as I will try to show below.

Prayer Warriors, Past Sins, and Promises of Deliverance

One afternoon, the regular Thursday healing ceremony at Overcomer's Christian Mission in Owerri included three women who were infertile, a young man who had gone "mad" while in university, and a married couple who were HIV positive. The pastor brought the afflicted individuals in front of the assembled "prayer warriors," members of the congregation who would assist in the prayer-induced healing. He explained the problems of each afflicted person and declared that these ailments were the work of the devil. They could only be reversed, he exhorted, by prayer and proper observance of the word of God. Then he asked those who wished to be healed to testify about their afflictions. They all told stories that suggested their suffering was not only the work of the devil but also that they had been in some way culpable in their past behavior, enabling their bodies and their souls to be captured by Satan.

One infertile woman explained how she had been promiscuous as a schoolgirl, became pregnant, and aborted "the child God had intended for me." Another told of her participation in the underworld of Mami Wata, a traditional deity now regularly associated with Satan in Nigerian Pentecostal preaching. The psychologically troubled young man spoke of his youthful plots to cheat his half-brothers out of their inheritance from a common father. The HIV-positive couple confessed rather cryptically that they had lived for many years "outside the house of God."

Following their testimonies, the individuals to be healed were led outside the church, where groups of prayer warriors worked on the afflicted individuals. They sang and danced and prayed over these wayward souls. Some of the prayer warriors went into trances and spoke in tongues. They symbolically beat the troubled individuals, shouting prayers that the devil should leave their bodies. Those being healed collapsed to the ground, some of them eventually convulsing and also speaking in tongues. At the end of it all, the barren women, the mad man, and the HIV-positive couple were brought back to the pastor in front of the congregation and declared to be on the road to healing—though the words of the pastor suggested that full

7. Some Pentecostal churches offer healing for AIDS and other afflictions, but often in exchange for testimonies that reinforce moral interpretations of the epidemic. Photo by Sasha Rubel.

recovery would depend on continued prayer and the observance, from that moment forward, of a good Christian life. Backsliding was always a risk. The devil lay in waiting.

At this and other ceremonies I observed, where the sick came for healing and new converts to Pentecostalism testified as part of becoming "born again," it always appeared that the more egregious the past sins, the more powerful the sense of salvation. The farther the fall from grace, the greater the redemption. The pastors seemed to welcome these cases the most, perhaps because they best demonstrated God's (and the preacher's) power. At the heart of all of the testimonies is always an acknowledgment of the person's prior failure to achieve Christian morality, exemplified by succumbing to the enticements of modern life in Nigeria, whether these temptations were money, power, greedy consumption, or wanton sexual satisfaction. Ironically, even as Pentecostal churches like Overcomer's condemn many of the trappings and traps of modern life, they go on to preach the "prosperity gospel," promising that material benefits will accrue to their followers, but of course only to those who live by the word of God.

The Pentecostal response to AIDS incorporates similar contradictory dynamics, at once condemning the sins believed to be behind the epidemic while offering hope and salvation for those infected who become born again. Pentecostalism is clearly important for understanding Nigerians' responses to AIDS, but religious reactions to the epidemic are, simultaneously, a revealing lens onto the appeal of Pentecostalism, its practices, and the consequences of such religious beliefs and behavior in contemporary Nigeria more generally. Pentecostal messages of moral clarity surrounding a litany of social changes are reflected in their stance on HIV and AIDS. Religion is not simply a social variable to be understood and manipulated to design more effective AIDS programs (as it is often treated in the public health sector). Rather, Nigerians' responses to AIDS and their embrace of Pentecostalism should be seen as windows on to the continuing salience of religion in how people grapple with the challenges of body and disease, society and social ills, and the individual and collective moralities with which everyday life is made meaningful (Klaits 2010).

Pentecostal Promises: Miracle or Hypocrisy?

Okey joined a Pentecostal church while he was a student at the University of Nigeria, Nsukka. He discovered his church through the campus branch of the Scripture Union, which is an umbrella organization of evangelical Christians that focuses on young people and is active in secondary schools and universities across the country. Scripture Unions are particularly attractive to young Christians on Nigeria's university campuses. This is partly because they offer university-age men an alternative to the often-violent fraternity-like cults on Nigeria's campuses that actively recruit new members, while providing young women some refuge from a highly chauvinistic and exploitative sexual environment in which harassment—and rape—are all too common.

I knew Okey because he was from Ubakala. On his visits home, I spoke with him often about life on the Nsukka campus, about being a born-again Christian, and about his views on politics, culture, and the future of Nigeria. To Okey and his born-again peers at Nsukka, Pentecostal Christianity bestowed a degree of discipline and predictability in an educational institution—and a wider society—that they viewed as veering out of control. On campus, the Scripture Union and Okey's own small church, Faithful Word of God, created a safe haven in which studying was valued and abstinence from alcohol and sexual intercourse was rewarded rather than ridiculed. Okey was a highly motivated and successful student. It was my impression that many of his fellow born-again Christians were also disciplined in their studies.

Of course, I heard conflicting stories about born-again Christians on university campuses. Some of the students and faculty I knew who were not born again asserted that Pentecostal enthusiasts used "rebirth" simply as a cover. Cloaked in the veil of pious Christianity, these people were committing the same sins as others, the skeptics asserted. Born-again Christians were having premarital sex, paying professors for better grades, and cheating on exams just like others students, or so it was said. I have little doubt that one could find born-again Christians doing the things their critics claim. But based on my observations, many of these young Christians tried hard to live up to the moral expectations of their faith. In the arenas of sexuality and alcohol use, it was my impression that numerous young born-again Christians abstained successfully. Okey said he was still a virgin when he graduated from Nsukka, and I had no reason to doubt him. Further, in his outlook on civic life, Okey struck me as precisely the sort of responsible citizen from which Nigeria would benefit tremendously by having millions more.

It is difficult to predict the long-term impact of these fast-growing born-again congregations on Nigeria's moral and political economies. At one level, Pentecostalism and other forms of charismatic and evangelical Christianity seem to be providing a certain degree of individual and collective self-discipline that most Nigerians lament is lacking in their society. But at the same time, these Christian worldviews enable, and even breed, various forms of intolerance, such as opposition to homosexuality and—in the Nigerian context, perhaps even more worrisome—to Islam, which is the dominant religion in the entire northern region of the country. Religious intolerance is a powder keg in contemporary Nigerian society, and many Pentecostal messages contribute to already-combustible dynamics.

Further, even as Pentecostal Christians, and especially their voluble preachers, rail against a range of social ills—from corruption to waning sexual morality to the persistent specter of witchcraft—some of the practices of Pentecostal pastors and their churches suggest bigger questions about hypocrisy that extend beyond whether individual worshippers continue to be sinners. Pentecostal churches, big and small, have become lucrative enterprises for their founders. Leaders of the biggest churches like Winners Chapel and Redeemed Christian Church of God have their own jets, fleets of luxury vehicles, and homes around the world. Even the overseers of smaller churches like Overcomer's live in mansions, drive expensive cars, and have the equivalent of hundreds of thousands of dollars in their personal bank accounts. What I had observed of preacher Emmanuel back-stage at the miracle crusade suggested that he, too, was accruing significant wealth. Pentecostal pastors are getting rich directly from the tithes of their followers, who are asked to contribute significant proportions of their in-comes to the church. Poor people contribute small amounts based on the promise of future miracles; wealthy people give large amounts to signify the God-given nature of their success.

As a result, many Pentecostal preachers are living in relative opulence. Even the pastor of Okey's small church drove a Mercedes-Benz. That church had only the modest campus congregation and a small church in the south-eastern city of Aba. When I visited the pastor's home with Okey, the pastor appeared to me to live quite comfortably. He had an air conditioner in his parlor, air conditioners in the bedroom windows, and a small generator that could provide electricity when the power went out. He clearly lived better than most of his flock. In conversations, I challenged Okey and many other born-again Christians as to whether Pentecostal pastors were benefit-ing unjustly from their followers. Certainly the Nigerian media has begun to focus on the massive wealth of some "new-breed" pastors. I have also read many editorials and blog postings and heard countless conversations in which Nigerians have complained about the hypocrisy of these men (and, increasingly, women). But although many Pentecostal Christians agree that the vast accumulation of wealth on the part of Pentecostal pastors in general is a problem, they often speak highly of their own church and their own pastor nonetheless.

Pentecostal preachers have a powerful narrative to justify their wealth and their continued requests for tithes: their success is evidence of the favor that God bestows on those who follow his word. Rather than criticizing their pastors, congregants are encouraged to emulate and support them, with the promise that they too will be rewarded. Further, Pentecostal preachers ap-peal to a widely held belief in Nigeria that there would be plenty of wealth to go around were it not stolen and squandered by corrupt politicians. As such, preachers of the prosperity gospel seem to easily convince their flocks that they can also prosper, even when promises of future wealth continue to prove elusive to most church members. Contributing to church coffers is presented as the means to save Nigeria and assure that, ultimately, the faithful shall be rewarded. Above all, perhaps, these preachers offer hope (Campbell, Skovdal, and Gibbs 2011).

In the last decade of the 20th century and the first decade of the 21st century, these churches have constructed a message that speaks with great resonance to Nigerians' sense that inequality is grounded fundamentally in immorality. Yet, ironically, many Pentecostal pastors in Nigeria seem to be creating new moral justifications for inequality rather than actually challenging inequality itself as morally problematic. Inequality connected to the state and to electoral politics is branded as evil, but the "God-given" wealth of church elites—even when their neighbors and fellow congregants have little or nothing—is portrayed as spiritually ordained. The conjunction of inequality and morality, and the question of whether Pentecostal responses are genuine and constructive or hypocritical and harmful, is central to understanding the connections between religion and AIDS in Nigeria.

AIDS as a Social, Moral, and Religious Crisis

Social scientists have already begun to examine connections between religion and AIDS in sub-Saharan Africa, including the increasingly significant role of Pentecostal Christianity (Pfeiffer 2004, 2011; Becker and Geissler 2007; Prince, Denis, and van Dijk 2009; Klaits 2010; Ashforth 2011). Much of this emerging literature, including work that addresses Pentecostal Christianity, focuses on how religion intersects with sexuality, morality, and preventive/risk behaviors, and on how religious communities, programs, and sensibilities affect contexts of treatment and support (Adogame 2007; Aja et al. 2010; Garner 2000; Takyi 2003; Pfeiffer 2011). Findings have been somewhat ambiguous. Some studies suggest that belonging to religious groups and absorbing religious messages about AIDS can be protective (Green 2003), while others find that moralizing religious messages can be counterproductive or contradictory (Smith 2004a; Pfeiffer 2004; Parsitau 2009). Many studies have tried to address practical public health questions about how best to incorporate churches and faith-based organizations into effective HIV and AIDS programming. Although these approaches may produce some innovative intervention strategies, a deeper understanding of the relationship between Pentecostalism and AIDS requires moving away from simplified notions of the causal effects of religion on AIDS and vice versa.

In an effort to better understand Pentecostal Christianity and its relationship to Nigeria's AIDS epidemic, I attended church services, watched evangelical TV programs, and read local Christian literature. In 2006 and 2007, with the help of a research assistant, I focused particularly on two popular Pentecostal churches in Owerri: Overcomer's Christian Mission and Winners Chapel. As indicated above, Winners Chapel is a huge international Pentecostal church started in Lagos and known as the quintessential proponent of the prosperity gospel. Overcomer's is also a prosperity church, and while it has congregations in Lagos and other cities and towns around the country, it has not achieved the megachurch status of Winners. In addition to observations at these churches and interviews with their members and pastors, I conducted a survey and ethnographic study in 2001 and 2002 among young Igbo-speaking rural–urban migrants in the Nigerian cities of Kano and Aba, as described earlier. The main focus of that study was to understand young migrants' behavioral responses to the AIDS epidemic; information about respondents' religious choices emerged as a significant secondary result.

As part of the Kano and Aba migrants' study, I conducted a survey of 863 young migrants (over 400 in each city), as well as in-depth interviews with subset of 40 young men and women, and several months of partici- pant observation. Only 5 young Igbos (out of 863) in Aba and Kano said they were not Christians. Although slightly less than 30 percent of my sam- ple reported formal membership in a Pentecostal or evangelical church, 66 percent in Aba and 72 percent in Kano identified themselves as "born again." That so many young Igbos described themselves as such indicates how pervasive and important the born-again identity has become among this youthful population. Even among people who said they were Roman Catholic (Catholic Church leaders in Nigeria have been the most resistant to adopting the language of being born again), about 70 percent described themselves in this way. In other words, even Christians who were not Pen- tecostal thought it was important to describe their faith in a way that was associated with Pentecostalism.

In southeastern Nigeria, a Christian moral framework is a common lens through which people make sense of the AIDS epidemic. This lens shapes how people conceptualize risk in relation to their sexual behavior. Religious views serve as reason for abstinence for some, a justification for the moral- ity of certain sexual relationships for others, and a source of ambivalence and denial for those who cannot legitimately fit their sexual behavior into a Christian framework but who are, nonetheless, affected by its powerful influence.

Before examining the complex ways religious understandings of the AIDS epidemic affect sexual behavior and the risk of contracting HIV, it is necessary to explain more about how Nigerians construe the epidemic religiously, contributing to a larger set of moralistic discourses about the disease. These interpretive understandings illuminate the cultural context and illustrate the symbolic frameworks within which Nigerians are making sexual decisions. The role of churches, particularly "new-breed" Pentecostal churches, has been profound in promoting these religious understandings of the etiology of HIV and AIDS and other social ills.

Pastors in churches like Overcomer's and Winners (and in some Protestant and Catholic churches, too) preach sermons in which HIV is tied to immorality. AIDS is blamed on the failure to live a good Christian life. Protection from HIV infection is promised only to those who obey Jesus' teachings. Similar to what I observed at the healing ceremony at Overcomer's, on many occasions—at various churches and in local TV evangelists' programs—I heard people who were HIV positive testify to their own past sins. While not all Pentecostal churches claim to offer spiritual cures for HIV and AIDS, and some churches provided support for HIV-infected converts, the larger religious message is that AIDS is the result of immorality and can only be prevented by being a good, moral Christian. This message contributes to a social environment in which the disease is highly stigmatized.

The strength of the stigma is illustrated by stories that circulate about the behavior of those who contract HIV. On several occasions, in Owerri and Umuahia, I heard versions of a rumor about someone infected with HIV who escaped from a government hospital and was raping young girls in order to "carry [infect and kill] others with him." The idea that people who have HIV might deliberately infect others (and therefore might need to be quarantined or killed) was prevalent in Nigeria in the first decade of the epidemic and still persists in some quarters (see Leclerc-Madlala 1997 for a similar phenomenon in South Africa). The image of an evil person devilishly planning to infect and kill others so that he does not die alone no doubt reflects public fears about AIDS, but it also serves to project blame onto a particularly immoral other. The stories place HIV-positive people outside normative morality and make it believable that they would harm others randomly and willfully. Although there is little or no evidence to suggest that HIV-positive Nigerians do, in fact, deliberately infect others through violent and antisocial means, the ubiquity and popular resonance of the rumor reinforce social anxieties about the epidemic and those infected with the virus. Such fears certainly inhibit testing and discourage disclosure on the part of those who learn they are HIV positive.

The dominant religious discourse about AIDS claims that it is a scourge visited by God on a society that has turned its back on religion and morality. Nnenna, a 19-year-old migrant in Kano who works in her uncle's small pharmaceutical shop, expressed a view that I heard frequently from young migrants and from many other people in the Southeast: "AIDS is a terrible thing. But this place is like Sodom and Gomorrah. Nigerians are being punished for their sins. If people did not have sex here and there, if the society were not so corrupt, there would be no AIDS. . . . Yes, it is God's punishment, but we have brought it on ourselves."

Chima, a 22-year-old man in Aba who sells shoes in the main market and who belongs to an "orthodox" Protestant church, discusses AIDS in terms that highlight the influence of the born-again view, even among Nigerians who cannot be formally classified as belonging to new-breed churches: "The fact that there is no medical cure proves that it is only through seeing God that one can prevent AIDS. AIDS is God's way of checking the immoral sexual behavior that is rampant in Nigeria now. I put my trust in God." It is within this larger cultural context, in which AIDS is clearly interpreted as a consequence of immorality, that young Nigerians must make their decisions about sexual relationships.

Sin and Sexual Behavior

Sexual behavior is clearly influenced by a whole range of factors that are not themselves directly attributable to religious or moral considerations. Nonetheless, the findings from my study of young Igbo-speaking rural–urban migrants in Aba and Kano suggest that the religious framing of the AIDS epidemic in Nigeria unfolds across at least three distinct patterns of sexual behavior (Smith 2004a). I label these three patterns as abstinence, moral partnering, and denial. Abstinence refers to the segment of the population that entirely refrains from (premarital) sexual intercourse. Moral partnering refers to those unmarried people who are sexually active but construct their relationships in the language of monogamy and religion. Denial refers to relationships that would be judged by society (and certainly by Christian churches) as obviously immoral but are somehow rationalized, hidden, or denied by the people who participate in them. Of course, these categories are fluid, as people who were once abstinent initiate a sexual relationship and people who were sexually active engage in "secondary virginity"—a newfound commitment to abstinence until marriage (and a common goal of young people in Nigeria who convert to born-again Christianity); as relationships evolve and are reinterpreted; and as people live in multiple and sometimes contradictory social and sexual worlds.

The most common of these sexual patterns is "moral partnering." About 70 percent of the migrants surveyed in my study reported that they had had sexual intercourse at some time in their lives, and slightly less than half of the respondents said they were currently in a sexual relationship. The vast majority described their partners as "boyfriends" or "girlfriends." In-depth interviews and participant observation made it clear that these descriptions had positive moral connotations. Young women like Ngozi, who worked in a tavern in Kano (as discussed in chapter 2), clearly expressed a view that longer-term and emotionally committed relationships were more morally acceptable—and, crucially, less likely to result in HIV infection—than sex for money or sex simply to satisfy physical desire. Single young people whose jobs were not so obviously connected to the sexual economy also sought to have and portray themselves as having moral partnerships. Marriage, of course, is the sexual relationship considered most moral by society.

Particularly significant for understanding the connections between religious understandings of AIDS and young people's sexual decision-making is the association of relationship morality with decreased risk, and the tendency to forgo condom use in moral partnerships. The dynamics of condom use in these sexual relationships are related to other issues besides religious morality, such as expectations about intimacy and cultural values about procreation (Smith 2003a, 2004b), but decisions not to use condoms were clearly connected in many Christians' minds to the morality of the relationship.

Young people who talked about condom use during in-depth interviews suggested that it was not as necessary in moral partnerships because the risk of contracting HIV in those relationships was minimal. Nneoma, a 23-year-old hairdresser's apprentice in Kano, put a religious spin on her explanation of why she did not use condoms: "I met my boyfriend in church. We are both children of God, and I know I can trust him. I only have sex with him because I love him, and I know that he is only with me. I protect myself from pregnancy [using birth-control pills], but I know he will not give me AIDS."

Numerous conversations with young migrants suggested that condom use is inhibited by the fact that condoms imply one's own or one's partner's infidelity. Just how protective these moral partnerships were is an open question, but clearly many young people in Nigeria perceived that their risk of contracting HIV was minimized if they and their partners were "good Christians."

Sexual relationships that fell into the category of "denial" were the hardest to assess, precisely because they were the most difficult to get young people to discuss. Men and women talked easily and frequently about the immoral sexual relationships of others, especially nameless others, but were much less likely to talk about their own "immoral" relationships—with the exception of commercial sex workers like Ogadimma, whose behavior was already so stigmatized that they spoke openly about matters of sex and HIV. Yet ethnographic data made it clear that morally dubious relationships, where money or carnal desires were primary motivators, were not uncommon even among devout born-agains. A few young people were open in talking about sexual partnering that flouted the Christian-influenced category of moral partnering, but most preferred to keep these relationships secret.

Not only young women's involvement in economically motivated sex, or men's participation in these relationships, fell into the category of denial. Through the rumors, gossip, and occasional confessions I heard during fieldwork, it was clear that many young men (and some, but seemingly fewer, young women) were, in fact, cheating on their "moral partners." Some people secretly had more than one "moral partner." Moreover, it was common for the beginning of one relationship and the end of another relationship to overlap, so, at least for a period of time, many people violated the supposed trust of each of these partnerships. Popular expectations about what a moral sexual relationship should be—shaped so powerfully in this population by Christian discourses—combined with the messy reality of what people's sexual relationships are really like, created a context in which the risk of HIV was difficult for young people to confront openly. Religious interpretations of sex and of AIDS decreased the perceived need for condoms in moral partnerships, but exacerbated the extent to which people denied being involved in other relationships and put out of their minds the risk from relationships that do not fit the moral model.

Religious interpretations of AIDS and moral judgments about sexual relationships clearly inhibit some sexually active young migrants from adequately protecting themselves. For some, however, as Cole (2010) found in Madagascar, fervent Christianity has created an alternative path for responding to social changes attributed to immorality and to the perception of crass consumerism and promiscuous sexuality among youth. In Nigeria, in the context of AIDS, this manifests most poignantly in Pentecostal discourse about the potential protection offered by abstinence. Abstinence was the most common response when young people were asked how best to prevent AIDS. Almost a third reported that they had never had sexual intercourse. Because a significant proportion of young people in any population are abstinent, it is hard to attribute the fact of abstinence to Christianity or to a strategy to prevent HIV infection. But interviews and participant observation left little doubt that in the minds of most young people abstaining from sex, their abstinence was religiously motivated. If nothing else, social pressures that connect premarital sex with being modern meant that youth had a difficult time justifying abstinence without recourse to a religious motivation.

Perhaps even more relevant, a large number of young migrants who said they had once had sexual intercourse now proclaimed a renewed abstinence in the name of religion. Uluchi, a 22-year-old migrant in Kano, explained her decision to embark on a new premarital abstinence in specifically religious terms, but with a nod to AIDS that seems to be increasingly common: "Since I found God I realized that I should save myself for my husband. Sex before marriage is against God. Now that I am off sex, I feel closer to God. Besides, you never know what might happen out there, with AIDS and everything."

Abstinence is imagined here not just as a mode of preventing transmission but as an ethical and religious choice that can combat the unchecked immorality believed to exacerbate the epidemic. I do not have (and I am not aware of) sufficient evidence to prove that the born-again cultural mores are increasing the prevalence or duration of premarital abstinence among young Igbo migrants in Aba and Kano, or more generally. But certainly young Christians believed it was so. Even if religiously inspired abstinence did protect some young people, this must be weighed against the stigma that this moralizing view of the epidemic exacerbates, and against the ways that moral interpretations of AIDS create obstacles to condom use and other protective behaviors like testing and disclosure.

Conclusion

Early in the epidemic, in the 1990s, young Nigerians frequently projected the risks of AIDS onto distant and foreign immoral "others." As the disease has spread and more people know or have heard of people who actually have HIV or AIDS, these psychosocial techniques of "othering" are being deployed with local referents. People frequently talk about AIDS as part of larger discourses about moral decline in Nigeria—discourses that explain and are promoted by the growing popularity and intensity of born-again Christian worldviews, especially among young people. Describing how AIDS is transmitted, adolescents typically say things like: "through wayward sex," "through lewd sex," "through promiscuous sex," "through sex with strangers," and "through immoral sex" (Smith 2003a). Of course, each of these behaviors characterizes *someone else's* sexual practices. Most people find ways to justify their own sexual practices as moral. When young Christians speak of immoral sexual behavior as the main risk factor for HIV, they frequently think of their religious devotion as immunizing them from immorality. Many young people are willing to leave the outcome in the hands of God. In his aptly titled *Infections and Inequalities*, Paul Farmer argues that

AIDS and other diseases must be understood as politically and economically produced. This is surely true in Nigeria, but the relationship between *infections* and *immorality* is also central to young Nigerians' interpretations of HIV. Indeed, it is untangling the intersection of inequality and morality that is elemental to understanding Nigerians' responses to HIV and AIDS, as well as their embrace of Pentecostal Christianity. Even as Pentecostal discourses condemn the forms of social immorality associated with AIDS and the wider problematic social changes it symbolizes, Pentecostal churches also offer the hope that these morally rooted problems can be overcome. Salvation is possible.

By looking at the parallels between discourses about AIDS and the religious messages of Nigeria's fast-growing Pentecostal churches, one can see how both are positioned in relation to Nigerians' ambivalence about rising inequality and other shifts in social relations associated with modern society (cf. Pfeiffer 2002 for Mozambique). Ever larger numbers of Nigerians, especially young people, are attracted to urban lifestyles, conspicuous consumption, global fashions, and modern forms of intimacy. But pursuing these material desires and modern identities frequently puts people in situations where they risk contracting HIV. Collectively, Nigerians blame these trends for the spread of HIV and AIDS. Further, in popular imagination and discourse, the connections between AIDS and morality extend beyond the notion that individuals make risky (and, in Nigerians' thinking, immoral) choices in the face of frustrated aspirations for more comfortable lives. The very trajectories of social change themselves are experienced ambivalently, as wealth, consumption, and individualism are seen as undermining core values and practices. Similarly, Pentecostal pastors promise prosperity in exchange for becoming born again and following the word of God, even as they rail against selfishness, greed, and corruption. Pentecostal Christianity's appeal in Nigeria is so strong precisely because it speaks to modern desires for wealth, consumption, and freedom from the obligations of kinship even as it condemns many of the social ills that Nigerians associate with these very transitions.

FOUR

"Feeding Fat on AIDS": NGOs, Inequality, and Corruption

One evening in 2004, a doctor in the Abia State Ministry of Health, whom I knew from my research but also from the local tennis club, phoned to say he wanted to have a discussion with me. We met at a local hotel. He bought us a couple of beers and led me to a corner of the bar where we could speak privately. After some of the usual pleasantries, he said he had a favor to ask me. "I'm thinking of floating [a Nigerian English term for starting] an NGO and I want your help," he said. He then went on to describe how so much donor funding was being funneled into AIDS and how his colleague who ran that sector of the Ministry was making money hand over fist. He explained how he had tried to persuade the Ministry's two highest officials to include him in the AIDS programs, but they continued to refuse. "They want to eat alone," he complained. The doctor concluded that the only way he would be able to benefit from the AIDS bonanza was to start his own NGO, tapping into international funds directly rather than continuing to be stymied by his colleagues in the Ministry who did not want to share.

The AIDS epidemic served as a major catalyst for the "mushrooming"—as Nigerians are wont to describe it—of local NGOs. By the early 2000s, AIDS money and the billboards, posters, and workshops it generated seemed to be everywhere. Government and NGO officials were chauffeured in donor-purchased four-wheel-drive vehicles with their logos on the side. Participants in AIDS seminars and training stayed in fancy hotels and collected handsome per diems. Many NGO personnel traveled abroad for conferences. No wonder people wanted a piece of the action. But as quickly as AIDS NGOs emerged all over Nigeria, so too did critical discourses about them and their founders.

In this chapter, I present three cases of local AIDS NGOs that I came to know well. The contrast between how people viewed the three NGOs and their respective leaders shows how Nigerians' assessments of inequality can turn on judgments regarding the quality of social relations as much as on material disparities. These cases illustrate the ways Nigerians evaluate NGO performance through an interpretive prism in which inequalities are continuously judged in moral terms. As I have discussed in the earlier chapters, for many Nigerians social inequalities appear to be becoming less tempered by the duties and obligations grounded in forms of sociality that privilege reciprocity and collective interests over individual enrichment and personal aggrandizement. These discontents are at the heart of people's ambivalence about the consequences of contemporary social changes and are crystallized in the perception that AIDS itself is the product of selfish and immoral behavior. The NGO efforts to address the epidemic are caught up in similar webs of moral anxiety about the shifting landscape of inequality.

AIDS and "NGOization"

In Ikoyi and Victoria Island in Lagos, Nigeria's commercial hub, in the rapidly growing subdivisions of the capital Abuja, and even on the crowded streets of much smaller cities like Umuahia in Abia State, NGO office signboards are ubiquitous: Stop AIDS, Action AIDS, Youth Against AIDS, Christian AIDS Charities, Naija AIDS Foundation, and the like. Signboards like these represent an explosion of NGOs over the past two decades. Probably no single social problem has produced more NGOs in Nigeria than the AIDS epidemic. Together, since 2002, the US President's Emergency Plan for AIDS Relief (PEPFAR) and the Global Fund for AIDS, Tuberculosis, and Malaria have channeled $2.25 billion to Nigeria, and much of the money is ultimately dispersed to NGOs. Other donors have contributed hundreds of millions of dollars as well.

"NGOization" is not unique to Nigeria. Scholars have documented the rise of NGOs and offered critical accounts of them in many settings around the world (Mercer 2002; Kamat 2004; Szeftel 2000; Watkins, Swidler, and Hannan 2012). Much of the literature, including that on Africa, has focused on NGOs' relationship to the state and to systems of governance (Bratten 1989; Kasfir 1998; Swidler 2006). From some perspectives, NGOs provide services that the state is unable or unwilling to support, and, depending on the case (or the scholar's point of view), this NGO work can either push the state to be more responsive to the people or provide the state continued leeway to perform ineffectively (Moyo 2009). In some instances, NGOs are seen as acting on behalf of government, solidifying its power; in others, NGOs are touted as challenging—or at least checking—state authority.

In the anthropological literature, attention has frequently focused on whether NGOs actually succeed in delivering the humanitarian and development benefits they promise (Bornstein 2005; Mosse and Lewis 2005; Igoe and Kelsall 2005). Very often the findings suggest they do not (Campbell 2003). Much has been learned by examining not just whether NGOs achieve their stated aims but also the effects they have beyond their ostensible purposes, in relation to institutional and organizational transformations (Ferguson 1990; de Waal 1997; Swidler 2006, 2009) and with regard to the lives of individuals working for or receiving NGO assistance (Kaler and Watkins 2001; Bornstein 2005; Dahl 2009; Mosse 2011; Maes 2012). This literature suggests that although NGOs are powerful agents that in some respects appear to create institutional homogeneity across diverse cultural settings, in other ways NGOs and the individual actors associated with them must constantly adapt to complex local realities (Smith 2003b; Swidler 2006; Meyer 2010). In Nigeria, this means that such organizations and their leaders must navigate a changing and often contradictory political and moral landscape in which individual and NGO actions are judged based on their degree of accountability in two competing systems: (1) emerging ideals of bureaucratic transparency and efficiency tied to a set of international norms and what some have argued is a growing, if often only tacitly acknowledged, form of global governance (Ferguson 2006) and (2) entrenched expectations associated with patron-clientism, which dictates that the resources of an NGO should be shared with others on the basis of personal and familial relationships (see Swidler 2009 for a more general argument along similar lines).

"Feeding Fat on AIDS"

Long before July 2004 when the Nigerian weekly news magazine *Tell* ran the cover story "Feeding Fat on AIDS," reporting on the country's lucrative AIDS industry, I had heard countless concerns, complaints, and conspiracy theories from friends, acquaintances, and others that AIDS was a boondoggle for many in government and especially in the NGO sector. As the epidemic advanced, more and more Nigerians recognized that HIV and AIDS were real problems, but even by 2012 it was still not uncommon to hear people speculate that AIDS itself was the concoction of a new local elite in cahoots with international partners, the latest form of fraud (known in Nigeria as "419") cloaked in the legitimacy of global humanitarianism.

Similar to what Vinh-Kim Nguyen (2010) found in Ivory Coast and Burkina Faso, where local AIDS NGOs and support groups for people living

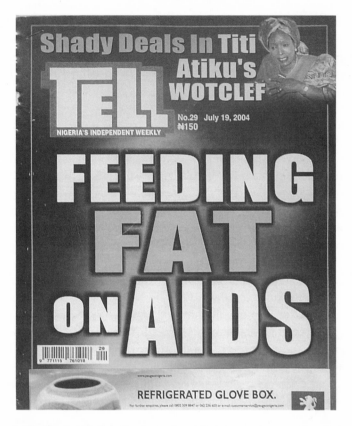

8. The Nigerian media both reflect and contribute to popular perceptions that
AIDS NGOs created to address the epidemic are boondoggles for their founders.

with HIV were often believed to be enterprises created to enrich their members, one of the most troubling versions of these popular rumors was the
suspicion that people who were HIV positive were benefiting from their infection. In some stories, HIV-positive individuals who spoke openly about their
sero status were believed to be pretending to have AIDS in order to secure
donor funds; in others, they were allegedly paid by European and American
sponsors to speak openly about their condition for their own and their sponsors' financial benefit. Why else, people reasoned, would someone openly
admit to having HIV or AIDS, which remain highly stigmatized in Nigeria?

That people afflicted with HIV or AIDS can be placed under a further
cloud of suspicion if they speak out about their status or simply participate
in programs designed to help them highlights the extent and power of such

stigma. But these rumors are more than manifestations of stigma; they are also a form of political critique. They are the product of widespread recognition and anger about the fact that many NGOs ostensibly created to address the epidemic are shams—fraudulent enterprises created to benefit from humanitarian AIDS money. People also know that even among those NGOs that are legitimate, many of their founders and staff receive handsome compensation for their good works (with expatriate employees of international NGOs exemplifying most obviously just how well one can do by "doing good"). Further, HIV-positive men and women who are receiving antiretroviral therapy or participating in donor-funded support groups and prevention programs *are* often receiving resources that are the envy of others. Envy about this form of "therapeutic citizenship" (Nguyen 2010)—the idea that people can demand and get access to rights and benefits of the state because of their health status, often in circumstances where they otherwise have little sway with their governments—is more a commentary on the precarious circumstances of ordinary Nigerians than on the extent of benefits accruing to people who are HIV positive.

At the heart of the widespread perception of NGO fraud is a lack of trust that feeds on decades of local experiences with corrupt and ineffective donor- and state-sponsored development interventions (Smith 2007a). With good reason, ordinary Nigerians do not always believe that the West has their interests at heart; they do not trust their government; and they often suspect the motives of their fellow citizens. Just as AIDS itself is seen as the consequence of moral crisis, so too are the efforts to combat it tainted with the perception that they are enterprises of greed and self-aggrandizement. But to divide Nigerian civil society's responses to the epidemic neatly into honest and corrupt NGOs, or Nigeria's HIV-positive population into innocent victims and opportunistic entrepreneurs, is far too simplistic. Nearly every NGO and NGO leader, regardless of how crooked or honest he or she might be, is caught up in popular critical moral discourses about the way these organizations exploit and exacerbate inequality. Much can be learned about the popular perceptions and political effects of these institutions by examining cases in which AIDS NGOs and their leaders are considered by Nigerians to be more or less corrupt. These organizations ostensibly operate to serve society, often especially the most vulnerable populations, with an implicitly moral mandate. But they frequently become embroiled in accusations of corruption that reveal the changing dynamics of inequality and morality as the very fabric of social relations in Nigeria is undergoing significant transformations.

A Poser, an NGO, and the Politics of Patronage

In the mid-1990s, Pius Okadigbo got a job working for a US-based NGO that ran a number of public health projects in Abia State. He was a university graduate, possessing a skill set that appeared to serve him and the NGO well. A friend of mine who was the Nigerian manager for the American NGO's projects in southeastern Nigeria spoke highly of Pius's work after he was hired. Based at the NGO's Umuahia office, Pius worked as a program officer, meaning that he ran training programs, supervised field staff, collected and analyzed project data, and helped draft reports for the NGO headquarters and for donors. Working for the NGO, Pius learned a wide range of skills relevant to running such an organization.

After several years with the American organization, Pius eventually left to run the office of a large Nigerian NGO. The local organization, United Against AIDS (UAA), for which Pius directed the Umuahia office, was one of the most prominent domestic NGOs created to address the country's HIV epidemic.[1] UAA's headquarters were in Ibadan in southwestern Nigeria, where it was supported by major grants from Western governments and multilateral donors. Nearly all of the big NGOs fighting AIDS, each of which can command many millions of dollars of international aid, are based in Nigeria's Southwest (and now, increasingly, in Abuja). Many of these mega-NGOs have regional offices around the country, like UAA's office in Umuahia in the Southeast.

It is no coincidence that the biggest and most well-financed NGOs are in the Southwest. Until the mid-1990s, Nigeria's capital was Lagos, and all embassies and nearly every major bilateral and multilateral organization had its headquarters there. In addition, the Southwest is home to three of Nigeria's best and most prestigious universities—University of Ibadan, Obafemi Awolowo University in Ile-Ife, and the University of Lagos. Over several decades, university faculty at these schools have created a full-blown industry of local NGOs that provide expertise for donor projects and tap into the millions in aid (and, in the past two decades especially, AIDS) dollars. These universities, their faculties, and the large number of other personnel who have experience with health and development programs provide international donors with an appealing base of human capital. From the donors' perspective, the experience and skills of these mega-NGOs promise more effective projects.

But, arguably, other reasons also explain the disproportionate flow of aid dollars in and through the Southwest. Many of my Nigerian university and NGO colleagues in the Southeast have observed that it is rare to see expatriate donor representatives visiting (much less working full-time in) other regions of the country besides the Southwest. The aid dollars stay in the Southwest not only because of the perceived expertise in the region but also because it is easier for the donors that way. My Nigerian friends and colleagues have observed that donors can conveniently oversee their portfolios of projects while staying in upscale neighborhoods and eating in the fancy restaurants of Lagos and Abuja, believing that their activities are reaching the grassroots through their local NGO partners. To hear my friends in the Southeast tell it, the international donors are also playing into sinister local politics, where elites in Lagos and Abuja keep control of aid dollars, allowing only a fraction of the millions in global assistance to reach places like Abia State, where people feel marginalized in Nigeria's ethnic, regional, and religious politics. But local criticism of inequality and corruption is not reserved for only the civil society elites of Lagos and Abuja. As the story of Pius will suggest, even on the smaller scale that characterizes local NGOs in Abia State, corruption is both a significant problem and a topic of intense popular discussion.

I saw Pius several times in the years when he ran the Umuahia office of UAA. He was always gregarious and polite. One day I ran into him during lunch at a restaurant in town, and he insisted that I accompany him back to his office. When we entered the reception area, two of his staff members quickly stood up and greeted him in English, "Welcome, sir!" One of the young ladies then opened the door for us to enter Pius's office, which boldly displayed "Director's Office" on a black-and-gold placard. Pius acted condescendingly toward his staff, ringing a bell when he wanted them to bring us cold drinks and loudly scolding a secretary for a mistake in her typing.

The office had all the accoutrements that I had long since become used to seeing in the offices of "big men" (and "big women") in government and NGOs: a chilly air conditioner, a computer and a printer, a phone (though cell phones have recently almost entirely displaced landlines), and a private refrigerator stocked with cold drinks. But in Pius's office the furniture was more expensive than is typical; the refrigerator was bigger than usual; the computer seemed to be the latest model of laptop; the printer was laser rather than inkjet; and Pius made a point of showing me that he had Internet service, which was at that time uncommon in private offices. Pius Okadigbo was enjoying his success.

From what I later heard from my colleagues at other Umuahia NGOs, Pius developed a reputation for ostentation and arrogance among his peers. I remember one mutual colleague telling me about Pius's participation in a consortium of AIDS NGOs in Abia State that met regularly to try to coordinate their activities. He said that Pius was always late to meetings and demanded that others defer to him in discussions, often boasting about how UAA was such a big player compared to the other, much smaller consortium members. This colleague said, "Pius would arrive carrying a pile of newspapers which he reads, or pretends to read, while his car is caught in traffic, dressed in a newly tailored traditional outfit, carrying the staff from his most recent chieftaincy title, and always acting as if he was busy and in a hurry." To many people, the idea that chieftaincy titles are for sale in Nigeria, creating a surplus of what Nigerians call "naira chiefs" ("naira" is the name of the Nigerian currency), is emblematic of social and moral crisis in the country. Even once-revered honors are reduced to commodities for sale in a prestige market where the corrupt try to legitimize their wealth by buying traditional symbols of social status.

Pius's NGO peers saw his chieftaincy titles as illegitimate, and they resented the way he flaunted his new wealth and position. They called Pius a "poser," a term Nigerians usually reserve for people whose conspicuous consumption and boastful personalities would have others believe they are more important than they really are. Pius had indeed made a lot of money from his job running UAA's Umuahia office, most of it rumored to be misappropriated. His salary was good, but not nearly enough to explain the car he had purchased, the house he was building in his village, or the traditional titles he had bought for himself. The dishonor of being perceived as a poser was not so much about the fact that Pius allegedly stole money from his NGO (though some people, of course, lamented that, too); it was much more about how he abused his new wealth and status to intimidate others. He was seen as an inauthentic big man, not because of the source of his money but because of the way he used it. Swidler (2009) has argued compellingly regarding the continued importance of patronage in the running of AIDS NGOs; Pius's behavior is a clear instance of how individuals can run afoul of implicit rules of conduct associated with patronage. Instead of sharing some of his money to cultivate social ties and build a network of followers in the manner that has a long and embedded history in Nigeria's clientelistic political economy, Pius was seen as aggrandizing himself at the expense of others, including those who had helped him along his path to success.

Yet Pius's story did not stop with his success and the discontent he generated in others. In a dramatic denouement that is unusual in Nigeria, Pius's ongoing theft of project money was publicly exposed, and he was eventually fired in the subsequent scandal. UAA initiated criminal prosecution, though I heard that the case was stalled in court, and most people suggested that

Pius would never actually be convicted. But he was thoroughly disgraced and seemed to have little hope of rehabilitating his reputation and career, at least in the NGO sector. Several friends speculated that Pius had been done in by his own staff—that the office accountant or others who knew of his corrupt dealings had quietly made sure that the UAA office in Ibadan discovered his malfeasance. They betrayed him, these stories suggested, not because he was stealing money (after all, many NGO bosses were doing that, my friends pointed out) but because he was so arrogant and selfish in his dealings with others, most especially his own staff. Pius was a poser. He was greedy and individualistic. Not coincidentally, these are the same traits that are seen as contributing to the larger social and moral crisis to which Nigerians attribute HIV and AIDS.

Naija Cares: A Good Christian Lady and the Nuances of Corruption

My friend Chidinma Alozie, who managed the American NGO where Pius first worked, eventually started her own local NGO called Naija Cares ("Naija" being common Nigerian shorthand for the country's name). For local NGOs in Nigeria, the key to success is garnering support from international donors. Naija Cares did quite well in this regard. By 2012 the NGO had survived for more than 15 years, receiving funding from multiple foundations, foreign government agencies, multilateral organizations, and the Nigerian government. Through a combination of social connections, successful project outcomes, and skill at proposal and report writing, Naija Cares has achieved exceptional durability in a context where the vast majority of local NGOs do not outlast the duration of a single funded project.

By examining the daily practices of NGOs like Naija Cares and the perceptions of these practices among ordinary citizens, the social effects and meanings of the NGO explosion accompanying Nigeria's AIDS epidemic can be fully understood.[2] Chidinma and her organization have been the subject of many rumors of corruption, warranted or not. I have no way of knowing the extent to which Chidinma has funneled money from her projects into her own hands over the years. But people around Umuahia assumed she benefited handsomely and well beyond her salary from the NGO. They knew that she built a small addition onto her relatively modest house in Umuahia; she was able to buy a nice (but used) car when her old one gave out; she joined with her siblings to build a new house for her mother in the village; and she has been able to provide well for her four children. (Chidinma was long ago divorced and, somewhat remarkably in the cultural context of southeastern Nigeria, raised the children as a single mother without her ex-husband's help.

The maximum amounts that most donors would tolerate for a local NGO director's salary in Nigeria would not enable Chidinma to afford a decent car, an added room on her modest house, or the cost of university education for her four children, even as the salaries of the expatriate personnel who award and supervise these donor funds easily exceed not only what someone like Chidinma is paid but also what she might manage to accumulate through "corruption." I am not saying that these inequalities justify corruption, or even that they are, in any simple way, the cause of such corruption, but such disparities are an important part of the context that one must recognize in order to understand the moral rules and social field in which Nigerian NGOs operate.

It would be easy to list the various means by which Chidinma could misappropriate donor money. But more central for my purposes here are questions such as how people like Chidinma understand their own motives and behavior, how these behaviors are interpreted by ordinary Nigerians, and what consequences all this has for the evolving relationship between inequality and morality in everyday life in Nigeria. Like ordinary Nigerians in all sectors of the economy, a large proportion of the people who work for the thousands of local NGOs in Nigeria can be seen as simply trying to survive in the world as they find it. But to the Nigerian public, NGOs are also symbols of precisely the kinds of things that are wrong with their society: partnerships between elites, the state, and international donors that benefit the few at the expense of the many; and widespread and all too widely accepted fraud and deceit, where even the noblest goals like helping the sick and the poor are perverted for personal profit. These are all made worse by an overall sense of intractability, where even the disenfranchised spend more time plotting or imagining how they can benefit from this system rather than trying to fix it (Smith 2007a).

Chidinma Alozie of Naija Cares offers an instructive example precisely because she and her organization can (and, I think, must) be analyzed both empathetically and critically. In contrast to a whole host of entirely fraudulent NGOs—which often have little more than a one-room office, or sometimes even just an email address, and have been created simply on the hope of landing one project from which the founders could steal all the money—Naija Cares carried out most of the activities it said it would in its project proposals. This alone separates it from a great many NGOs in Nigeria. From many long conversations with Chidinma, I know that she genuinely hopes that her NGO's work can make a difference for the sick and the poor, especially poor women. She is a devout born-again Christian and often justifies her humanitarianism in the language of religion. Nonetheless, over the years Chidinma definitely used some project resources for personal purposes. I witnessed instances of it myself and heard about a lot more from her staff.

It is important to note that many of the ways Chidinma used NGO money and assets for her own needs drew little scrutiny from her staff. This is partly because, in the Nigerian context, Chidinma was widely perceived as the "owner" of Naija Cares. As such, many considered her to be entitled to use staff labor, project vehicles and resources, and even, to some extent, project money for her own benefit. The quid pro quo for this latitude was that she was expected to care for her staff in the manner that a good patron should—for example, granting time off when a staff member had a personal problem or a burial to attend, providing loans or salary advances when they were requested with good reason, or using her political connections to help someone in her social network get a job or a child gain admission to a school. Part of the difference between Pius and Chidinma was the divergent manners in which they conducted themselves as patrons.

Chidinma has mostly inspired and maintained the loyalty of her staff by being a decent and caring patron, but this has not been the case in every instance. She expected members of her staff to be obedient, even obsequious, in their behavior toward her. Over the past 15 years, I have observed at least half a dozen staff members fall out with Chidinma. Her version of the story almost always included a description of how the staff member had behaved disrespectfully or exceeded his or her authority. I knew almost all these individuals, and most of the staff members who were fired (or forced to quit) said that they had become increasingly unable to bear the way Chidinma dictated to them. Most interesting to me, several of these former employees went on to start their own NGOs. I suspect they had learned the benefits of NGO "ownership," and over time their aspirations and resentments became too much for them to remain under Chidinma's command. Indeed, it was from these former employees that I heard the most detailed accounts of corruption at Naija Cares. While I believe that some of what they told me was true, I always took these stories with a grain of salt, knowing they could be driven partly by bitterness or jealousy.

The issue of jealousy is a powerful one in the lives of NGO "owners." Chidinma was regularly worried about people trying to "bewitch" her, or, as she put it after she became born again, "use the devil against" her. Indeed, one motive for all of the NGO resources she channeled to her church may have been her hope that these good works would assure that God would protect her against enemies. I heard her make this prayer explicitly many times; it is a common entreaty in Nigeria, where people feel that jealous enemies are a constant threat to their own well-being and prosperity. For Chidinma, the sense of insecurity was not entirely imagined. In the 1990s, she received a series of extremely threatening letters accusing her of all kinds of terrible acts and threatening her with retaliation, both physical and spiritual. Perhaps not coincidentally, it was around this period that she became born again.

The juxtaposed examples of Pius and Chidinma—where one engaged in corruption solely for personal gain and one engaged in corruption that benefited a wider social network—speak to the complexity of the ways that inequality and morality intersect in the course of everyday life in contemporary Nigeria. Like the AIDS epidemic that so many NGOs have been founded to fight, these organizations sit at the center of these intertwining strands of social life, the subject of critical moral discourses about corruption but also implicated in the material reproduction of inequality. They are institutions created, in part, to help manage difficult processes of social change, but they are also implicated in furthering social disparities and more firmly entrenching the power of those whose wealth and authority place them in control over others.

People Living Positively (and Suspiciously Well)

So far I have presented two cases of local AIDS NGOs in Nigeria run by people who were not, so far as I knew, HIV positive. As I indicated at the beginning of the chapter, people living with HIV are themselves sometimes suspected of benefiting inordinately from AIDS money. Nowhere is this more widely assumed than in arena of AIDS support groups, many of which have gone on to register themselves as NGOs.

In 2002, the Federal Medical Centre in Owerri, the capital of Imo State, became one of the pilot sites for the implementation of Nigeria's initial program to deliver antiretroviral therapy to people living with HIV and AIDS. A local NGO I knew in Owerri, Community & Youth Development Initiatives (CYDI), helped people receiving treatment start the region's first support group. The director of CYDI, Benjamin Mbakwem, had training and experience in HIV counseling and worked closely with doctors running the clinical program at the hospital. Benjamin is a close friend and colleague of mine, and a person whose integrity I have admired for years. He used his counseling experience and clinical connections to help a number of people in the treatment program to start a support group, Association for Positive

9. The staff of Community & Youth Development Initiatives (CYDI), an NGO in Owerri, Imo State, Nigeria, has worked since 2000 to prevent AIDS and assist people living with the virus. Photo by Sasha Rubel.

Care (AsPoCa). Initially, AsPoCa met once a month on one of the main clinic days when people came to the hospital to collect their antiretroviral drugs.

In many respects, forming AsPoCa was one of the most significant achievements of the first years of work at CYDI. In Nigeria, the vast majority of people who know they are HIV positive learn their status because they are sick and get tested by a doctor based on their symptoms. Testing among people who are not obviously sick is uncommon, even since the wider availability of treatment. In the context of the stigma still associated with the disease, it is extremely challenging for people who discover they are HIV positive to decide whether and to whom to disclose their status, how to manage treatment when many people in their lives do not know they have HIV or AIDS, and how to adjust to the reality of their illness. The support group gatherings offered welcome opportunities to share anxieties, relate common experiences, seek advice, and benefit from collective support.

Over time, however, it became clear that AsPoCa would encounter problems. Significant conflicts emerged over leadership. Gender inequalities similar to those in the wider society created obstacles for women in the group, both with regard to adequate representation in leadership and in terms of sexual harassment. These conflicts were the result not only of interpersonal and gendered dynamics but also of the emerging awareness that the group might be able to attract resources from the government or international donors. These issues came to a head during a competition for World Bank money.

In 2001, the World Bank loaned Nigeria approximately $90 million to fight HIV/AIDS. The money was targeted to benefit 18 states, including Imo State. The Imo State Action Committee on AIDS (SACA) used part of its multimillion-dollar portion of the loan to support the efforts of NGOs working to combat AIDS. In 2004, the Imo SACA issued a request for proposals through which local NGOs could compete for grants of up to $30,000 to finance their activities. At best, no more than a handful of NGOs in Imo State had been doing any serious work on HIV/AIDS in the past decade. But the competition attracted 79 applications, including many from organizations created purely in order to apply for the World Bank/SACA grants.

Community & Youth Development Initiatives had assisted AsPoCa in registering as an NGO precisely so that the association could become viable and independent. With Benjamin's help, AsPoCa crafted and submitted a proposal for a $30,000 grant. In the process, significant rifts occurred in the group, and some members left to form their own support group, driven largely by competition to control possible government and donor resources. AsPoCa won funding under the World Bank/SACA mechanism, and after they received their grant, Benjamin heard numerous complaints from members about how the leadership was spending the money. In Nigeria, it is always hard to judge the veracity of accusations of corruption. On the one hand, experience demonstrates that corruption is extremely common and so one is predisposed to believe such accusations, based as much on the presumption that corruption is ubiquitous as on the merits of actual evidence. On the other hand, allegations of corruption are the common currency of complaint, including among people who are envious of others. Regardless of the relative integrity or culpability of the accusers and the leaders, it was striking how deeply embroiled AsPoCa became in the machinations of corruption.

In the years since the initial SACA grant competition, several more factions of AsPoCa split from the original support group to form their own organizations. According to Benjamin, the main reason for these splits was so that particular individuals and their supporters could establish their own NGOs and reap the benefits of AIDS funds from PEPFAR, the Global Fund, and the Nigerian government. By 2010 at least half a dozen local support groups had registered themselves as NGOs, and most were receiving some kind of donor support.

Not surprisingly, the flow of dollars to NGOs "owned" by people who were HIV positive contributed to local perceptions that many were indeed "feeding fat on AIDS." Rumors circulated that the leaders of these support-group NGOs were buying themselves nice cars and building houses in their villages. A conversation I had with a recent secondary school graduate about his prospects for employment and income represents a wider spectrum of similar interactions with Nigerians who suggested that AIDS had become a profitable enterprise and that NGOs were the means to such riches. The young man said, "In this Nigeria I would be better off carrying [contracting] AIDS and starting an NGO than parading from office to office with my secondary school result [diploma]."

Anthropologist Miriam Ticktin (2011) writes of rumors she encountered while doing fieldwork among undocumented migrants in France—many of whom were African—which implied that asylum petitioners were seeking ways to infect themselves with HIV so as to gain permission to remain in Europe through France's medical humanitarian exemption. Whether those rumors are based on any genuine attempts by individuals to contract the virus, and whether any Nigerian actually would take to heart the young man's claim that infection with HIV might be a more successful means of access to a livable wage than his attempts to find honest labor, is perhaps beside the point. In both the young man's comment above and Ticktin's account, the claim or rumor that a person might wish to infect him or herself with AIDS is a potent moral metaphor for the breakdown of proper access to social and economic opportunities and valued life trajectories. AIDS and the discourses it spawns conjure up and respond to new inequalities, even as they build on old ones.

Conclusion

A considerable literature suggests that AIDS (but also more medicalized conceptions of bodies and persons generally) has reconfigured the relationship between the individual and the state, creating what Nguyen (2010) calls "therapeutic citizenship," something others have written about in similar ways (e.g., Biehl 2007; see also Petryna 2002, 2009). While the details may be different in specific cases, the general argument is that access to health care (and in the case of HIV and AIDS, access to antiretroviral therapy) has emerged as an arena in which people can make claims on the state—and international donor support—in ways that simultaneously circumvent, reinvent, and also reproduce the inequalities that have typically characterized the relationship between ordinary people and their governments. The picture painted in these accounts is both hopeful and depressing. In some instances, resorting to therapeutic citizenship has enabled people to claim and receive benefits from the state that they have not otherwise been able to effectively demand or access (Nguyen 2010; Petryna 2009). However, only some patients are able to leverage their medical conditions and suffering for recognition and assistance, and rarely are they able to translate therapeutic citizenship into broad political representation and rights (Biehl 2005).

In this chapter I have focused on the centrality of Nigeria's burgeoning AIDS NGO sector as a social space where problems of inequality, morality, and social change associated with the epidemic are being expressed, reconfigured, and, in many respects, more deeply entrenched. When organizations and individuals—including people who are themselves HIV positive—who have mobilized to combat the epidemic are perceived as benefiting from their purported good work, it reinforces the popular perception that AIDS is the result of social and moral crisis. Similarly, when so many AIDS-related NGOs (and, by implication, so many HIV-positive individuals) are believed to be corrupt, it only adds to the stigma of the disease and the perception that people who have contracted it somehow brought it on themselves by their immoral behavior.

But the phenomenon of AIDS-related NGOs in contemporary Nigeria is also part of a larger story about new forms of inequality, particularly in the relationship between international donors, the Nigerian state, and ordinary citizens. Nigerians (especially Nigerian elites) have appropriated the NGO model, introduced by Western donors as a means to circumvent the perceived inefficiencies and corruption of the state, and used it for their own purposes. While donors might laud the work of local NGOs, the fact is that many NGOs in Nigeria are created by their "owners" to maximize their own profits. Even though such organizations create opportunities for Nigerians to harness international donor resources for their own upward mobility, they frequently end up being enterprises that ultimately re-create and exacerbate inequality, rather than remediate it in any meaningful way. Further, the major Western donors are often unaware of genuine and effective organizations like CYDI. They instead tend to channel funds to big NGOs based primarily in Lagos and Abuja, "mega-NGOs" that become fiefdoms for their "owners" and top officials. Thus the donors are often complicit in reproducing inequality. Indeed, NGO elites are by most measures (where they live, how much money they make, how connected they are politically) far removed from the people they are ostensibly trying to help.

The fact that NGOs in Nigeria are often mechanisms for the reproduction of inequality is not all that surprising, and it is an occurrence not confined to Nigeria (Haller and Shore 2005; Igoe and Kelsall 2005; Swidler 2006, 2009). But perhaps more interesting is how these NGOs provoke popular political imagination. The stories that circulate about "feeding fat on AIDS" speak to ordinary Nigerians' awareness that the dynamics of domestic disparity are tied to the larger global system of inequality. People are certainly cognizant of these connections when it comes to the oil industry, the country's largest source of revenue (Watts 2004; Smith 2007a; Peel 2011), but they are also well aware of the importance of access to donor dollars as the linchpin for success in the arena of health and other development-related enterprises.

It is commonly (and correctly) believed that most of the money in NGO work in Nigeria comes from abroad and that those who get rich in this "business" are those with the best connections to foreign funds. Interestingly, many ordinary Nigerians believe that their compatriots who profit from AIDS and other development NGOs dupe their foreign backers, and they think that outsiders would be more likely to use aid money honestly than their fellow citizens. While I am less charitable than most Nigerians in my assessment of the motives of US and European foreign aid in Africa, Nigerians retain at least a partially positive perception of the motives of foreign aid donors.

In addition to the commentary they offer regarding the role of global powers in the reproduction of inequality in Nigeria, the stories about NGOs feeding fat on AIDS also reveal Nigerians' awareness, anger, and ambivalence about a moral economy in which practices of patronage undermine and outweigh competing rules based on bureaucratic accountability. On the one hand, the stories and widely expressed discontents about NGO corruption suggest that Nigerians are fed up with politics and economics of patronage. On the other hand, the distinction between Pius and Chidinma suggests that there are still many moral pressures and social rewards for using "ownership" of an NGO to build one's career as a patron. Pius was condemned not so much because he benefited financially from his position at UAA but because of the way he mishandled himself in his relationship with fellow staff, peers, and his various publics. He was seen as greedy and self-aggrandizing, whereas Chidinma was mostly seen as a good patron and a moral person. Nevertheless, even Chidinma was the subject of rumors, jealousy, and defamatory gossip, suggesting that the position of a good patron is itself becoming suspect in Nigeria's changing political economy (Gore and Pratten 2003; Daloz 2005; Smith 2007a).

Indeed, Nigerian NGOs are not just objects of discontent in popular discourse. They also sit at the nexus of significant processes of social and political change, perhaps contributing as much to reproducing inequalities as remedying them. But both their rhetoric (sincere or not) and the existence of many committed people and NGOs like Benjamin and CYDI offer hope for change—and a basis upon which to critique the status quo and demand change. The very fact that some NGOs—and the elites who benefit from them—are popularly acknowledged as illegitimate, and even fairly good ones like Naija Cares are the subject of critical rumors, suggests that inequality sits uncomfortably with collective morality, whether the moral economy is grounded in patron-clientism, a more bureaucratic neoliberal order, or some mix of the two. AIDS NGOs are both bellwethers and active participants in these changing dynamics.

FIVE

Returning Home to Die:
Migration and Kinship in the Era of AIDS

During a brief visit from Ubakala, I stayed as a guest of Zebus Ogbonnaya and his family in the Oshodi area of Lagos. We were all just about ready to sleep when there came a knock at the door at around 9 P.M., just a few minutes after Zebus had snapped closed the padlocks on the metal gate that reinforces the front door against intruders. Oshodi is one of the most crowded sections of Lagos, Nigeria's commercial capital, which has a population of well over 10 million people. Hundreds of thousands of Igbos from the Southeast live in Lagos, and many will reside there for most of their lives. But even lifelong Igbo residents often feel a pervasive sense of insecurity in Lagos. The reasons for this are many. For one thing, Igbo migrants to Lagos, which is situated in the Yoruba-speaking Southwest, are, in some senses, forever "foreigners" there. For another, economic hardships and fear of rampant crime pervade daily life in Lagos, as in many of Nigeria's urban areas. As the country's biggest city by far, Lagos conjures up the plethora of images Nigerians share regarding the struggles and crises—but also the opportunities and possibilities—associated with contemporary urban life.

But neither Nigeria's internal ethnic tensions nor the specter of economic adversity and violent crime fully account for the feeling of anxiety that seems to loom large in the lives of so many rural–urban migrants. Lagos, like other cities to which millions of Nigerians are flocking in search of opportunities for education and employment, is a place perceived to contain and represent numerous deeply worrying hazards, many of which are expressed in moral terms. Rural–urban migrants in Nigeria commonly see city life as threatening to long-cherished values of family and community. The allure of consumption, the pursuit of money, and the relative anonymity of city living create a sense that selfishness and greed constantly jeopardize commitments to the primacy of human social relationships. These worries are crystallized perhaps most powerfully in perceived threats to the institutions of kinship. The AIDS epidemic produces diseased bodies that seem to stand for these larger dangers to family and community.

The knock at the Ogbonnaya family apartment in Oshodi proved to be the opening scene in one family's experience with AIDS and the ways that efforts to cope with the disease become embroiled in larger anxieties about a changing society. Zebus answered the rap on the door with a cautious query in Pidgin English, "Na u dat?" ("Who is it?"). In the Igbo dialect of Zebus's home community of Ubakala in Abia State, a woman responded, "O wu nwi gi" (literally, "It is your wife"). Zebus and his wife, Akudo, who was dozing on the sofa across from him, knew immediately that the visitor was from Zebus's natal community almost 500 kilometers away in south-eastern Nigeria, as the abbreviated form (*nwi*) of the Igbo word for wife and, more generally, for female in-law (*nwunyi*) is specific to Ubakala and other nearby communities. Unlocking the gate, Zebus and Akudo heartily greeted Chioma Amechi, a sixtyish woman who is married to one of Zebus's uncles in the village. Visitors from "home"—often unannounced—are frequent in Zebus and Akudo's Lagos flat. Relatives from both Zebus's lineage in Ubakala and Akudo's lineage in Ohuhu, a neighboring community, often use the small two-bedroom flat as a base during trips to Lagos for business, family, or personal matters.

That night, no one asked Chioma Amechi the purpose of her visit, and she did not volunteer it. Given how early the Ogbonnaya household had to be up and out for work and school the next morning, it was clear that we would not know the purpose of Chioma Amechi's visit until the next evening. In the morning, I walked with Zebus to his small photocopying shop on Agege Motor Road, about a mile from the family's flat. On the way, Zebus speculated about the purpose of Chioma's visit. The arrival of village relatives inevitably creates some anxiety that they might be delivering bad news. He was able to rule out a number of possibilities. None of his kin at home had died, he concluded, because a male relative would normally deliver such news. Besides, if there had been a death, Chioma surely would have said something by then.

It also seemed highly unlikely that Chioma was coming in the hope of asking Zebus and Akudo for assistance in migrating to Lagos or finding a job. Relatives wanting to migrate had come before, seeking short-term accommodation while they looked for a job or a place to live. Such visitors were among the most burdensome because the duration of their stays were indeterminate, and it was a huge strain on household resources and relationships to host visitors for extended periods. A year or so earlier, Zebus had eventually asked one of Akudo's relatives to leave after he had spent almost two months in their flat with no prospect of finding either employment or his own accommodations. Although Akudo too was fed up, Zebus's action had created some tension between them, not least because Zebus had recently agreed to take in his own nephew while he attended secondary school in Lagos. But Chioma Amechi was well beyond the age of a typical aspiring rural–urban migrant.

During our conversation that day, I asked Zebus what might bring a senior woman like Chioma to see them. The possibilities seemed endless. Perhaps she wanted help with one of her children—some of them were of the right age to want to migrate to Lagos for employment or higher education. Perhaps she wanted to secure the support of Lagos-based community members for some kind of church or women's association project back home in the village. Zebus had recently been president of the Lagos branch of his village's development union. These speculations reflected just how deeply embedded Zebus and his family remained in the affairs of their extended families and communities of origin, a situation that is normal for Igbo rural–urban migrants in Nigeria.

Despite the burden of obligations to "home" and "home people," these ties formed Zebus and Akudo's most important social network. They relied on home people (*ndi ulo*) for access to all kinds of resources. They found their current flat, a big improvement on their previous tenement, through a tip from a relative. Zebus supplemented his meager income from his struggling photocopying business by pursuing government contracts to supply stationery and office supplies, contracts most often awarded on the basis of kinship connections and community allegiances. Their daughter had recently started secondary school at the Federal Government Girls College back home in Umuahia, and Zebus relied on the help of his cousin to make sure his daughter received provisions and pocket money.

Notwithstanding the lengthy speculation about the purpose of Chioma Amechi's visit, Zebus and Akudo were unprepared for the news she would reveal. That evening, after dinner, Chioma began to cry. Zebus and Akudo comforted her and assured her that whatever it was, God would see her through. Finally, through inconsolable tears, Chioma told them that her son, Ufomba, who had been working as an auto mechanic in the central Nigerian town of Makurdi, had returned to Ubakala two weeks earlier terribly sick. He was extremely thin, had a wracking cough and frequent diarrhea, and was perpetually weak. He confessed to his mother that he had been diagnosed with AIDS. Neither Chioma nor Ufomba had told Udo, her husband and his father, about the reason for Ufomba's condition. Thus far, Ufomba's diagnosis was known only to Chioma, though I would later learn when I returned to Ubakala that rumors swirled in the community about the source of Ufomba's sickness. Chioma begged Zebus to come home and tell his uncle, Udo, the truth of Ufomba's condition. She feared that her husband would react angrily and might even expel their son from their home. Zebus had always been especially close to Udo, and she hoped that his influence would enable the family to manage this tragedy in some harmony.

Much of my focus so far in this book has been on moral discourses about AIDS and the ways they are indicative of widely prevalent anxieties about the consequences of inequalities associated with contemporary social changes in Nigeria. To put it more concisely, I have concentrated more on AIDS in the social imagination, as it relates to other aspects of everyday life, than on the disease as a lived medical condition. In this chapter I examine the ways families cope with the reality of AIDS and the manner in which rural communities react to the homecoming of an urban migrant kinsman who is sick from the virus. These responses are emblematic of larger changes in kinship. In contemporary Nigeria's shifting cultural landscape, the processes of social reproduction—how a society reproduces persons, families, and institutions, and what kinds of persons, families, and institutions these are—seem up for grabs. The specter of AIDS both symbolizes and exacerbates these uncertain times and processes. The profound importance of kinship, felt perhaps even more acutely as it appears stretched and strained by multiple trajectories of social change, heightens the degree to which AIDS affects so many lives in Nigeria. In addition to looming large as a symbol of social and moral crisis, AIDS arrives literally at the doorsteps of many more Nigerians than the nearly three million who are estimated to be infected with the virus.

The story of Ufomba's illness illustrates the intimate links between kinship, rural–urban migration, and Nigeria's AIDS epidemic. Further, rural–urban migration and the transformations in social relations associated with city life are deeply implicated in popular understandings of the nature of the moral crisis that is seen as underlying AIDS. The intersection of inequality and morality as it plays out in the spheres of migration and kinship shows some of the clearest parallels between Nigerians' understandings of the ultimate causes of the country's AIDS epidemic and their interpretations of the reasons for what is perceived to be a larger social crisis. But despite the challenges posed by contemporary social changes, kinship ties remain vital, not only as people grapple with AIDS but as family life and livelihood strategies extend from village communities to Nigeria's ever-growing cities.

In real and imagined ways, rural–urban migration, city life, and the continuing tug of kinship obligations create the context in which understandings of AIDS are constructed. The nature of family ties in this period of rapid
social change also affects the manner in which those who contract AIDS are
received by their families. This process frequently involves return migration,
where migrants who contract HIV and develop AIDS in the city come home
to the village in hopes of finding kin who will care for them. I draw inspiration in this chapter from the ways Julie Livingston connects caregiving for
the sick or disabled to norms surrounding kinship and the moral imagination more generally. In her history of debility in Botswana (2005), Livingston details the past century's pattern of contestations within families over
how best to care for individuals who have been handicapped physically or
mentally through accident, illness, or birth abnormalities. Even as new lines
of tension are cleaved among kin and in-laws over allegations of witchcraft,
expressions of jealousy and blame, and attempts to adjudicate responsibility for rehabilitation or maintenance, Livingston attends to the emotional
bonds and good caregiving practices that continue despite extreme poverty
and inequality.

In southeastern Nigeria, when a rural–urban migrant returns home with
AIDS, the specter of stigma looms large and wider threats to kinship posed
by a changing society are illuminated. Nonetheless, families mobilize to
care for their sick kin, reinforcing the very bonds that seem threatened. Later
in the chapter, I return to the case of Zebus's nephew, Ufomba, as an example of how AIDS and the challenges of caregiving for people infected with
the virus reveal the burdens of and challenges to the institutions of kinship
that are so fundamental to everyday life in Nigeria. I also describe how
Ufomba's family sought to cope with his illness. First, however, I provide
some background and context regarding kinship, rural–urban migration,
and their relationship to ongoing social changes more generally.

Rural–Urban Ties: Kinship and Community in a Clientelistic Political Economy

In Nigeria, and across sub-Saharan Africa, the central role of kinship networks in social and economic life and the enduring importance of people's
ties to their ancestral village communities suggest that the relationship between migration and other contemporary social transformations is intimate
and far-reaching. The movement of people between rural and urban areas
is fluid, as individuals and families move back and forth to fulfill a wide
variety of personal, economic, and cultural interests and obligations. As

briefly noted in chapter 2, the effects of migration on behavior also run between the village and the city. Social reproduction in rural and urban areas is mutually constituted, with the links between such communities being particularly important in a context where the political economy is dominated by patron-clientism, and kinship ties remain the most reliable means to navigate the system. A growing literature in African studies emphasizes the continuing importance of rural–urban connections as a special feature of urbanization in sub-Saharan Africa (Gugler and Flanagan 1978; Geschiere and Gugler 1998; Simone and Abouhani 2005; Simone 2011). Africanist scholars have described how urban Africans reproduce the social institutions of their ancestral rural communities in the city, maintain life-long ties with those communities, and themselves have great influence over the gradual transformation of rural institutions and practices (Trager 2001; Gugler 2002).

Among the Igbo in Nigeria, the strength of ties between rural and urban areas is profound. Igbos who migrate to urban areas remain heavily involved in the affairs of their natal communities (Gugler 1991; Smith 1999; Chukwuezi 2001). They build their first (and often only) house in the village. They return "home" to participate in traditional festivals and rituals of the life cycle. They contribute to village development projects and maintain membership in local development unions. They pay dues and continue their affiliations with village churches. They mediate local disputes and participate in local politics. And, almost without exception, they are buried at home (Smith 2004c). Perhaps less noted in the literature, but equally important, is the degree to which rural Igbos maintain ties with their urban kin. As highlighted in the anecdote that opens this chapter, these relationships are not just about urban Igbos returning home but also about rural Igbos going to the city for aid (Chukwuezi 2001).

The strength of the link between city-dwelling Igbos and their natal communities was intensified by the historical experience of Biafra, Nigeria's civil war from 1967 to 1970, in which the Igbo nation attempted unsuccessfully to secede. The roots of the conflict stemmed from regional, religious, and ethnic cleavages and a desire on the part of the Igbo for political and economic control over their homeland. As the events leading to the declaration of secession unfolded (including a bloody, mostly Igbo-led military coup and a brutal counter-coup by Muslim northerners), tens of thousands of Igbos were killed in other regions of Nigeria before they could flee home. In the aftermath of the war, during which approximately one million people were killed or starved to death, Igbos lost land and property they had acquired outside Igboland before the war (Kirk-Greene 1971; Graf 1988). Although Igbos have resumed their entrepreneurial and migratory customs in the years and decades since Biafra, they have not forgotten. Staying connected to home is considered important for safety as well as for success (Smith 2005; Harneit-Sievers 2006). But these days it is equally important for rural Igbos to cultivate ties to urban relatives in order to assure access to social and economic resources.

Like many other African ethnic groups, most Igbos share an intense sense that ties to home—and kin—are important for personal and political safety. Rural–urban ties are vital for gaining access to resources and opportunities and for the maintenance of cultural identity (Berry 1985; Bayart 1993; Chukwuezi 2001). People commonly depend on their lineage, clan, and ethnic identities, and associated social networks to negotiate the institutions of the state and the wider economy (Geschiere 2009). In this context, the ties between urban migrants and their rural kin are highly valued and laden with obligation. Even for those urban migrants who might feel discontented with the extent of their obligations to rural kin, the possibility of opting out is almost unthinkable (Bastian 1993; Geschiere 1997, 2009). Urban migrants are expected not only to send remittances but also to participate fully in the economic, social, cultural, and political life of their ancestral communities (Geschiere and Gugler 1998; Lambert 2002; Cliggett 2005).

Yet the relationships between migrants and their relatives at home are by no means always smooth. These relationships are the topic of constant discussion and negotiation, are often fraught with tension, and, not uncommonly, form the basis for accusations of witchcraft and sorcery (Geschiere 1997, 2009). Recurring patterns in relationships between rural–urban migrants and their communities of origin provide a window onto larger processes of continuity and social change that characterize Igbo customs and, arguably, much wider arenas of African social life. Notions of kinship are central to understanding these processes because expectations about who constitutes one's kin, what obligations kin have to one another, and how kinship relations move or extend across geographical space are both central to the construction of rural–urban ties and part of what gets renegotiated and reconstructed as people live out their multisited lives.

The things Igbo people want are surely "modern"—good schools for their children, government services for their communities, more money for themselves. However, in Nigeria, the way to get them is by having allies, townspeople, and especially kinfolk who are strategically placed to secure a share of the nation's political and economic resources. One cannot succeed in Nigeria, most Igbos will tell you, without the aid of reliable kin-folk (Smith 2001c, 2007a).

In analyzing the place of this system of patron-clientism in processes of social change, it is particularly important to recognize the degree to which patrons are often as dependent on and as morally bound to these webs of obligation as clients are. Remember from chapter 4 that the source of Pius's downfall was ultimately in his refusal to spread his success to his "clients"—to those individuals who were dependent on him and who felt entitled to a share of his prosperity. In Igbo society, one does not gradu-ate from the obligations of kinship via economic success or migration. To become wealthy and successful is to incur even greater obligations to those who have helped you along the way. Indeed, for an Igbo person, the great-est motivation to become affluent is to enjoy the recognition of being an important patron—as friends, colleagues, and interlocutors have told me time and again. It is true, patrons routinely complain that clients expect too much, and clients regularly grumble that patrons do not do enough. But these complaints, in addition to demonstrating the strains in relationships created by the conflict of individual aspirations and group obligations, also testify to the continuing power of such ties. Despite their burden and indi-cations that they increasingly compete with other priorities, the obligations and affective bonds of kinship cannot be ignored. Further, I think few Igbos would genuinely wish to break off such ties completely, even if given the freedom to do so.

As kin move across the Nigerian political and economic landscape, so does HIV. The virus follows and exploits the movement of people (Setel 1999; Dilger 2006; Thomas, Haour-Knipe and Aggleton 2010). Much of the literature on the epidemiology of HIV focuses on southern Africa, where infection rates are much higher than in Nigeria, and where entrenched pat-terns of labor migration suggest a significant role for migration in spread-ing the virus (Clark et al. 2007). Some evidence also suggests the impact of migration may be less straightforward than conventionally portrayed (Lurie et al. 2003), with spouses left behind sometimes infecting returning migrant partners rather than vice versa. Relatively few epidemiological stud-ies have been conducted in Nigeria, but some scholars suggest that rural–urban ties are an important pathway for infection in Nigeria as well (Oladele and Brieger 1994; Orubuloye 1997; Mberu and White 2011). Although the conventional view is that migration serves to spread the virus, it is also true that AIDS morbidity and mortality can trigger migrations, as people move to cities to seek treatment, people return "home" to die (Whyte 2005), or households dissolve and disperse in response to AIDS-induced crises (Hosegood et al. 2004).

Ufomba was infected after moving to the city. Given that when he came home he was already sick, it seems unlikely that he spread the virus at this point, but he may have done so during other visits to Ubakala before he became symptomatic. More relevant for my focus here, the community's responses to his illness illustrate how perceived connections between migration and AIDS reflect people's experiences and anxieties about contemporary processes like urbanization, a changing economy, and the monetization of many aspects of social relations, particularly as they affect kinship.

The Celebrations, Expectations, and Burdens of Home People

Despite—or perhaps in part because of—widespread awareness that succeeding in the city is not easy, migrants feel tremendous pressure to represent their life trajectories positively when they return home for visits. The continued strength of ties to extended families in communities of origin creates collective expectations that are constant topics of discussion. On the one hand, migrants often postpone or try to avoid visits to their natal villages and towns when they feel they do not have the financial resources to make a trip home viable. On the other hand, when migrants do go home, they often try to craft their visits as triumphal, depicting their lives in the city as more successful than they really are.

In the Igbo-speaking Southeast, it is a tradition that migrants return home during the Christmas period, and rural communities are abuzz with activity during these weeks, much of it fueled by the returnees' conspicuous consumption. Many migrants I know saved for months in advance of Christmas in order to be able to adorn themselves with several new and appropriately fashionable outfits, purchase suitable gifts for their relatives, and have enough money to spend generously while at home. It is difficult to demarcate behavior that is generous from behavior that might more accurately be labeled as ostentatious and self-serving. Indeed, "home people"—the residents of migrants' natal communities—are themselves often ambivalent and contradictory when it comes to the consumptive and distributive behavior of their migrant kin. They pressure their urban brothers and sisters to show off their success and share their wealth, admiring those who do and deriding those who do not; but they also commonly condemn ostentatious behavior as self-aggrandizing. Migrants are seemingly damned if they do and damned if they don't. But ultimately, the pressures to prove success, to show off their urban fashions, and to share the fruits of their labor outweigh the complementary fears of resentment. Christmas in the Igbo Southeast is a show, and migrants are the main protagonists.

It is not only at Christmas that migrants feel the pressure to prove that their economic journeys have been successful. Family weddings, burial ceremonies, and other rituals are also centripetal events. In the life of an Igbo community—indeed, in the life of any particular lineage—there are far more family and community ceremonies than any individual migrant can possibly attend. Migrants thus choose their participation strategically, based on assessments like the prestige of the person marrying or being buried or the strength of ties (affective and otherwise), but also based on whether they were—as I heard many migrants say—"buoyant." By this they meant whether they had enough cash on hand to be able to participate at a level "befitting" the status they aspire to maintain among kin and other home people. As at Christmas, migrants who attend these events demonstrate their success—but also, importantly, their continued loyalty to kin and community of origin—through displays of conspicuous material consumption and through generous cash and in-kind gifts to friends and relatives.

Despite the hoopla around the Christmas season, burials are arguably the most important ritual in Igbo family and community life. Certainly if one measures a ritual's importance by the time it takes to plan, the money spent, the level of expectation for attendance, and the degree to which people feel they are required to meet collective expectations, there is no other ceremony that exceeds funerals in social significance. While many people in contemporary southeastern Nigeria bemoan the degree to which burials have become prohibitively expensive, escalating in a kind of arms race of lavish spending and conspicuous displays of wealth, modernity, and social connections, few families are willing to risk the social opprobrium associated with the failure to bury one's kin well. The result is that bodies are embalmed or refrigerated and commonly stored in mortuaries for months as families try to plan and assemble the resources for a suitable burial. The costs of hired vehicles, canopies, musicians, electricity generators, and copious amounts of food and drink can sometimes overwhelm families, leading to the incursion of heavy debts, the exacerbation of long-simmering conflicts, and intense personal anxieties. Indeed, many of the fundamental social aspirations associated with modernity and people's ambivalence about the inequalities that go along with ongoing social changes are on prominent display in the dynamics of Igbo burials (Smith 2004c).

Migrants are deeply implicated in Igbo burials, both when they are the relatives of the deceased and when they die themselves. As the opening anecdote about Chioma Amechi's visit to Zebus's family in Lagos suggests, migrants are constantly reminded of their ties to home through the specter of death. News about a death among home people (the term "home people," again, signaling anyone whose lineal or marital ties are to the place of origin, regardless of where they may reside) spreads quickly in Igbo migrant communities. Further, death mobilizes ties among migrants forcefully and effectively.

A hallmark of Igbo migrant communities is the "hometown associations" of people from the same rural place of origin that they have developed and maintained in their urban locations (Uchendu 1965; Smock 1971; Wolpe 1974; Chukwuezi 2001). These associations (sometimes also called development unions or improvement unions) serve many functions—including supporting development projects in rural communities of origin, serving as channels for migrant political influence "at home" in the village, and offering networks of social support and communities of identification for fellow migrants—but one of their main purposes is pooling resources to support burials. Hometown associations collect dues and levies from their members. Although migrants occasionally allow their dues to lapse, they are least likely to default on the component of their membership fees allotted for burial dues. These dues act as a kind of insurance: when a migrant dies away from home, the hometown association pays to transport the body home (not an insignificant sum for Igbos living in far-flung destinations like Lagos and Kano). Even in Igbo communities in the United States and Europe, such contributions toward burials are part of the international incarnations of Igbo hometown associations. In addition to paying to transport a body, hometown associations make significant contributions to the burials. The specific structure of dues versus levies and the amounts that these associations contribute vary significantly across communities, but in every Igbo migrant community that I am aware of the role of migrants in supporting the burials of fellow home people is significant. During my research in Kano, I remember few stories told with as much lament as those about the (exceedingly rare) Igbo man who let his ties with his hometown association and home people lapse to the point where, upon his death, he was buried without fanfare in the city cemetery.

In a context where migrants' success is measured above all in their place of origin; where returns home are performed, even in death, in the idiom of triumph; and where visits are delayed or avoided when circumstances suggest something less than success, it is not surprising that returning home with AIDS amounts to a calamity beyond its health implications. I do not mean to suggest that all visits home by Igbo migrants are in this triumphal idiom, or that there are not many reasons that bring family members home to visit, including the poor health of family members or migrants themselves. Such visits are indeed common, and they often occur without fanfare, rumor, or scandal. Much of social life—including much of migrants' relationships with their kin at home—unfolds underneath and without the fanfare associated with major community rituals and events such as weddings, burials, and the Christmas holidays. But I would argue that it is important and appropriate to set up a discussion of the experience of a return home with AIDS in the context of this more public aspect of migrant–home relations because, in significant measure, local interpretations of AIDS are constructed in relationship to these more performative elements of the relationships between migrants, their kin, and the communities to which they belong. Migrants may undertake a permanent return home for many reasons, both triumphal and ignoble—ranging from the attainment of sufficient wealth to retire in splendor, to spectacular financial failure necessitating renewed dependence on rural kin. However, a return home with HIV, with the moral stigma of AIDS attached to it, is among the most shameful manifestations of migrant failure imaginable.

I return now to the story of Ufomba Amechi. Ufomba's story encapsulates many aspects of young rural–urban migrants' experiences more generally, including powerful aspirations for a better life; struggles to survive and succeed in Nigeria's changing and increasingly urban economy and society; continued expectations to support family at home; and the pressure to represent the migration journey as beneficial. More specifically, his experience in Ubakala also represents a number of elements characteristic of the challenges faced by rural–urban migrants who come home with AIDS. The problem of disclosure, which precipitated Ufomba's mother's trip to Lagos to recruit Zebus's help, is one of many anticipated difficulties of living with the stigma of AIDS. But Ufomba's story also attests to the extent that families still provide love and support for their sick and dying kin, even in the face of stigma and stereotypes about AIDS that they may not only share but also perpetuate.

Returning Home with AIDS

Ufomba Amechi was the third of six children and the second of two sons. Born in 1979, he spent his childhood and adolescence in Ubakala, where he attended and completed both primary and secondary school. He tried over several years to gain admission to a university but never succeeded. Just before 2000, he migrated to Makurdi, the capital of Benue State, in what is known as Nigeria's "middle belt" (because it is situated geographically, culturally, and religiously in between Nigeria's heavily Muslim north and its heavily Christian south). There, he worked first as an apprentice to an auto mechanic to whom he was somehow distantly related on his mother's side. After two years with his master, he opened his own small workshop and was making a living at his trade, albeit a relatively meager one.

When Ufomba returned home sick, I was doing research for the "Love, Marriage, and HIV" study (Smith 2007b; Hirsch et al. 2009). I was working closely with CYDI, the NGO in Owerri (mentioned in the preceding chapter) with close ties to the Federal Medical Centre (FMC). At that time, FMC operated the only antiretroviral therapy program in the region. I offered to use my connections to help Ufomba get enrolled in the FMC program. Unfortunately, Ufomba died less than three months after I met him, before he completed the various tests and protocols that might have enabled him to start taking antiretroviral medications in the Owerri program.

Over those months, I talked with Ufomba on multiple occasions and also observed how his return to Ubakala unfolded among his family and in the community more generally. The secrecy, stigma, and denial that marked Ufomba's experience in Ubakala have been widely documented in Nigeria and elsewhere (Parker and Aggleton 2003; Campbell et al. 2005; Rankin et al. 2005; Niehaus 2007). The literature on AIDS stigma is vast, spanning psychological, sociological, and anthropological perspectives. Here, I wish to build primarily on the attention that has been drawn to the connections between social inequalities and stigma (Parker and Aggleton 2003; Castro and Farmer 2005). Approaches that attend to the political economy of stigma have pointed out that that the stigma associated with HIV infection exploits and exacerbates existing social inequalities based on, for example, class, race, gender, and sexual orientation. I extend this perspective by focusing on the ways in which the moral interpretations of the AIDS epidemic in general (and of individual infections in particular) are connected to broader moralistic understandings of the social changes that produce and heighten inequality. In other words, the stigma associated with HIV is not simply the product of moral judgments about the presumed individual sexual behavior that resulted in infection; it is inextricably linked to broader categories of related moral violations. It is from its associations with larger societal transformations that are seen as potentially, and sometimes patently, immoral that AIDS stigma derives its power.

One of the questions I asked Ufomba was whether he knew how he had become infected with HIV. He acknowledged that he did not know for sure—he had had unprotected sex with a number of women over the years—but he speculated about a particular woman who he learned had been having sex with other men while telling him that she was intimate only with him. "There was this lady from Otukpo," he said, "and she played me 419 [meaning she deceived him]. I think she was the one. Girls from Otukpo are one kind, and they say AIDS is rampant there." Ufomba was repeating a popular view I had heard from many others about the relationship between Nigerian regional cultures, women's sexual morality, and HIV risk. Benue State (where both Makurdi and Otukpo are located) has indeed been identified through epidemiological surveillance as a relatively high prevalence area in Nigeria's quite diverse regional epidemics. In everyday discourse in southeastern Nigeria, places like Otukpo are identified as bastions of infection, where high risk is purportedly explained by "loose" (and by implication inferior) cultural mores around women's sexuality. It is telling that Ufomba felt that he had most likely contracted the virus from a woman he suspected of engaging in multiple concurrent partnerships. Although statistically this may have meant her risk of contracting the infection was relatively high, it also reflects widespread assumptions that "good" women who have serially monogamous relationships do not carry the virus because they are engaging in more moral sex; even though the epidemiological reality often belies that stereotype (Lurie and Rosenthal 2010). The resort to blaming women's (and to a lesser extent men's) failed sexual morality is common in many settings besides Nigeria (Setel 1999; Simpson 2009; Cole 2010). In Nigeria, it maps powerfully onto wider cultural stereotypes through which ethnic and religious groups tell moral stories about others to explain problematic features of political and social life in the country. The Igbo themselves serve this stereotypical function for other groups in Nigeria on a variety of issues.

Of course, elided in this predominant focus on women's sexual morality, and on the cultural failings of whole ethnic or religious groups, are (1) the role of men in producing Nigeria's AIDS epidemic and (2) the significance of political-economic factors like poverty, inequality, poor health services, and other structural underpinnings of health-related behavior and outcomes. This is not to say that Nigerians are entirely uncritical of men's role in HIV transmission. As I indicated in chapter 2, I have heard many people, usually women, condemn various aspects of men's behavior, especially in the context of the relationship between masculinity and the changes associated with a modernizing society (on masculinity and AIDS, see Setel 1999 for Tanzania, and Hunter 2005, 2010 for South Africa). Further, many Nigerians are well aware of the structural connections between AIDS and poverty and inequality. Nevertheless, as should be evident by now, it is striking how commonly and how forcefully interpretations of individual cases of AIDS, and of the national epidemic itself, turned on moral judgments. The specter of being judged morally shaped Ufomba's return to Ubakala and the way he and his family tried to manage impressions in the community.

This impression management began at home, within the family. Ufomba's father, Udo, was eventually told, with Zebus's help, that Ufomba had been diagnosed with AIDS. He reacted angrily at first, lashing out at both Ufomba and Chioma for the shame this would bring to the family—a disgrace grounded in the perception that AIDS infection is indicative of moral failure. For Udo, Ufomba's HIV infection signaled a failure on the part of his whole family, and he knew that his community would judge Ufomba's AIDS in moralizing terms. Udo had heard the stories told about others in the community suspected of being sick or dying from AIDS. Most of them attributed infections to sexual behaviors associated with monetary greed, unbridled desires, and the failure to follow the word of God. Implicit in each of these assessments was the presumption that the infected individual had become unmoored from the social (and moral) ties that would have prevented the kinds of personal conduct that lead to infection. The stigma of HIV infection was also a tacit criticism of the inability of individuals to resist (and to some extent of the failures of families to enable them to resist) the temptations of modern life associated with AIDS.

A few weeks after he learned of his son's infection, I asked Udo about his reaction to the news. He said he feared that people would think his son contracted AIDS because he was unable to refrain from the temptations of city life. Udo himself worried that his son had given in to sin. But it is important to recognize that the perceived sins and temptations associated with AIDS are not simply about sex; they are about sex associated with the lure of money, consumption, the individualistic freedoms of city life, and about perceived threats to kinship and collective values. In a world where family, community, and prosocial behaviors are still highly prized (even as they appear under siege), in Udo's mind Ufomba's infection reflected on him and his entire kin group.

As a consequence, the Amechi family did everything they could to keep secret the nature of Ufomba's illness. They told more distant relatives and neighbors that he had typhoid and malaria, and his mother even contributed to rumors that someone had bewitched her son. It is telling that being seen as a victim of witchcraft is preferable to being seen as suffering from AIDS (see also Rödlach 2006). An explanation based on witchcraft leaves open the question of whether the victim is innocent or deserving of his predicament. One can be a target of witchcraft fairly or unfairly. Further, blaming witchcraft for the misfortune of infection is not necessarily incompatible with recognition of the biomedical reasons for transmission; witchcraft explains the ultimate reason why a person had the misfortune of contracting HIV, without necessarily denying the proximate cause of unprotected sex. Sometimes people infected with HIV go out of their way to construct a story of innocence around their infection—for example, in Nigeria getting infected by blood transfusion is seen as less blameworthy than getting infected through sex. All of these strategies attest to the power of moral stigma surrounding AIDS in Nigeria.

By the time Ufomba returned to Ubakala sick with AIDS in April 2004, a small number of other people had already come back to this community of 11 villages to die of AIDS. I have no idea how many, but I had seen a few cases myself and heard rumors about more. Without very intimate knowledge (which I had in Ufomba's case, but rarely in others), it is impossible to know for sure whether someone who was rumored to have died of AIDS really did. Indeed, the fact that AIDS is such a morally stigmatizing explanation for sickness and death means that it can be mobilized socially even when there is no real evidence to support it. Rumors about people sick with AIDS have to be seen in their political context. Saying someone has AIDS can be a weapon in intrafamily and intracommunity conflicts (Farmer 1992; Yamba 1997; Thomas 2007).

For example, in one instance a woman who had been a successful trader was rumored to have died of AIDS. The woman, known as "Thick Madam" for her prodigious girth as well as her ample wealth, had built a booming business that began with transporting foodstuffs to Lagos and bringing back products like cosmetics and children's clothing to sell in Ubakala and nearby areas. As her business grew, she expanded to other areas; at the time she died, she was said to have owned several trucks. Along the way she and her husband divorced. When she died, people attributed her purported HIV infection to the consequences of her greed, which people said led to her divorce and thereby enabled her supposedly promiscuous behavior. I was in no position to judge what actually killed her, much less whether the stories about her behavior were true. But there was no doubt that the moral interpretations of her death, via the accusation of AIDS, served to express and criticize how the single-minded pursuit of wealth in Nigeria has affected marriage, transformed established gender roles, and diminished people's ability to control their desires. In this example, gender inequality was obviously an important component; a man pursuing wealth and along the way leaving his spouse might be criticized, but not nearly as vehemently as a woman doing the same.

That so many of these rumors circulated about migrants who got sick—seemingly more so than about permanent residents of the community—suggests that these stories spoke to worries about the threats to kinship embodied in migration and its associated social and cultural transformations. As Ufomba's case illustrates, rumors about AIDS need not be false in order to participate in this collective unease about the connections between infection, inequalities, and immorality.

Despite the Amechi family's efforts to conceal the true cause of Ufomba's illness, rumors inevitably circulated that he had AIDS; his rapid weight loss alone had provided sufficient fodder for such gossip. I heard a range of stories that implicated various moral failings, from those that surfaced long-simmering micropolitical rivalries between the Amechis and other families in Ubakala, to much more sweeping indictments of the immoral behavior associated with urban life and a whole generation of young people. For example, several people from the Amechis' village speculated that Ufomba's infection was the result of his grandfather's failure to obey customs associated with the family's origin. Apparently Udo and Ufomba's paternal ancestor, like the ancestors of a number of families I knew in Ubakala, had first come to Ubakala as a slave several generations back. Later, with the abolition of slavery, the man's progeny became incorporated into the slave owner's kin group. But memories had been passed down and so too were some restrictions on marriage within that kin group. In the wake of Ufomba's illness, I learned that Udo's father allegedly had broken those rules, and some said Ufomba's susceptibility to HIV was a consequence of his grandfather's transgression. The moral lapses that explain AIDS are mainly linked to contemporary problems, but the social imagination also at times implicates the transgressions of individuals in prior generations in the transmission of the virus.

Also common in the wake of Ufomba's illness were much more general accusations. Typical in these broader accounts was an indictment of the individualism, sexual liberty, and greedy desires for consumption regularly attributed to both young people and city folk. Even among villagers who were sympathetic to Ufomba's individual plight, the specter of AIDS provoked considerable expressions of anxiety and discontent about the consequences of the materialism and individual liberties associated with modern, urban life. Only rarely was there any overt acknowledgment that people in Ubakala shared almost all of the same aspirations that propelled Ufomba to migrate. Nor did people confront the fact that continued ties to home people contributed strongly to the pressures on young migrants to pursue money and the modern lifestyles that, when they do not result in HIV infection, are in many ways highly rewarded by kin in communities of origin.

Nonetheless, while Ufomba's family tried hard to maintain secrecy in order to forestall the stigma and shame they feared from public knowledge of his HIV status, and while the community at large trafficked in rumors that were negative and hurtful, throughout the last months of Ufomba's life many members of his family—especially his mother and sisters—and some friends and neighbors offered loving care and support. Certain people in the community shunned him and his compound during those months, but many did not. At one point, Ufomba joined his mother's Pentecostal church, and several members of the congregation came frequently to pray with him and his mother.

That same year, I interviewed more than 20 people who were on antiretroviral therapy (ART) in Owerri. While they were luckier than Ufomba, who died before he could enroll in the ART program, many recounted similar stories of difficult disclosures and community stigma. But they also told of specific examples of generous caregiving by close relatives. For example, one young woman told me that her mother left her father's compound to take care of her when her father's people ostracized her and refused to allow her to convalesce in the family house. Another woman praised her husband for staying with her and taking care of her during her illness even after he learned that he was not HIV positive. While everyone feared the consequences of disclosure and most recounted instances of stigma and mistreatment by some who had learned of their status, it was striking how many people also had family and friends who stuck by them, often heroically.

Ufomba was buried in a modest service. As he died young, unmarried, and without children, it would never have been expected that he be given a grand burial, even had he not died of AIDS. But his service was particularly small and subdued, a fact that some people in the community attributed to the cause of his death. No mention was made of AIDS in the service, even though the pastor who conducted it was the Pentecostal preacher who had prayed for his cure and every speaker surely knew or believed that Ufomba had died of AIDS.

It has been widely speculated and hoped that the availability of treatment would diminish the stigma of AIDS by removing its status as a definite death sentence, thereby reducing the degree of anxiety around how to morally orient oneself toward people on a fast path toward their ultimate end (Farmer 1999; Bunnell et al. 2006; Niehaus 2007). This does not appear to have happened yet in Nigeria. Perhaps this is in part because treatment is new and its capacity to cheat death is still not seen as certain. But stigma around HIV and AIDS is produced not only because of the specter of death but also because AIDS remains firmly connected to people's apprehensions about forms of social change that are seen as undermining cherished values and practices associated with extended families and communities of origin. Particularly troubling is the perception that social relations have become unmoored from the reciprocal ties of kinship. In the era of AIDS in Nigeria, preserving and promoting the value of families is paramount, and individuals living with the virus are still viewed as emblems of the larger threats to families and kin groups. The importance of marriage and childbearing becomes especially poignant for people living with HIV, a phenomenon I explore in chapter 6.

Conclusion

It is hard to overstate the significance of rural–urban migration—perhaps especially in its effects on kinship—among the constellation of processes contributing to social change in contemporary Nigeria. These patterns of migration are part of a transformation of the national economy from a mostly rural, agricultural base to a more commercial, service-oriented, and urban-based system. Indeed, while Nigeria's economic trajectory might accurately be attributed to the growing penetration and expansion of capitalism, it is the pain and perceived shortcomings of that process (little manufacturing, overreliance on oil, high unemployment, the need resort to informal sector occupations, a rapacious state, and much more) that contribute not only to Nigerians' discontent but also to the ways these changes alter everyday practices of sociality. Further, rural–urban migration produces powerful connections between national and local politics, arguably reinforcing the ethnic, regional, and religious character of Nigeria's divisions. Although internal migration does deepen some aspects of identity politics in Nigeria, in other ways it contributes to integration, as the lives and livelihoods of communities throughout the country are tied to urban places across the nation. Socially, migration to cities has created new forms of association and has played a part in the evolution of different kinds of communities and families in settings where people live more individualized everyday lives. But it is important not to exaggerate these trends. Indeed, as the case examined in this chapter attests, rural–urban migration among the Igbos of southeastern Nigeria creates powerful circuitries that connect rather than separate rural and urban lives, communities, and social processes.

Migration is perhaps foremost among those processes of change to which people are inexorably attracted and about which they are also apprehensive. The reasons for the attraction and the anxiety are many and complicated, and they certainly do not unfold in the same way for everyone. Nonetheless, my research in Nigeria suggests that shifting pressures on kinship relations are at the core of these changes as they are experienced and interpreted by ordinary citizens. On the one hand, people perceive migration as threatening both the affective and the obligatory bonds of kinship. The perception that city life undermines these ties is much more worrisome than the distances that make face-to-face relations between home people and migrant kin infrequent. Individualism, greed, and unbridled ambition are seen as antithetical to a more collective orientation in which sharing, duty to family, and loyalty to community are prized values.

On the other hand, however, there can be no doubt that families encourage, depend on, and in many ways celebrate the migration of their members. Economic livelihoods, political influence, and social status in Nigeria are inextricably intertwined with rural–urban migration, whether one is a migrant or a relative in a rural village. People cultivate these kinship ties in no small part because they are perceived as essential to navigating Nigeria's clientelistic political economy, in which access to resources often depends on who you know and who might feel obligated or compelled to help you. But as several of the case studies in this book have shown, this situation itself is experienced ambivalently. Even as kinship relations are nurtured and mobilized to take advantage of the patronage system, this economy of favors is condemned as corrupt.

A confluence of forces puts young migrants in a difficult situation: economic and gender inequality; aspirations for modern commodities, fashions, and lifestyles; pressures to stay connected, supportive, and loyal to kin and community of origin; and a broad sense that a changing Nigeria poses threats to fundamental moral values. Moral and material economies are tightly linked. Gripping inequality is lamented as both the cause and consequence of a moral crisis. Nigeria's AIDS epidemic sits prominently at these fault lines between inequality and morality. As I have tried to show in this chapter, the nexus between rural–urban migration and kinship is both a powerful component of local understandings of the causes and meanings of AIDS and a significant aspect of how people must navigate the epidemic, whether they are managing their own risk, trying to live with the disease, or caring for a loved one who is sick.

Inequality and the moral code are deeply intertwined in every society, and there is probably nothing unique about the fact that Nigerians think about inequality—and virtually every aspect of social life—in moral terms.

Undoubtedly, pressures and aspirations to be and appear moral are part of the human condition. Moral norms can act as a means of challenging inequality and yet also serve to perpetuate it. But it seems that moralizing discourses as a mode of interpreting and responding to anxieties produced by rising social inequality have become especially prevalent in this period of rapid and dramatic social change in Nigeria. The threats that new and growing inequalities pose for kinship, community, and widely shared values about proper conduct are among people's greatest worries. Nigeria's AIDS epidemic has become emblematic of these wider anxieties.

Certainly in many respects the interpretation of AIDS in moral terms has contributed to—indeed must be seen as at the core of—the continuing stigma of the disease. Navigating the risk of infection, much less trying to live with the virus, is profoundly affected by this larger social and moral landscape. Ufomba's experience returning to Ubakala, sick with AIDS, was made all the more difficult by the rumors and stories, tinged with moral judgments, that his situation provoked—although many of his kin still rallied behind him. While much of the worry about AIDS stigma focuses on this detrimental aspect of moralizing the disease—and my own data certainly support this concern—it is important to note that the social and moral crises that Nigerians invoke to explain AIDS have their roots in processes of social change that reach well beyond the disease. Explaining the nature of these changes and the tensions they produce is central to understanding the social consequences of the epidemic itself.

SIX

Living with HIV: The Ethical Dilemmas
of Building a Normal Life

Ufomba Amechi died—as have many others—with no opportunity to benefit from the wider availability of antiretroviral therapy (ART) in Nigeria over the past several years. For those who do manage to access the country's expanded treatment program, the possibility of living life with HIV (instead of almost certainly dying from it) does not negate the reality of the stigma and the moral anxieties surrounding AIDS. In fact, my experience with people receiving ART suggests that they face intense pressures to construct lives for themselves that minimize—and, if possible, hide entirely—their own symbolic status as carriers of a disease that, in popular consciousness, stands for so much of what is wrong with society.

In practice, this means that people who are able to take antiretroviral drugs to prolong their lives are constantly worried about building social, not just biological, futures for themselves that appear and feel normal. They are equally concerned with portraying their lives as normal to their families, friends, and communities. This is most poignant in their aspiration to marry if they are unmarried, to remarry if they are widowed or divorced, or to remain married if they have a living spouse, and, perhaps above all, in their desire to have children. The impulse among people living with HIV to have a family is by no means unique to Nigeria (Thornton, Romanelli, and Collins 2004; Cooper et al. 2007). But as I will show below, the notion that "normalcy" is ultimately rooted in family-making must be understood in the context of the moral discourses that link AIDS to the popular perception that social reproduction—the very future of society—is under siege in contemporary Nigeria.

As the stories in this chapter will illustrate, for people living with HIV, navigating fears about being judged as perpetrators and carriers of social immorality pushes them to make choices that threaten their own health and the health of others—for example, not adhering to their medication regimen, failing to disclose their positive status to uninfected spouses or sexual partners, choosing to have unprotected sex, or initiating a pregnancy despite considerable risks to the child. Without taking into account the power of the moral discourses that connect AIDS to the widespread perception of social crisis in Nigeria, and without recognizing that the stigma attached to AIDS is linked to the most fundamental aspects of social reproduction, the behavior of people living with HIV can appear not just irrational (putting their own lives in jeopardy) but even highly unethical (putting others in harm's way). While I do not intend to minimize the health hazards and ethical conundrums associated with the secrecy and lies that are integral to the lives of many HIV-positive people in Nigeria, I hope that by situating their decisions in a broader context it will be possible to see their decisions more empathetically. Further, perhaps this perspective can contribute to designing HIV and AIDS policies and programs that treat not only diseased bodies but also the negative social consequences associated with the moralizing responses to the epidemic.

ART Access in Nigeria and the Challenges of Treatment as Prevention

As in many parts of the world, lifesaving antiretroviral drugs have only recently become more widely available to Nigerians. The Nigerian federal government launched a small-scale treatment program in 2001 that enrolled fewer than 10,000 people (only about three-tenths of 1 percent of people in Nigeria estimated to be HIV positive) over four years. In late 2005, in conjunction with the increased support for ART provided by international donors such as the Global Fund and the US President's Emergency Plan for AIDS Relief (PEPFAR), Nigeria's then-president Olusegun Obasanjo announced that all people in the country who need ART (defined in Nigeria as people with CD4 counts below 200 or who present with full-blown AIDS, not just HIV) would receive drugs free of charge.[1] The initial goal was to reach 250,000 people by June 2006. This ambitious target was not achieved by that date, but 2010 estimates indicated that approximately 300,000 Nigerians were receiving treatment through the scaled-up program (National Agency for the Control of AIDS 2010).

As ART has expanded, attention in the public health literature has begun to turn to the effects treatment has on prevention-related behaviors, specifically the sexual behavior of ART recipients (Moore and Oppong 2007; Lurie et al. 2008; Seeley et al. 2009). From the point of view of medical and public health experts, part of the motivation for studies of the sexual behavior of people on ART is a fear that successful treatment will lead to sexual "disinhibition"—that is, with the availability of successful treatment, people may eschew protective behaviors because they feel infection can be managed with medicine. Recent studies have also considered the sexual behavior of people on ART from the perspective of their marital and reproductive goals (Myer, Morroni, and Rebe 2007; Homsy et al. 2009). This trajectory of research supports a view that the conduct of people in treatment for HIV must be understood through a lens that connects sexuality—and health-related decisions and behavior—to gender, reproduction, and larger social contexts (Hirsch 2007; Gruskin et al. 2008; Persson and Richards 2008; Laher et al. 2009). In this chapter I build on this emerging literature, taking into consideration the decisions of people living with HIV not only in terms of health implications but also in the context of broader social realities that explain their behavior.

My findings are the result of several years of work and study with patients receiving ART from the Federal Medical Centre (FMC) in the southeastern Nigerian city of Owerri. Until recently, FMC-Owerri was the only facility in the region offering ART. The hospital initially enrolled 450 adults living with HIV, and from 2002 through 2005 these individuals received drugs at a highly subsidized rate. In 2006, following the new policy of free drugs and the plans for a massive scale-up, FMC-Owerri began expanding its government-supported program with a target of 2,000 patients, which it achieved by 2007.

I did much of the research for this chapter, and have coauthored findings elsewhere (Smith and Mbakwem 2007, 2010), with my colleague in Nigeria, Benjamin Mbakwem, whom I first introduced in chapter 4. Benjamin founded the Owerri-based NGO called Community & Youth Development Initiatives (CYDI) in 2001 with the principal aim of addressing Nigeria's AIDS epidemic by mobilizing local people and resources to increase effective prevention, offer counseling, and provide care and support for individuals living with the virus. CYDI has worked to organize prevention activities for hard-to-reach populations like urban nonschool youths, has created the most prominent and popular center for counseling and information about HIV and AIDS in Owerri, and, as explained earlier, helped to found the first support group in Imo State for people living with HIV, called the Association for Positive Care (AsPoCa), which is made up of dozens of individuals who receive ART through the FMC-Owerri program. Benjamin has counseled scores of people who are HIV positive. In what follows, I draw on Benjamin's and my own experiences working with people who are HIV positive. Their perspectives and experiences add another layer of understanding in the exploration of the ways the epidemic's effects must be situated in relation to wider social realities, particularly the popular perception that Nigeria's economic, political, and social problems are rooted in the same collective moral failings that explain AIDS.

AIDS and Anxieties about Reproduction

Until the availability of ART, the conventional experience in Nigeria was that HIV delivered not only a biological death sentence but also a social death sentence, as stigmatization of the disease was bound up in the fact that a life cut short by AIDS was often a life without reproduction. Niehaus argues that in South Africa the stigma of AIDS has less to do with an association with sexual promiscuity and more to do with the fact that people with AIDS are (or at least were before the availability of ART) perceived to be "dead before dying" (Niehaus 2007, 848; see also Ashforth 2002). Similarly, I argue that the social death associated with AIDS is directly connected to the fact that it prevents (or at least makes much more difficult) people's participation in social reproduction. It is possible to hide one's HIV status, but it is not possible to hide whether or not one is married or has children, a point that will emerge repeatedly in the stories that follow. I chose these cases for the ways that they illustrate and represent more general themes about how many individuals balance their concerns about reproduction with their antiretroviral treatment, as they seek restored possibilities for social normalcy. Each example highlights threads that were common across our larger subject population, as well as the ways seemingly contradictory or risky choices can best be understood in the wider social context of people's lives.

Pathways to Marriage

Ifeoma's story is emblematic of some typical dynamics that unfold as a person on ART begins to reconstruct a normal life. Ifeoma was looking to marry but struggling with whether or how to reveal her status and how to take her drugs while in a relationship with a man who did not know that she was HIV positive. Twenty-eight years old at the time, Ifeoma came to the FMC-Owerri in December 2002 desperately sick. She had large ulcers in her mouth. She couldn't eat and appeared severely wasted, even on the verge of death. Ifeoma tested positive for both HIV1 and HIV2 (different strains of the virus) and was immediately started on ART. Over time she recovered remarkably well, to the point where the staff at CYDI said that her plump figure and smooth skin were prime examples of the astonishing effects of ART and of the often-cited AIDS message in Nigeria, explained already, that "AIDS no dey show for face" (you cannot tell if someone has HIV by looking at him or her).

A couple of years prior to her illness, Ifeoma had been separated from her husband. Shortly after their first child was born, they had had a serious conflict that led her to return to her family and her natal community without her child (in most of Igboland, lineage is patrilineal, and children are considered to "belong" to their father's family). The separation lasted several months, and at one point during this estrangement she heard that her husband and her infant son were sick. Before she could arrange to visit, she learned that they both had died. Rumors circulated that the man died of AIDS. At that time, Ifeoma's mother urged her to get an HIV test, but she refused. She felt perfectly fine and did not believe—or did not want to believe—that her husband and child had died of AIDS, much less that she could feel so healthy and also be infected.

About seven months later she became ill with a fever and diarrhea and went to a local hospital. Without her knowledge or permission, the hospital conducted an HIV test. She recalled being summoned to the doctor's office, without any of the preparations of pretest counseling. The doctor began by saying things like "you know, in this world man proposes but God disposes" and "some news can appear to be too bad, but over time we realize it's not the end of the world." He then revealed that she was HIV positive. Ifeoma reportedly fainted and remembers waking up with water being thrown on her face and a crowd of doctors and nurses surrounding her.

After her husband's death but prior to learning of her HIV status, Ifeoma had begun a relationship with a man in a nearby city. When she got sick and learned of her HIV status, she hid it from her new partner, returning to her natal home until her health improved. Prior to her illness, Ifeoma and her boyfriend had frequent unprotected sex, and the man was encouraging her to get pregnant to "fast-forward" a marriage. He wanted evidence of her present fertility before formalizing their relationship. When she learned she was HIV positive, Ifeoma felt she could not tell him without jeopardizing the relationship. She believed that once he found out he would make inquiries about her past and discover that her first husband and child had died of AIDS. This news, she thought, would make him suspect that she began having unprotected sex with him while knowing full well that she was HIV positive, which would have made her look far more blameworthy than she had been. Further, she felt it was impossible to introduce condoms into their sexual relationship given their shared desire for her to get pregnant. There would be no reasonable way to explain her sudden request for protection. In her anxiety over being accused of having been cavalier in exposing her boyfriend to HIV, Ifeoma chose to continue practices that would, in fact, put him at continued risk of contracting the virus.

She required vigilance to maintain her secret. Each of Ifeoma's three antiretroviral drugs was a separate pill and each had to be taken twice a day. Combined with the various vitamins she also took, it meant that a monthly supply was more than 200 pills. To mitigate this problem, Ifeoma took advantage of one aspect of household gender inequality. She hid the pills under the sink in the kitchen, a room her boyfriend almost never entered. Further, she would time her dishwashing—a task he never undertook—to coincide with when she needed to take her medications. In this way she managed to keep her secret and stay on her drugs. At the time that Benjamin and I lost contact with Ifeoma—she moved to the city of Port Harcourt with her boyfriend and planned to try to collect her drugs there—she was still hoping to get pregnant, marry her boyfriend, and eventually find a way to disclose her status.

Many people on ART face similar issues of disclosure that are central to the endeavor of navigating sexual and romantic relationships, and these issues frequently come to a head around plans for marriage. With the increasing awareness of the risks of HIV in Nigeria, many individual churches and denominations, including the Catholic Church, now require couples to undergo HIV tests if they wish to be married by the church. The prospect of being tested before marriage creates great anxieties for individuals who are HIV positive (and, undoubtedly, for people who fear they might be). People create all kinds of ways to deal with this problem, including using premarital testing as a way to gracefully disclose their infection without revealing that they have previously kept it secret. The fear of disclosure is driven as much by an awareness of the moral stigma associated with AIDS as by the realities of how loved ones treat people who are HIV positive. In fact, partners, spouses, family members, and friends frequently become allies, not only in people's struggle to live with the disease but also in their efforts to construct normal lives.

The case of Chinyere is illustrative. On World AIDS Day in December 2003, Chinyere came to CYDI's office in search of help. After crying until she was exhausted, she narrated her story to Benjamin. Early in 2003 she had gone to the hospital very sick. Unbeknownst to her, she was admitted at an institution notorious for its unwillingness to treat HIV cases. After a short stay at the hospital a nurse asked her to follow her to the doctor's office. Barely able to walk, Chinyere dragged herself into the doctor's consulting room. As she sat down he held up her lab result and shouted, "Look at you! The sin of fornication has finally caught up with you! Before I open my eyes I want you out of this building. We don't treat people like you here." While the willingness of health professionals in Nigeria to treat HIV has improved dramatically in recent years, some doctors still refuse to care for AIDS patients, and hospitals and clinics can be venues for the perpetuation of discrimination. Banished from that hospital, Chinyere eventually sought treatment from another doctor who willingly treated HIV patients. She got well and for many months felt perfectly fine. She put her HIV status out of her mind.

The following August, an Igbo man named Obi, who was based in Europe, came home for a visit. Chinyere's family wanted her to marry him, and his homecoming was partly to see whether Chinyere was the right woman for him. As indicated in chapter 2, young people in contemporary southeastern Nigeria increasingly choose their own spouses independent of family preferences, often based on an ideal of romantic love, but the role of families in suggesting possible spouses and advocating for (or rejecting) particular unions remains prominent. Igbo men who have migrated overseas are particularly liable to look for their families' help in finding "a good girl from home" to marry. When Obi returned to Nigeria, he and Chinyere got along well. They traveled around the country and Chinyere enjoyed his company. Eventually, they started having sex. Then, just before he was to return to Europe, she fell sick—so sick that she could not even escort him to Lagos for his departure.

When Chinyere arrived at CYDI, she was frightened about her future. During Obi's visit things had gone so well that they had initiated the first steps in the traditional marriage ceremony, and Chinyere had moved in with her future mother-in-law. CYDI helped her enroll in the ART program. She began to get well physically, but in Chinyere's mind she had bigger problems—the possibility that her HIV infection would derail her marriage. Obi was a wealthy man. He was sending money home to build a big house in his village. Chinyere was handling some of the money, meaning that she always had cash. Her future mother-in-law liked her. She and Obi seemed to genuinely care for each other. There was the added enticement that she might eventually join her husband overseas. The possibility of losing it all if her HIV status were to be revealed was terrifying.

Not too long after Chinyere started on her drugs, Obi arranged to have the next steps of the traditional wedding ceremony undertaken in his absence. The traditional wedding, where the two extended families come together to perform the customary rituals, is often completed in the absence of one or both of the betrothed, especially in this era of far-flung migration. The plan was that they would also be married in the church when Obi next returned to Nigeria. In the week leading up to the traditional ceremony, Chinyere experienced terrible rashes all over her body, a common reaction to nevirapine, one of the first-line drugs in the combination provided in Nigeria's ART program. She came to CYDI frantic about her appearance, worried that someone might guess that she had HIV and fretting that she couldn't possibly wear a turtleneck at her traditional wedding ceremony, where the bride is expected to dress in the latest fashions. She eventually told her mother-in-law that she had an allergic reaction to an everyday medication, and this was the story conveyed to the larger wedding party. Chinyere made it through the traditional wedding without her HIV status being discovered, but she still faced the fact that Obi would soon come home for the church wedding, and she had not revealed her status to him.

The impending church wedding hastened her dilemma. She and Obi were Catholic and, as mentioned above, HIV tests are required of all couples wanting to marry in the Church. Chinyere came to CYDI pleading for assistance in either obtaining a fake HIV lab result or finding someone who was HIV negative who could take the test in her name. It is widely known that in Nigeria fake lab results are sought and sometimes issued to enable church weddings. When she was told that CYDI would not facilitate such a scam, she discussed other possibilities with her counselor. She settled on the idea that she would go together with her fiancé for pretest counseling, pretend it was her first test, and feign horror when her result was revealed. She banked on the hope that now that she and Obi were traditionally married, he would stick by her when her status was revealed and that she would avoid the worse consequences of his discovering her longer-term deception.

On the appointed day, when she and Obi went for their results, Chinyere fainted dramatically at the revelation of her status. Her gamble paid off. Although Obi tested HIV negative, he did not threaten divorce as many Nigerian men do when they find out their wife is positive and they are negative. CYDI staff attributed Obi's seemingly enlightened response to all the time he had spent in Europe. I'm not sure this was the reason. Partners, spouses, families, and friends of people living with HIV or sick with AIDS are often far more supportive than popular rhetoric suggests. In fact, some people become allies not only in helping care for the sick but also in protecting people living with HIV from the stigma associated with the disease. Perhaps the most illuminating aspect of Chinyere's case is that once her status was known to Obi, he became her coconspirator in figuring out how to get married in the Catholic Church. He could accept his wife's HIV status, believing her claims of having always been a good faithful woman who had been unknowingly infected by an immoral sexual partner in the past, but he could not live without the social recognition of a church wedding. He personally arranged to secure a fake result for Chinyere.

Chinyere eventually became pregnant, and with the aid of prophylactic treatment her child was born HIV negative. When she did not breastfeed the baby boy, she again had to invent an explanation to cover her unusual behavior. Over time she lost contact with CYDI, but at last report her marriage remained amicable, her child was healthy, and only she and Obi knew her HIV status.

Looking for a Child

It is hard to exaggerate the importance of childbearing in southeastern Nigeria and throughout much of Africa. As the renowned anthropologist Meyer Fortes argued long ago, "Parenthood is regarded as a *sine qua non* for the attainment of the full development of the complete person to which all aspire" (1978, 125). Little has changed since Fortes's day. Having children in Nigeria is not only a means to achieve full individual personhood but also a fulfillment of one's obligations to kin and community. Biological reproduction is part of social reproduction. Through marriage and parenthood, one not only reproduces and replaces individuals; one also creates and builds the social networks through which people survive and prosper. Every Igbo person assumes he or she will marry and have children, and childlessness is the greatest of calamities. Personal lives are devastated by it and popular culture is obsessed with it, a fact illustrated by the frequency with which infertility is a central theme in films produced by Nigeria's booming video industry (McCall 2002; Haynes 2007; Abah 2008).

In this context, it is no wonder that one of the predominant aspirations for people on ART is to have children. Many ART patients embark on or resume childbearing, but the process is fraught with social obstacles and potential health consequences. A particularly poignant case of a young woman named Ukachi exemplifies the social and symbolic importance of children in Igbo society in general and for people living with HIV in particular.

Ukachi periodically attended the Monday ART clinic at FMC-Owerri to collect her drugs, but she did not join the support group and seemed to have little or no interaction with other people on ART. One day, she approached a CYDI counselor. She did not know her boyfriend's HIV status and was worried that she might infect him, or if he was positive, that he might have reinfected her with another strain of the virus. They were hoping to marry and have children, and she did not know what to do.

It turned out that Ukachi was already a single mother. She had a four-year-old son to whom she gave birth long before she discovered she was HIV positive. The boy's father was a cousin with whom Ukachi had fallen deeply in love, although they were absolutely forbidden to marry. After several years of pining for her cousin, Ukachi set her mind to marrying someone else and starting a more traditional family. She commenced a relationship with a man who she thought might make a good husband. Several months into that relationship, one of her relatives was in an accident and she traveled to the hospital to donate blood. As part of that process her blood was screened and she was informed that she was HIV positive. She had never been sick and for several months she tried to ignore the result, continuing her relationship with her boyfriend. Finally, she decided to travel to Owerri to seek a confirmatory test at the FMC. She was indeed HIV positive. She followed up with more tests, and when it was revealed that her CD4 count was low she started on ART.

Her boyfriend had recently been sick but had claimed it was malaria. She wanted to persuade him to do an HIV test but didn't know how without making him suspect she was infected. He wanted her to get pregnant before they set a date for marrying, so she was as worried about getting pregnant as she was about protecting her health. With time, the boyfriend decided they should proceed with the traditional wedding even though Ukachi was not pregnant. Shortly after they married she became pregnant. She stopped coming to Owerri for her drugs and for a long time we lost contact.

When she returned, seven months pregnant, we learned that Ukachi had moved to the city of Enugu with her new husband and had stopped taking her medication. She had gone for antenatal care in Enugu, but the clinic staff would not agree to assist her delivery unless she had an HIV test. Faced with the possibility of exposure, as her husband still did not know her status, she traveled to Owerri so that she could give birth at the FMC. Once one of the most beautiful and healthy looking of all the patients in the ART program, Ukachi looked sickly and wasted. She stayed in Owerri long enough to have her baby but returned shortly thereafter to Enugu. When we asked why she had stopped taking her medication, she said she feared she could not hide or explain all the pills (as a patient coming from Enugu—two hours away—she was entitled collect a three-month supply of pills, which, including vitamins, would amount to over 600 tablets). Rather than risk the consequences of revealing her HIV status and possibly undermining her marriage, she chose to have a child who would solidify the relationship and stopped taking her drugs, even though these actions posed potentially disastrous health consequences for her, her baby, and others. It is impossible to understand Ukachi's choices without accounting for the primacy of marriage and reproduction in the socially shared conceptions of why one would care to be alive in the first place. For people who are HIV positive, fears of disclosure and awareness of the stigma associated with the moralized understandings of AIDS heighten the urgency of constructing a life that looks normal to partners, family, and society.

Concerns about appearing normal extend beyond people who are infected to include their spouses and families. Benjamin and I have both observed numerous cases where an uninfected spouse who knew his or her partner was HIV positive nevertheless exerted tremendous pressure to procreate. One example was the wife of Nnamdi, a founding member of AsPoCa, the Owerri support group. He learned he was HIV positive after becoming extremely sick. At the time that he was diagnosed with HIV he tried numerous treatments, including various traditional doctors, without improving significantly. When the FMC-Owerri pilot ART program began in 2002, he was one of the first to enroll. He told his wife of his problem immediately—in fact, he had no choice because when he first received his lab result several family members were with him in the hospital and the indiscreet staff revealed his HIV status to him in front of the visitors. His wife stuck by him steadfastly. She tested negative for the virus. At the time of his diagnosis they had two young sons.

Nnamdi said that when he was sick he never even thought of sex, much less of having another child. But when he became better after beginning ART, he and his wife resumed a sexual relationship. Nnamdi reported that he always used condoms. About a year or so after he had started on ART, he sought counseling at CYDI because his wife had begun putting pressure on him to have another child. As a leader of AsPoCa, he was well versed in the most up-to-date information about risks, prevention, and treatment. He said he did not want to expose his wife to HIV, and he was not inclined to risk unprotected sex to produce a pregnancy when they already had two HIV-negative sons. Because of the patrilineal structure of Igbo lineages, people are greatly concerned with having sons to whom they can pass on their names, land, and property. Normally, Nnamdi would have been eager to have another child and happy to have a daughter, but under the circumstances, he said, "I am OK with two sons."

His wife, Ogechi, was, however, intensely desirous of having a third child. Nnamdi wasn't sure how to negotiate her increasing insistence, so he asked if he could bring Ogechi to CYDI for counseling. At CYDI she was told about the dangers of unprotected sex for herself and about the possible risks of mother-to-child transmission. She knew the facts already yet still wanted to get pregnant. She explained that her friends and relatives had been asking for some time why she had not had another child. She said, "Everyone is always asking about my next issue [offspring]. I do not feel normal with only two children. I can't tell them why we are not having more issues [children]." In addition to the social pressure to have more children, she also expressed a strong desire for a daughter. Regarding the possibility of contracting HIV herself, she simply said, "My husband is healthy now that he is taking his drugs. If I become infected I will also take drugs." The fervent desire for more children eclipsed any perspective on long-term health risks to her. In short, it mattered more for her to continue living a normal life by the standards that felt most important to her than it did to remain healthy and have a longer life without any additional children.

CYDI referred Ogechi to the doctor in charge of the ART clinic at FMC-Owerri to make sure that she fully understood the medical risks. The last I knew, Ogechi had not had another child. But the reason was not from an altered understanding of the health risks; it was due to a change in her perception of her marriage, particularly the behavior of her husband, whom she discovered had been cheating on her. Had Nnamdi not resumed a pattern of extramarital relationships that Ogechi found reprehensible, she would likely have continued to insist on another child.

While marriage and reproduction are among the most important dimensions of forging a normal life in southeastern Nigeria, as across the world social norms are by no means monolithic. A "normal" life is not reducible to the duties promulgated in formal social conventions. Nnamdi's resumption of habitual extramarital sex is emblematic of the multiple forms of normalcy and the kinds of resurrected life projects that must be understood in the context of the availability of antiretroviral treatment. In his public persona as an AsPoCa leader and in private conversations with friends at CYDI, Nnamdi presented himself as someone who steadfastly adhered to conventionally prescribed moral and medical codes, both of which prohibit extramarital sex. To people who knew he was HIV positive, he spoke with great authority—and personal conviction—about all the things that one must do to protect one's own health and that of others.

But over time we began hearing stories from women who joined AsPoCa that Nnamdi was one of a number of men in the group who preyed upon single or newly widowed women, taking advantage of their vulnerability to entice them into sexual relationships. Ogechi eventually came to CYDI to complain about her husband's behavior, as she was worried about protecting herself. In the words of one CYDI staff member, "She no longer sees him as a loving husband for whom she will do anything in his time of need. Now she sees him as the man she's living in the same house with whose actions she cannot predict or control." In her words, "He is back to normal," with all the unhappy connotations that implied. Yet Nnamdi's apparent sexual "disinhibition" needs to be understood in context. Rather than simply a deviation from medical advice (and from the normative life projects of marriage and reproduction), his behavior is in fact part of common pattern among married men in Nigeria (as discussed in chapter 2), who reinforce their social status through extramarital relationships with younger women. For Nnamdi, his health brought about a return to normal sexual life, both within and outside his marriage. Ogechi, however, viewed his actions in different moral terms, and her judgments affected the choices and desires she'd felt were crucial to her life plans so short a time before.

Conclusion

For most people who are enrolled in Nigeria's expanding ART program, the opportunity to resume a normal life is cherished and ardently pursued, even as living with HIV continues to pose social predicaments, public health risks, and existential dilemmas. The vast majority of people receiving ART at the FMC-Owerri are mindful of these continued risks and are committed to keeping themselves and their loved ones safe, but the physical risks to personal and public health are factored into a larger equation in which the very reasons for wanting to be alive are always paramount.

In southeastern Nigeria, marriage and parenthood, the principal tasks of biological and social reproduction, reign supreme in the hierarchy of social expectations and individual aspirations. For people who are HIV positive, the importance of these life goals is felt even more sharply because the stigma of AIDS derives from the popular perception that infection is indicative of moral failings—like sexual promiscuity and weakening ties to kin and community—that are seen as responsible for threatened social reproduction. To avert the stigma associated with HIV, seropositive people try to commit themselves wholeheartedly to marriage and childbearing, thereby asserting their contributions to family, community, and society. By pursuing normative life projects, people on ART mark themselves as morally legitimate despite their HIV status—in other words, they contradict the stereotype surrounding HIV while also in many cases hiding their status. Ironically and tragically, these very endeavors often put them and others at further risk of infection.

As the cases of Nnamdi and Chinyere demonstrate, when individuals pursue the prosocial life projects of childbearing and faithful marriage, many spouses become allies in overcoming the stigma of their partners' HIV-positive status and are willing to overlook the risks that their marriages pose to their own health. Although I do not have statistics to verify it, from what doctors and counselors in Owerri told me, spousal support in serodiscordant marriages was far more common when the uninfected partner was the woman than in the opposite case. However, when a seropositive person's actions look like the kind of behavior that is stereotypically believed to be the cause of HIV and AIDS, as Nnamdi's extramarital sex appeared to his wife, not only does it produce a greater sense of risk on the part of the spouse or partner; it also reduces their willingness to be supportive.

For many people on ART, the dilemma of how to make families while living with HIV is resolved, or at least addressed, by seeking partners from within support groups like AsPoCa. At FMC-Owerri, AsPoCa has been a principal meeting ground for people seeking sexual partners and possible spouses. Several other support groups have been established in the region and recent scholarship suggests that support groups across Nigeria have become arenas for sexual networking and marriage markets (Rhine 2009). As in the larger society, not all of what goes on in the support group is laudable—for example, as in Nnamdi's story, members of support groups are sometimes subject to pressure from other members to engage in sexual relationships. But overall, the emerging communities of people living with HIV seem to be a positive development, enabling people to build futures, including reproductive futures, in ways that make it easier to address both social and medical realities.

The availability of drugs restored the possibility of normal lives for people with HIV, an option that not long ago had been perceived as impossible given the social and biological death sentences associated with AIDS in Nigeria. But stigma remains powerful. As a result, people on ART continue to try to manage their treatment mostly in secret. They simultaneously craft public lives that are seen as upholding the values of creating and perpetuating families, securing the future of society through marriage and childbearing. In so doing, they hope to mitigate potential stigma if or when their status is discovered. There is probably no way to avoid the fact that the fulfillment of personal aspirations and social expectations sometimes directly conflicts with public health interests. But as the stories described here attest, people on ART are highly attuned to these issues; most of them take all of this into account to the extent that they can. The lives of people on ART are complicated, contradictory, and messy. Perhaps we should not expect much different; treatment allows people infected with HIV to live normal lives, with all the complexities this entails.

It is no coincidence that this book includes many stories of young people: men and women in their teens, 20s, and 30s. In the eyes of Nigerian society, and I think even in their own minds, these youth represent the perils and promises of the future. They make up the population that is moving to the city in the largest numbers in search of education, employment, and modern urban lifestyles. As Jennifer Johnson-Hanks (2006) found with regard to young unmarried mothers in Cameroon, young Nigerians of both sexes are postponing marriage and having premarital sex in an era when doing so can simultaneously be a necessary means of survival, a strategy to stay in school, a rewarded measure of modern identity, and a marker of immorality. To find answers in a world filled with contradictions, young people in Nigeria are joining Pentecostal churches by the millions. An entrepreneurial few start their own churches or "float" an NGO. This same generation is most likely to become infected by HIV. Their lives, seemingly more than those in other age groups, are the subject of constant discussion about social and moral crisis in Nigeria. I have argued that the prevalence and force of these discourses are related to the consequences of rising inequalities generated by ongoing patterns of migration, the fitful penetration of capitalism and the rise of a cash economy, altered employment opportunity structures, and other associated social changes in Africa's most populous country. And of course the AIDS epidemic feeds into and exacerbates this collective angst about the future.

The moralizing discourses about AIDS that I have traced in various forms throughout this book, attached as they are to people's larger anxieties about the way things are going in Nigeria, have affected people's lives as much as—and in many cases more than—the virus itself. Even among people who are HIV positive, many say that the moral stigma associated with infection is even harder to live with than the effects on their health. An assortment of outside forces contributed to the creation and growth of these moralizing discourses: from the international community's fascination with the African origin of HIV; to Western representations of the continent, in which AIDS became just the next big crisis of African culture; to bad or exaggerated data and estimates that inflated the epidemiological threat; to a plethora of donor-supported interventions that portrayed both individual risk and the wider epidemic as rooted in the ethical choices Africans make regarding their sexual behavior. Each of these external influences enabled and exacerbated Nigerians' moralizing interpretations of the epidemic. But ultimately the energy and power of these discourses are derived from their connection to Nigerians' experiences with and ambivalence about the consequences of wider transformations in their country, and specifically anxieties about how these trends have deepened existing inequalities and created new ones. Whether it is an individual's infection, the epidemiological profile of a particular region, or the sense of societal catastrophe associated with the epidemic, AIDS is understood by Nigerians as the consequence of a moral crisis. Similarly, a whole host of political, economic, and social problems are explained as failures of spirituality, culture, and sociality. These moral interpretations of AIDS, and of a wide range of social problems related to inequality, not only underpin people's understandings; they animate their responses.

What makes AIDS particularly emblematic and evocative as a symbol of people's anxieties about the contemporary moment in Nigeria is its direct relationship to social reproduction—to the way that a society reproduces persons, families, social institutions, cultural traditions, and so on. Reduced to its most basic form, and in its most common mode of transmission globally, HIV is a virus that kills people for an act—sexual intercourse—that is absolutely necessary for human reproduction. Analogously, Nigerians also see the AIDS epidemic and the larger social problems it represents as a threat to the social aspects of reproduction. AIDS imperils the processes that produce the kinds of people, social relations, institutions, and values that constitute an effective and good human society. In contemporary Nigeria, the character of these most foundational elements of society feels like it is transforming rapidly, with little certainty of how things will turn out and significant concern over what is being lost in the process.

Given the centrality of the younger generations in these processes of transformation, one might imagine that the tensions around the rising inequalities associated with social changes in Nigeria are the result of an intergenerational conflict, with the older generation lamenting the ceding of the control they once had over social reproduction to a younger generation with different aspirations, values, and lifestyles. Spronk (2012) argues that such intergenerational tensions are central to understanding the dynamics of social change in Nairobi, Kenya. There is some truth to this view for Nigeria, too. I've heard many elders complain about the wayward lives of youth, decrying and demonizing everything from the loss of respect for elders to the rise of individualism and the failure of collective morality to rein in crime, promiscuity, and other social ills. This discourse is one that resonates in many parts of the world today (Cole and Durham 2007).

But the ambivalence about rising inequalities and other consequences of social change in Nigeria is by no means limited to the older generation. Young Nigerians, whom I have spent so much time studying over the last decade, are also deeply worried about their society. In part, they are frustrated because the promises of urbanization, modernization, education, democracy, and development have not been fully realized. But they are also anxious about what the changes they aspire to are actually producing. Young people are equally as adamant as their elders—and in many cases even more adamant—that things are going wrong in Nigeria. Positioned at the cusp of these changes, they are acutely aware of the consequences.

I conclude this book with some final thoughts about the relationship between inequality and morality in contemporary Nigeria, revisiting each of the spheres of social life I have explored, and summarizing the reasons why ongoing changes produce so much apprehension in Nigeria. I have tried to make this book more about people's experiences and of responses to the consequences of social change than about AIDS, and more about Nigeria and Nigerians than about health and disease. But I believe that understanding Nigerians' moral responses to various dimensions of the widely shared sense of social crisis has much to teach us about better managing the AIDS epidemic. After offering some concluding thoughts about the arenas of social change I have examined in this book, I end by suggesting how this wider perspective can contribute to more effective interventions.

"Johnny Just Come": The Aspirations and Anxieties of Urban Life

One of the more popular actors in Nigeria's video film industry, Nkem Owoh, frequently plays a now widely known comic character called Osuofia. Osuofia embodies urban Nigerians' stereotypes of rural people—illiterate, superstitious, and backward—but he also represents aspects of "traditional" rural culture that urbanites find endearing. Perhaps the most renowned of these films is *Osuofia in London*, about this bumbling but disarmingly candid village man's first visit to the capital of the United Kingdom, Nigeria's former colonial ruler. The film is so popular, I think, because it pokes fun at aspects of their society that Nigerians recognize and mostly—but not entirely—wish to transcend. It also mocks British culture and society, providing an implicit critical commentary about where the growing forces of formal education, urbanization, and global/Western cultural influences might be leading Nigeria. It is at once a critique of the past and a warning about the future, albeit in a genre that mostly just enables the Nigerian public to laugh uproariously. In 2009, almost as if to remind Nigerians that no one is safe in Nigeria's troubled times, Owoh was kidnapped by a criminal gang that demanded a huge ransom for his eventual release.

The Osuofia character built on an image that long preceded Nollywood, Nigeria's huge video film industry: the naïve and wide-eyed villager discovering big-city life for the first time. In Lagos, such newcomers are known as "JJC"—"Johnny Just Come," a now well-known Pidgin English phrase marking a migrant who has just arrived in the city and doesn't know anything. Jokes about JJCs are plentiful in Lagos, and they signify the superior knowledge, sophistication, and savvy that longtime Lagos residents pride themselves on having in comparison to recent migrants and rural folk. But some of the stories about JJCs are meant not just as jokes; they serve as warnings about the dangers of Lagos life—be it fraud, burglary, or violent crime—or simply the risk of being undone by the fast pace, anonymity, and cutthroat ways of urban living. That Nigerians continue to arrive in Lagos, and in every city around the country, in such large numbers is a testament to the fact that the appeal—and the perceived opportunities—of the city still outweigh the fears, anxieties, and sense of social loss associated with rural–urban migration.

Africa remains the most rural continent in the world; a slight majority of the population still lives in villages (White, Mberu, and Collinson 2008). But this profile is changing rapidly. For well over a decade, Africa has been urbanizing faster than any other part of the world. In Nigeria, 44 percent of the overall population now lives in urban areas, and it is estimated that within a decade, a majority of Nigerians will live in cities and towns (Population Reference Bureau 2006). It is impossible to generalize about the impact of migration and urbanization in a way that does justice to the diverse spectrum of experiences in a country of over 160 million people and tens of millions of rural–urban migrants. But certainly for many Nigerians, including most of the Igbo people whom I know best, their lives in the city remain connected to rural communities of origin in a complex circuitry. Village life—both in its nostalgic and idealized form and in its image as a place of hardship, backwardness, petty jealousies, and endless obligations—serves as a constant foil against which people judge the transformations associated with the city.

As the lives of *okada* drivers in cities like Owerri and Umuahia illustrate, many migrants find that the lure of opportunities in the city does not translate easily into better lives. For the majority of Nigeria's urban population, everyday life involves hard work (if one can find it), low pay, and the constant reminder of escalating inequality, as a consequence of which, in front of one's eyes, some people are outlandishly enjoying their riches while others suffer. This inequality and the changes in sociality that accompany it keep people from fully embracing the social shifts that their choices and behavior contribute to creating.

Social Reproduction and Gender Inequality

Among the populations I studied, migration and urbanization are experienced ambivalently, regardless of gender. But for women the challenges are greater because of the dynamics of gender inequality and the fact that, for many female migrants, urban economic realities also include adjusting to an imbalanced urban sexual economy. Like men, migrant women must navigate the trials of surviving in the city even as they are expected to help their kin at home in the village. Unlike men, women face an almost impossible set of contradictory pressures regarding their sexual behavior.

In the hardscrabble circumstances that many young female migrants find themselves in, transactional sex can be one of the only ways to survive. The spectrum of transactional sex is wide. More than simply trading sex for money in the stark terms associated with prostitution, it often involves socially acceptable partnerships where men's economic support is seen as the normal expression of caring and affection, building on a long tradition in which love is expressed, in part, through material support (Cole and Thomas 2009). For both married men who are unfaithful to their wives and the (mostly) unmarried younger women who are their partners, the intersection of emotion and economics is central to maintaining a sense of morality in relationships that risk being perceived otherwise. Most of these transactional relationships sit somewhere between romance and commercial sex.

The structural and symbolic systems of gender inequality in Nigeria assure that women are perceived as dependent on men. Consequently, women, even more than men, must constantly navigate the nexus of morality and materiality in their sexual lives. The desire to be in a "moral partnership" in the way that I described in chapter 3 reflects the power of societal expectations. Men also seek social approval—most men who visit commercial sex workers, for example, do not broadcast such practices—but for women, the consequences of being judged as outside the boundaries of moral sexual behavior are much greater. It is no coincidence that there are no purely derogatory masculine words in Igbo (or in English) that are analogous to harlot, whore, or slut.

Of course, gender inequality and the social surveillance of women's sexuality long precedes the AIDS epidemic, and it happens not just in Nigeria but in many societies—probably every society. But in Nigeria's era of AIDS, where widely circulating discourses suggest that people are sick and dying because of a society-wide moral crisis, it is women's sexuality—especially single young migrant women's sexuality—that rises to the top of the collectively imagined list of the causes and emblems of the crisis. Men in particular fear the demise of a system of gender inequality that assures a division of labor and power, defining men's and women's social, economic, and political roles quite strictly and to men's benefit. Formal education, a changing economy, rural–urban migration, and many other forces of social change are challenging and eroding this entrenched system of gender inequality— even as new strictures sometimes emerge.

As much as migration, urbanization, and many other intersecting changes offer women unprecedented opportunities, the moral interpretations of Nigeria's AIDS epidemic serve as a reminder that the surveillance of women's sexuality remains a powerful enforcer of gender inequality. The case of "Thick Madam," described in chapter 5, clearly illustrated this point. When Thick Madam died it was widely rumored that she had AIDS. I had my doubts, given her apparent good health and the suddenness of her demise. Nonetheless, Ubakala residents—mostly men, but also some women— explained that her death from AIDS was the consequence of a woman having too much money and too much independence, which had resulted in promiscuity. Illustrating a common pattern, the case was an example of nontraditional behaviors and social trends being explained as moral failures, especially women's moral failures. AIDS is inextricably bound up in these perceived failings as they figure in the Nigerian social imagination.

The Pentecostal Revolution and the AIDS Epidemic

That the HIV virus emerged in Nigeria in the same decades that Pentecostal Christianity became so popular is a coincidence. But the spread of moralizing explanations for the AIDS epidemic in the same era as the growing appeal of born-again Christianity in Nigeria is not. The same social circumstances that attract people to Pentecostalism's messages about modern social life—promising its benefits, condemning many of its consequences, and putting it all in a moral perspective—also energize the moral interpretations of and responses to AIDS. Further, Pentecostal pastors both take advantage of and contribute to people's imaginative interpretations of AIDS to better make their point about social and moral crisis in Nigeria and the need for a spiritual revolution.

I have aimed to show how Pentecostalism's appeal builds brilliantly on Nigerians' ambivalence about the inequalities associated with recent social changes. By promising prosperity, justifying wealth, and providing new social networks to enable people to realize their material and spiritual ambitions, Pentecostal Christianity addresses and expands people's modernizing aspirations. By condemning crime, corruption, and greed; by promising to cleanse Nigeria of its ills; and by offering new communities of fellowship, these churches confirm Nigerians' perceptions that social change has brought unwelcome consequences. Pentecostal Christianity's popular prosperity gospel promises something better and assures people that the rewards will accrue to followers now, and not just in the next life.

Regarding Nigeria's AIDS epidemic, the Pentecostal message seems to promote stigma more than it provides protection, care, and support. By harnessing and feeding popular interpretations of the epidemic, where individual infection is blamed on sin and the national epidemic is explained in terms of a society-wide failure of morality, Pentecostal pastors and churches contribute to a moralizing view of the disease that makes condom use difficult, disclosure deeply problematic, and care and support a succor offered only in exchange for testimony about one's sins.

However, much as I have come to see many (but certainly not all) of these Pentecostal preachers and churches as agents in the creation and reproduction of moral opprobrium, it is overly simplistic to reduce their role to nothing more than purveyors of stigma. I've met many HIV-positive people who converted to Pentecostal Christianity *after* they were infected and others who have sustained their born-again beliefs from the first hint of sickness until death, finding their faith to be the most valuable gift in their lives. Seeing their own predicaments as the consequence of past sins is a small price to pay, it seems, for the meaning and the hope that comes with turning oneself over to the hands of God. In Nigeria, where the social and economic realities of everyday life stymie opportunities daily, a religious movement that draws so many people in so completely offers something that is desperately needed—hope.

An Epidemic of NGOs

Unlike the burgeoning popularity of Pentecostal Christianity and the spread of the HIV virus in Nigeria, which were simply coincident, the AIDS epidemic clearly accelerated the explosion of NGOs in recent years. The impetus for channeling donor funds to NGOs has sources besides AIDS, of course. Donor preoccupation with civil society and the fantasy that NGOs would somehow protect people from the state and improve governance all at the same time is explained by other historical forces, including the push on the part of Western governments for democracy in the developing world after the fall of communism and the emergence of the neoliberal world order (Mercer 2002; Kamat 2004; Szeftel 2000). NGOs would have proliferated even without AIDS. But in Nigeria—and in much of Africa—the massive flow of AIDS dollars in particular has irrigated the NGO world and led to the unprecedented "mushrooming" of local NGOs over the last couple of decades (Watkins, Swidler, and Hannan 2012).

The cases presented in chapter 4 show how NGOs sit precariously at the evolving nexus between power and social inequality. Donors often view the problem of Nigerian NGO corruption as a consequence of the pull of traditional culture—nepotism, patronage, and other forms of personalistic social ties—against bureaucratic accountability. For ordinary Nigerians, however, what bothers them about NGO corruption has more to do with the erosion of accountability associated with kinship and patronage than the perpetuation of these traditional social bonds. As the example of Pius's overly selfish corrupt practices illustrated, for Nigerians the exacerbation of inequality through corruption is at least as much about the collapse of shared morality associated with reciprocal social relations as it is about the failure of official transparency. And as with the AIDS epidemic itself, in assessing NGO corruption Nigerians frequently reverse the Western view: the problem is not a lack of modernity, as donor discourses suggest, but rather too much modernity, at least when contemporary social changes are perceived to undermine proper sociality and morality.

But even this view—that Nigerians' frustrations and anxieties about ongoing social changes and concomitant problems like corruption are a product of a yearning for inequality-tempering forms of social relations associated with kinship and personalistic patron-clientism—is too simple.

New values and aspirations are in competition with old ones, even as they often share certain features. The Nigerian state, Western donors, and local and international NGOs promise better forms of accountability without fully delivering them. Nonetheless, these modern ideas have some traction. After all, it is not as if kinship, patronage, and reciprocal social relations ever produced social equality. The idea that the state and institutions like NGOs might serve as more neutral arbitrators, redressing inequalities rather than just tempering them, holds appeal for many Nigerians. In this context, drawing on these alternative idioms of accountability, even relatively good patrons like Chidinma, who ran one of the NGOs discussed in chapter 4, can face accusations of corruption, or at least the fear of such charges.

In addition to thinking about local AIDS NGOs as institutions where the changing face of social inequality in Nigeria can be observed, it is important to realize that they can also be engines for the dissemination of the interventions that reproduce harmful interpretations and responses to the epidemic. In their efforts to please donors by parroting policies like ABC, but also in their concern not to challenge the prevailing moralistic discourses around AIDS circulating in Nigeria, AIDS NGOs can all too often be more of a problem than a solution. As I will discuss further in the final section, countering the deleterious consequences of these moral understandings of AIDS must be one of the top priorities of AIDS NGOs if they truly wish to mitigate the infections, sicknesses, and deaths caused by the disease.

Kinship: Stretched and Strained, but Not Broken

In southeastern Nigeria, no arena of social life is more important to people—both morally and materially—than kinship. I cannot count the number of Igbo proverbs I've heard that express the importance of kin. For example, people commonly say "*onye were madu were ike*" and "*onye were madu were aku*," which translate literally as "somebody who has people has power" and "somebody who has people has wealth." These proverbs are not simply a cultural or historical curiosity. They express how people think the world works, even now. Indeed, one of the curious aspects of kinship in Nigeria is that its importance appears not to have diminished significantly despite the apparent assault from a changing political economy, urbanization, and people's exposure to global media.

There is little doubt that village life in Nigeria is changing—some might even argue eroding. After all, people are moving to cities at a furious pace. Many rural communities are disproportionately both very old and very young because so many young adults have moved away. Further, ever fewer households in rural villages sustain themselves through subsistence agriculture alone. Certainly in Ubakala—and throughout many rural communities in Nigeria—nearly every household has a diverse livelihood strategy, often combining agriculture, wage labor, small businesses, and remittances from migrant members in the city. One might imagine that the imperative of high fertility, big families, and unbreakable ties to community of origin would be disappearing. But while fertility rates have declined slowly, there is little evidence of the final demise of kinship.

In part, this is because access to social resources in Nigeria is still mediated through patronage and social connections, and kinship remains a privileged sphere in which one can count on others for help (Berry 1989; Smith 2001c, 2007a). Kinship is the social-relational bedrock for the moral economy that is so much on people's minds as they worry about social change and grapple with the AIDS epidemic. The assertion that there is no reason to predict the final demise of the extended family system and its primacy in social life is based, in part, on the vehemence with which Nigerians react to perceived threats to it. One way—and in my view quite an accurate way—to explain the resonance and influence of moral interpretations of the AIDS epidemic is to understand that these discourses find their power in the ways that AIDS is seen as standing for the threats to kinship and social relations posed by ongoing changes. Although many popular understandings of AIDS are indicative of people's anxieties about the future of kinship and the moral economy that it undergirds, the passion with which Nigerians express their discontent with the country's perceived moral crisis is also evidence of the extent to which they wish to preserve and defend forms of sociality that appear to be eroding.

The relationship between kinship and social change is more complicated and contradictory than an all-too-easy dichotomy between tradition (often associated with kinship) and modernity (often associated with kinship's demise). As much as people feel that kinship is under siege in contemporary Nigeria, it should not be forgotten that many of the aspirations and behaviors that appear to threaten the extended family system and its moral economy are in fact driven by people's desire to do well for and by their kin. Whether it is the desire to migrate to the city, further one's education, get a good job, make a lot of money, or acquire new things, people's individual motives are, in part, efforts to meet the expectations of their kin. This does not mean that the worries about growing inequality, greed, and unbridled individualism are unfounded. But the moral discourses critical of these trends indicate that kinship and the values it embodies are still prevalent and powerful, even as Nigerians themselves participate in producing the very changes they find so worrisome.

Morality and Inequality

I have argued in this book that Nigerians commonly respond in moral terms to inequalities associated with various dimensions of contemporary social change. Further, Nigerians interpret AIDS as a symbol, a cause, and a consequence—albeit one among many—of the troubling transformations unfolding in Africa's most populous country. The meaning of the disease and the spectrum of social responses—from individual to institutional—are heavily influenced by people's perceptions of larger trajectories of change. The moralistic interpretations of individual infections as well as the nationwide epidemic have been reinforced by some of the messages and approaches of internationally supported initiatives—what I have called "iatrogenic interventions." But the primary foundation of Nigerians' moral lens for understanding AIDS lies in Nigerian society.

Research and scholarship on the AIDS epidemic has demonstrated time and again, in settings around the globe, the extent to which the virus exploits inequality (Farmer 1999; Ojikutu and Stone 2005; Fassin 2007). People who are poor, who lack economic and political resources, and who are marginalized by society suffer disproportionately (Piot, Greener, and Russell 2007; Padilla et al. 2008). What is more, even in circumstances where it is not the poorest people who are most affected, inequality acts as a significant driver of the epidemic and offers a compelling explanation for who gets infected and who does not. In Nigeria, as elsewhere, sexual behavior that puts people at risk for HIV infection is often more about trying to achieve aspirations for a modern and middle-class lifestyle than about stark choices related to survival (Hunter 2002; Leclerc-Madlala 2003; Smith 2010).

The moralistic lens applied in local interpretations of these behaviors has had many deleterious consequences for AIDS prevention, for testing and treatment programs, and for care and support of people infected with or affected by HIV and AIDS. The idea that AIDS is a marker of—or even punishment for—individual and collective immorality has generated misunderstandings, silences, and scapegoats. Rather than addressing the root inequalities that actually drive the spread of the disease, Nigerians have been obsessed with the moral crisis that is perceived to encourage the spread of the epidemic.

Similarly, when popular discontent about the consequences of social change—and resulting inequalities—is expressed in moral terms, it sometimes protects rather than resists the processes, institutions, and actors responsible for reproducing Nigeria's deep disparities. When Nigerians attribute the country's ills to the ethnic, religious, regional, and cultural differences that divide them, the realities of class inequality are obscured and ever-starker exploitation by elites is perpetuated. The moral idiom for voicing discontent with social change frequently seems to inhibit the emergence of a political struggle that might effect lasting structural transformations: a classic case of antipolitics (Ferguson 1990; de Waal 1997). Rather than trying to transform social structures that inequitably and often "immorally" distribute power and wealth, most ordinary Nigerians seek means to manipulate the system to their own benefit, thereby upholding the social scaffolding on which disparities have been constructed.

But recognizing the antipolitical aspects of people's moral interpretations of Nigeria's problems is only part of the story. In other ways, the moral lens is so powerful precisely because it expresses Nigerians' ambivalence about real political and economic changes unfolding in their society. Rather than the moral lens simply obscuring class interests, the resulting laments about greed, criminality, anonymity, and individualism also express an acute awareness of what is lost with the transformations associated with the penetration of capitalism, urbanization, and development. These moral anxieties point to a troubling aspect of social change that one misses if inequality is viewed only in terms of money and access to political power. For Nigerians, just as problematic as economic and political forms of inequality are changes in the fabric of social relations. Contemporary transformations threaten kinship, face-to-face sociality, and the inequality-tempering forms of patron-clientism in which "haves" and "have-nots" had real social obligations to each other. While I believe that certain things stay hidden and protected when Nigerians express their ambivalence about new inequalities and other troubling consequences of ongoing social changes in moral terms, the moral lens also points to aspects of social life that we might miss—and that Nigerians clearly value—if we only see the world through the lens of economics, or, for that matter, through epidemiology and the objectives of public health programs.

Addressing the Social Face of AIDS

At the beginning of this book I employed the common Nigerian Pidgin English prevention slogan *AIDS no dey show for face* to help introduce my argument that looking at Nigeria's AIDS epidemic only through the lens of health and disease misses its social dimensions. I have tried to offer a perspective on AIDS in Nigeria that focuses on what we can learn about Nigeria

and Nigerians, particularly how they are experiencing inequalities associated with contemporary social transformations. I have argued that in many
ways the social responses to the AIDS epidemic have been as consequential
as the biomedical effects of the disease for the well-being of the infected and
for the epidemic's meaning in the public sphere, precisely because understandings of AIDS in people's imaginations are so bound up with their ambivalence about the troubling consequences of wider social changes. When
looked at only as a medical or public health problem, AIDS doesn't show its
face; but if understood socially, we learn not only more about the epidemic
but also about society as a whole. Having studied AIDS in Nigeria this way,
I believe there are some lessons from understanding the social responses
to the epidemic that might contribute to better addressing the medical and
public health aspects of the disease.

With regard to prevention, the single most important task is undoing
the moral stigma associated with condoms. But this challenge is connected
to the larger problem of how shared moralizing interpretations of the disease have impinged on people's decisions about sexual behavior. The "A"
(Abstinence) and "B" (Be faithful) components of the ABC approach could
not be much more widely known in Nigeria than they are now. In the surveys and interviews I conducted with Nigerians, mostly young adults, more
than 90 percent knew and could correctly identify the meanings of these
messages. But as I have tried to show, in addition to reducing the problem
of AIDS prevention to individual choice (and by implication to individual
culpability), these messages frequently have the unintended consequence
of producing behavior among sexually active people that actually increases
their risk of infection. Perhaps most notably, in an effort to construct images
of their sexual behaviors as moral—for themselves, their partners, and society—people eschew condoms, as they are so strongly associated with the
kinds of sex that immoral people have. This pattern is reinforced by rumors
and conspiracy theories that circulate about condoms, making them stigmatized symbols of the very disease they are supposed to prevent.

I see two main options for rehabilitating condoms as a prevention strategy in Nigeria: one is long-term, difficult, and maybe unrealistic; the other
may not be easy, but is more feasible. The long-term strategy would seek
to undo the moralizing discourses about AIDS. Public health messages
would need to encourage Nigerians to see the epidemic less as an emblem
of problematic social change and more as a virus that exploits inequality
and poverty, but from which people can protect themselves, even before
those bigger social problems are ameliorated. Such an approach would be
difficult because the moral view of AIDS—and of troubling consequences

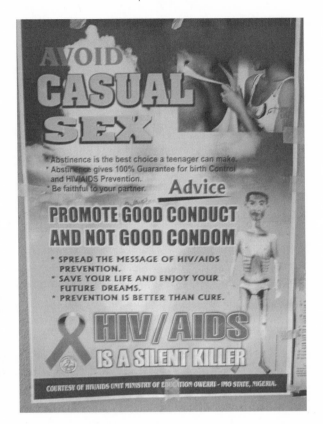

10. The stigma associated with condoms is a primary example of how moral interpretations of Nigeria's AIDS epidemic have been detrimental to effective prevention.

of contemporary social changes more generally—is deep-seated and reflects genuine concerns as well as misconceptions.

More realistic, I think, would be a campaign to emphasize the moral and ethical benefits of condoms in order to help people see condom use as something one employs to protect oneself, one's partner, one's family, and society more generally. Countering early images of AIDS in which condoms were depicted as a means to protect oneself only in the event of immoral sex with a dangerous other, AIDS prevention programs should try to create and disseminate messages about condoms that connect their use to values and practices that Nigerians cherish rather than with those they find problematic and threatening. To better promote condoms, public health messages could associate them with caring, respectful, reciprocal social relations, in which social connections are validated and affection is expressed through observing duties and obligations to others. The challenge is to make condom use the moral choice, not the immoral choice. This strategy would take advantage of Nigerians' moralistic view of AIDS rather than trying to counter it.

As the examples in chapter 6 showed, even in treatment programs, the moral discourses surrounding AIDS pose obstacles. Although antiretroviral treatment is still not available in Nigeria to many who need it, the situation improved dramatically beginning in 2005. At this writing, upward of 300,000 people are receiving drugs. The advent of large-scale treatment programs in Nigeria—and across Africa—is an achievement worth celebrating. But treatment has not mitigated stigma in Nigeria in the way that many had hoped. People on antiretroviral drugs cannot easily disclose their status to their friends, families, communities, and workplaces. To maintain their secret, they sometimes fail to take their drugs as prescribed, and they often face difficult decisions about whether to tell sexual partners about their status. Further, in the eyes of the public health programs and medical providers that give them their drugs, they are more AIDS patients than people, making it difficult to address and actualize their ambitions to live more normal lives—marrying and having children being paramount among these aspirations.

The plight of people in treatment is a reminder that popular perceptions of the perils of AIDS are ultimately rooted in the disease's perceived threat to social reproduction. In an era of rapid social change, where the future seems up for grabs, AIDS stands poignantly for this uncertainty, and for the sense that ongoing transformations are tearing at things people dearly value. No wonder, then, that for people who have HIV and AIDS, marrying and having children—the most basic and biological foundation of the larger processes of social reproduction—are among the most common aspirations, motivating many of the decisions they make in terms of disclosure and treatment of their infections. Unfortunately, these are desires that current public health programs and the stigma associated with the disease have made more difficult. For people on antiretroviral medications, perhaps the most important improvement in current programs would be to help rather than hinder their reproductive aspirations, thereby allowing them to participate in the larger processes of social reproduction about which Nigerians are so anxious. Some of this would require public health innovation: for example, the recent availability of single-dose pills that amalgamate the several combination-therapy drugs should increase adherence to antiretroviral treatment by eliminating the anxieties associated with hiding bulky supplies of ART pills. More readily accessible ART dissemination centers and more reliable supplies of the drugs are also necessary. Access to Prevention of Mother-to-Child Transmission (PMTCT), one of the easiest and cheapest modes of prevention available, is extraordinarily low in Nigeria. By increasing the numbers of people on ART and ensuring that pregnant women have access to PMTCT, two huge obstacles to the management of Nigeria's epidemic could be redressed, and public health advances, like those seen in the last decade in countries such as Botswana, could be achieved. After all, people on ART have vastly lower viral loads and are thereby less likely to infect an HIV-negative partner, even when having unprotected sex. Serodiscordant couples like Chinyere and Obi and Nnamdi and Ogechi have a higher likelihood of remaining that way while on ART, even when attempting to have children.

Nigerians' moral interpretations of and social responses to the epidemic have tremendous implications for AIDS prevention and treatment. Ultimately, however, these interpretations and responses express the truth that AIDS is not their biggest problem. Increasing social disparities, growing threats to the inequality-tempering and personalizing ties of kinship and community, and a sense that social relations are less governed by acceptable morality than in the past: these are the issues that give the prevailing understandings of the epidemic their power, and they are what most profoundly trouble Nigerians in the era of AIDS.

ACKNOWLEDGMENTS

As everyone who has written a book—especially an ethnography—knows, many people and many institutions contribute to the journey and to the final product. Observers often conceive of anthropologists' trade as one in which a single person does most of the work, but along the way we depend on, learn from, and accumulate a great debt to numerous others. I owe many thanks to those who helped me in this project and can only gesture to the extent of my gratitude here.

The research upon which this book is based extended for more than a decade, and it would not have been possible without funding from multiple sources. Awards from the National Institutes of Health (3 P30 HD28251-10S1; 1 R01 41724-01A1; P30 AI042853; 1 R01 HD057792-01A2) supported much of the fieldwork in Nigeria, as did grants from the National Science Foundation (BCS-0075764) and the Wenner-Gren Foundation for Anthropological Research (6636). Most recently, a grant from the Pentecostal and Charismatic Research Initiative, through the Center for Religion and Civic Culture at the University of Southern California, funded by the John Templeton Foundation (Grant #13893, Subcontract #143426), enabled me to continue my research on AIDS in Nigeria with a specific focus on the impact of Pentecostal Christianity. To all of these sponsors I am most grateful.

Some of the chapters in this book draw on material I have published previously in journal articles. Although none of the articles is reproduced in its entirety or exactly as it appeared previously, I want to acknowledge which pieces I have drawn on and where, and thank the publishers for permission to incorporate this material. Chapter 2 includes some material drawn from "Modern Marriage, Men's Extramarital Sex, and HIV Risk in Nigeria," which appeared in *American Journal of Public Health* (97[6]: 997–1005) in

2007. I thank the journal for permission to use parts of that article. Part of chapter 3 includes material adapted from "Youth, Sin and Sex in Nigeria: Christianity and HIV-Related Beliefs and Behaviour among Rural-Urban Migrants," published in *Culture, Health & Sexuality* (6[5]: 425–437) in 2004. Thanks to Taylor & Francis for permission to draw from that article. Chapter 4 draws extensively from "AIDS NGOS and Corruption in Nigeria," published in *Health & Place* (18[3]: 475–480) in 2012, and from "Corruption, NGOs, and Development in Nigeria," which appeared in *Third World Quarterly* (32[2]: 243–258) in 2010. I want to thank Elsevier and Taylor & Francis, respectively, for permission to use material from those articles. Finally, chapter 6 draws significantly on "Antiretroviral Therapy and Reproductive Life Projects: Mitigating the Stigma of AIDS in Nigeria," an article I coauthored with my Nigerian colleague Benjamin C. Mbakwem in *Social Science & Medicine* (71[2]: 345–352) in 2010. Thanks to Benjamin and to Elsevier for permission to use some of that material here.

As I was working on the book, I presented iterations of various chapters in invited lectures at several universities, colleges, and conferences. At these events many colleagues provided valuable feedback. I presented an early version of chapter 1 at George Washington University's Institute for Ethnographic Research, and I want to thank in particular Stephen Lubkemann, José Muñoz, and Roy Richard Grinker for their questions, comments, suggestions. I presented another earlier version of chapter 1 at the seminar series on "Gender, Sexuality and Health" at the Mailman School of Public Health at Columbia University. Special thanks to Constance Nathanson and Jennifer Hirsch for their valuable feedback. Papers that led to chapter 2 were presented at the Program of African Studies at Northwestern University, with thanks to Richard Joseph and Adam Ashforth for their comments and suggestions; at the Population Council in New York; and at the University of the Witwatersrand in South Africa, where I owe thanks to Stephen Tollman, Kathleen Khan, Clifford Odimegwu, and other colleagues there.

I delivered papers that led to chapter 3 at the Yale Council on African Studies at Yale University, where I received helpful comments from Kamari Clark, Mike McGovern, and Catherine Panter-Brick; at Lafayette College, where Allison Alexy and her colleagues and students offered lively input; and at the University of Copenhagen at a conference entitled "Religious Engagements with HIV/AIDS in Africa," organized by Rijk Van Dijk, Hansjörg Dilger, and Ruth Prince. Many colleagues at that conference offered interesting perspectives on religion and AIDS that influenced my thinking, and I have continued to benefit in unanticipated ways from the connections I made there. My perspective on the relationship between Pentecostal Christianity and AIDS has also been enriched by colleagues who were part of the Pentecostal and Charismatic Research Initiative. At group meetings in Quito, Ecuador, and Nairobi, Kenya, interactions with these scholars helped me better understand my observations in Nigeria. In particular, I am grateful for discussions with and insights offered by Febe Armanios, Zainal Bagir, Chad Bauman, Karen Brison, Richard Burgess, Robert Dowd, Paul Freston, Musa Gaiya, Henri Gooren, Andrew Johnson, William Kay, Karrie Koesel, John McCauley, Danny McCain, Donald Miller, Alexander Panchenko, Patrick Plattet, Robin Shoaps, Yusuf Turaki, Timothy Wadkins, and Richard Wood.

Chapter 4 benefited from constructive responses to papers delivered at Dartmouth College, where I owe special thanks to James Igoe and Sienna Craig; at Mount Holyoke College, where Holly Hansen organized an engaging workshop about corruption and accountability in Africa; and at the London School of Economics, where Catherine Campbell and her colleagues hosted a stimulating conference at which many colleagues pushed my thinking. I presented versions of chapter 5 at Colby College, where I owe special thanks to Catherine Besteman, and at Emory University, where I want to thank in particular Peter Brown, Carla Freemen, and Craig Hadley. Various iterations of chapter 6 were delivered at a workshop organized by Abigail Harrison and Sangeetha Madhavan prior to the annual meeting of the Population Association of America in San Francisco in 2012, where I received useful comments from many, including Susan Watkins; at the Munk School of Global Affairs at the University of Toronto, where I owe particular thanks to Michael Lambek; at the School of Medicine at Johns Hopkins University, where I want to thank both Randall Packard and Lori Leonard; at the University of California, Berkeley, where I am grateful to Jennifer Johnson-Hanks and Daniel Perlman for their comments; and at the HIV Center for Clinical and Behavioral Studies, the New York State Psychiatric Institute and Columbia University, where I thank Jennifer Hirsh for organizing a great workshop at which I benefited from the input of many participants. Finally, I profited from participants' comments on a talk I gave about some of the general themes of the book at a conference at the University of Kansas called "Medical Anthropology in Global Africa," organized by my former graduate student, Kathryn Rhine.

In addition to those mentioned already, conversations and collaborations with many other colleagues have contributed to this book. Those people include Rogaia Abusharaf, Caroline Bledsoe, Sylvia Chant, Jennifer Cole, Joanna Davidson, Pamela Feldman-Savelsberg, Ellen Foley, Peter Geschiere, Mark Hunter, Marcia Inhorn, William Jankowiak, Carola Lentz, Sangeetha

Madhavan, Ruth Marshall, Sanyu Mojola, William Miles, Vinh-Kim Nguyen, Ebenezer Obadare, Kristin Peterson, Lisa Ann Richey, Rosalind Shaw, Ann Swidler, Lynn Thomas, Susan Watkins, Michael Watts, and Susanna Wing. In addition, for almost a decade I worked with a wonderful group of scholars on a project we called "Love, Marriage, and HIV," a comparative ethnographic study, the results from which are mostly published elsewhere. But those collaborators have constituted my dearest and most important intellectual community and they are among my best friends in the academy. While this book is not about that research, at least not directly, the collective influence of that group on my thinking is immeasurable. They are Jennifer Hirsch, Constance Nathanson, Shanti Parikh, Harriet Phinney, and Holly Wardlow. I wish everyone could find such wonderful collaborators in their academic careers.

At Brown University, where I have been since 1999, many colleagues have been intellectual interlocutors and an even wider array of people has supported my work and career. In the Department of Anthropology, I want to thank in particular Paja Faudree, Lina Fruzzetti, Matthew Gutmann, Sherine Hamdy, Marida Hollos, Stephen Houston, David Kertzer, Jessaca Leinaweaver, Catherine Lutz, Patricia Rubertone, Andrew Scherer, William Simmons, and Kay Warren. The department has been a wonderful intellectual home, but also a warm community. During most of the time I wrote this book, Catherine Lutz was chair of the department, and I want to thank her in particular for being so supportive. In recent years we have had a wonderful cast of temporary young faculty—postdoctoral fellows and visiting assistant professors—and many of them have been fantastic colleagues, adding to my thinking and enriching our intellectual community. In particular, I want to thank Ellen Block, Rebecca Carter, Bianca Dahl, Melissa Hackman, Saida Hodzic, Kenneth Maes, and Becky Schulthies. Their vitality and scholarly creativity have been an inspiration to me. I owe special gratitude to Bianca Dahl, who read a full draft of the book manuscript and provided insightful comments and incredibly helpful feedback. As many in our department discovered, Bianca has a special talent for constructive criticism and she provided remarkably astute suggestions.

My graduate students, current and former, have read and discussed many aspects of my work and often have provided constructive criticism and stimulating comments, questions, and suggestions. Keeping up with them is both challenging and inspirational. I want to thank former students Caroline Archambault, Jan Brunson, Lacey Andrews Gale, Maya Judd, Susi Keefe, Elisaveta Koriouchkina, Inna Leykin, Rebecca Warne Peters, Kathyrn Rhine, Harris Solomon, Salome Wawire, and Bruce Whitehouse. I am also grateful to current students Paula Dias, Susan Ellison, Chelsea Cormier-McSwiggin, Kendra Fehrer, Alex Jones, Karen Jorge, Andrea Maldonado, Katharine Marsh, Maya Mesola, Coleman Nye, Mohamed Yunus Rafiq, Stephanie Savell, Derek Sheridan, Kristin Skrabut, Stacey Vanderhurst, and Laura Vares. Coleman Nye merits special thanks because she worked for me for a semester as a research assistant and helped me find and digest much of the literature relevant to this project.

Over the years I have taken a number of Brown undergraduates to Nigeria to conduct research and to work on AIDS-related projects with some of my local collaborators. Those students included Alexandra Bachorik, Heather Clark, Sora Chung, Bathsheba Demuth, Rahul Kamat, Sarah Kimball, Nayla Khoury, Sasha Rubel, Emily Timm, and Rachel Weston. All of them pushed me with their questions and added to my understanding of Nigerians' experience with the AIDS epidemic. I am especially grateful to Sasha Rubel, who helped launch my work on Pentecostal Christianity with her own excellent research one summer. Sam Krinsky, another former Brown student, spent a year in Ibadan on a Fulbright and his work on Pentecostal Christianity has also contributed to my knowledge and curiosity.

Brown's Anthropology Department staff—Matilde Andrade, Katherine Grimaldi, and Marjorie Sugrue—has provided invaluable support and assistance. The only thing more magical than Kathy's magic wand, which is waved over almost every student and faculty manuscript or grant proposal before it goes out for review, is her tireless good nature, the glue that holds our community together.

Beyond the Anthropology Department, many others at Brown have become valued intellectual interlocutors, including Susan Alcock, Peter Andreas, Gianpaolo Baiocchi, Keith Brown, Nitsan Chorev, Andrew Foster, Nancy Jacobs, Patrick Heller, Glenn Loury, Nancy Luke, Wendy Schiller, Susan Short, Hilary Silver, Richard Snyder, Barbara Stallings, Leah VanWey, Corey Walker, and Michael White. The staff at the Population Studies and Training Center has been vital in supporting my research and grants, especially Priscilla Terry and Tom Alarie. Kelley Smith, whose editorial skills are only the tip of the iceberg of all she offers the Brown community, provided superb suggestions in a careful read of the manuscript. Thanks to her—again.

Many people in Nigeria deserve to be acknowledged and thanked because, more than anyone else, they made this book possible. A good number of Nigerian academic colleagues are located in other settings around the continent, but they are central members of my Nigerian scholarly community. They include, among others, Alex Ezeh, Chimaraoke

Izugbara, Blessing Mberu, and Clifford Odimegwu. In the academy in Nigeria many scholars have helped and influenced me. I want to thank in particular Igwe Aja-Nwachuku, Pat Ngwu, Oka Obono, Akachi Odoemene, Ogwo E. Ogwo, Chuks Okereke, and Morenike Ukpong. I was lucky that Akachi, Chimaraoke, Clifford, Oka, and Morenike all spent time at Brown, and so I benefited from having them in Providence as well as in Africa. I worked with superb research assistants in Nigeria over the past decade, including Chidozie Amuzie, Ugochukwu Anozie, Frank Ehuru, Jane Ibeaja, Chinkata Nwachukwu, and Elizabeth Oduwai Uhuegbu. Probably my greatest intellectual debt for making this book possible belongs to Benjamin Mbakwem, my longtime friend and collaborator in Owerri, one of the places I spend my time when I do research in Nigeria. Benjamin founded a nongovernmental organization, Community & Youth Development Initiatives, in 2000 and has been at the forefront of AIDS prevention and efforts to assist people living with HIV in Nigeria. In addition to his heroic work in public health and community development, Benjamin is the savviest observer of Nigerian culture, society, and politics that I know. I have spent countless hours listening to his stories about and interpretations of the world in which he lives and works. I can only hope this book is half as interesting as the things Benjamin has to say.

Many people who are not directly involved in my research have made my extended stays in Nigeria possible and enjoyable, and in various ways they have contributed immensely to this book. At home in Ubakala they include Jemmaimah Agoha, Moses Agoha, Eze Raphael Mbagwu, Chief Israel Iroabuchi, Prince Udo Ogbuehi, Chief and Lolo Ufomba Ihenacho, and Okwuchukwu Amuzie. As I write these acknowledgments, I have learned that Okwuchukwu recently died too young from diabetes, a reminder that many other health problems in addition to AIDS accompany Nigeria's fitful growth and development. In Owerri, I want to thank especially James Anukam, Jane Ibeaja, Bishop M. N. Nkemakolam, S. K. Okpi, Chibuzo Oriuwa, and Ukay Wachuku for what are now lifelong friendships. In Umuahia, my second home since 1995 has been Umuahia Sports Club, and my friends there continue to teach me about Nigeria while also providing the camaraderie that makes my time there so enjoyable. My friends are too many to name, but I want recognize especially C. C. Anyalebechi, Emeka Emeh, Dr. James Ifediora, Kalu Ire Kalu, Goddy Nwogu, Ike Obgokiri, Ferguson Onuoha, and Lawrence Ukattah. To them and all my other friends I say again, "Ahi Club!"

I am eternally grateful to the many people who shared with me parts of their life stories, whose identities are concealed in the book with pseudonyms. To all of them, but particularly to those who are HIV positive, I hope the book does at least small justice to their lives, struggles, and courage. I cannot thank them by name, but they know who they are.

At the University of Chicago Press I want to thank David Brent and his able editorial associate, Priya Nelson. David's unfailing enthusiasm for and support of the book project, though various ups and downs, helped keep me moving forward. Thank you. I am indebted to Jenni Fry, who provided superb copyediting that greatly improved my writing. I am also sincerely grateful to three anonymous reviewers, one of whom saw the manuscript twice, for insightful and constructive suggestions, which I tried my best to take to heart in the final revisions. The reviewers, and so many other people mentioned already, deserve much of the credit for whatever is good about this book. It is clichéd to say so, but it is nonetheless true that any shortcomings are solely my responsibility.

Finally, I want to thank all my family and friends, extended and near, for being such a boundless source of strength and affirmation, including Mom, Don, Derek, and Story, but also Ada, Ngozi, Chidi, Chisara, and Okechukwu. I am lucky and grateful. Kimmy, I hope that you continue to grow up with the same experience of love and support from which I have benefited so immensely. Your enthusiasm for life is my inspiration.

NOTES

INTRODUCTION

1. Throughout this book, I have disguised the identities of individuals and some organizations with pseudonyms. In addition, in individual cases where simply disguising a name might not be enough to protect people's privacy, I have slightly altered small details.
2. One of the reasons why sentinel surveillance data is considered less accurate is because the group it surveys—pregnant women seeking health care—is both an unrepresentative population and one that by definition has been engaging in unprotected sex. One would therefore expect that the group would exhibit a higher prevalence rate than the general population.

CHAPTER TWO

1. One might suggest (and I believe) that strong connections exist in every society between emotional and economic support (and between love and money), to a greater degree than is often acknowledged. For an illuminating exploration of these issues in American society, see Zelizer 2005.
2. The five-country study "Love, Marriage, and HIV" was funded by the National Institutes of Health (1 R01 41724–01A1). I am grateful to Jennifer Hirsch, Shanti Parikh, Harriet Phinney, and Holly Wardlow, my collaborators on the project, whose intellectual contributions to my thinking about these issues have been invaluable.
3. The high cost of getting married is contributing to a perceived crisis of masculinity in many African settings, including southeastern Nigeria. Important scholarship on this issue includes Hunter 2005, Masquelier 2005b, and Isiugo-Abanihe 1994.
4. That most men want to keep their affairs secret from their wives is partly a result of husbands knowing there will be consequences if wives find out——consequences that the women themselves can impose. Several men and women in the "Love, Marriage, and HIV" study recounted the ways wives punished their husbands' infidelities, including withholding food, withdrawing financial support, preventing sexual access, and, on much rarer occasions, publicly humiliating them or even retaliating with an affair of their own. Women are by no means powerless pawns in these modern Igbo marriages, but they do have good reason to keep secret or stay silent about their husbands' extramarital sexual behavior.

5.   For more on married women's responses to their husbands' infidelity, see Smith 2009 and 2010. On the same issue in other settings, see Hirsch et al. 2007; Parikh 2007; Phinney 2008; and Wardlow 2007.

CHAPTER FOUR

1.   United Against AIDS is a pseudonym, as is Naija Cares, the name of an NGO highlighted later in this chapter. Some details about the organizations are slightly altered to protect the privacy of various people associated with them.

2.   For valuable ethnographic accounts of NGOs, see Bornstein 2005; Hilhorst 2003; and Schuller 2009.

CHAPTER SIX

1.   Counts of CD4 cells are a measure of the body's immunological strength, and they decrease as HIV multiplies. Even when an HIV infection has not produced full-blown AIDS, low counts are an indication that sickness may be imminent. Measuring CD4 counts is simpler and cheaper than measuring viral loads, and cut-off marks below which treatment is indicated have generally been used to determine who is eligible for ART in poorer countries like Nigeria. It is an instructive reminder of the consequences of global inequality for health to know that richer countries tend to have higher CD4 count thresholds for triggering treatment than do poorer countries. In other words, one has to be more immune-compromised to qualify for treatment in a poor country than in a rich one. As mentioned previously, many Nigerians do not test for HIV until they are sick. People with full-blown AIDS are automatically eligible for treatment, in theory, but drugs are not, in fact, always available.

REFERENCES

Abah, Adedayo. 2008. "One Step Forward, Two Steps Backward: African Women in Nigerian Video-Film." *Communication, Culture & Critique* 1 (4): 335–57.

Adogame, Afe. 2007. "HIV/AIDS Support and African Pentecostalism: The Case of the Redeemed Christian Church of God." *Journal of Health Psychology* 12 (3): 475–84.

Aja, Godwin N., Naomi N. Modeste, Jerry W. Lee, Suzanne B. Montgomery, and Juan C. Belliard. 2010. "Perceived Church-Based Needs and Assets for HIV/AIDS Prevention in an Urban Nigerian Community." *Journal of Religion and Health* 40: 50–61.

Altman, Dennis. 1998. "Globalization and the 'AIDS Industry.'" *Contemporary Politics* 4 (3): 233–45.

Anthony, Douglas. 2002. *Poison and Medicine: Ethnicity, Power and Violence in a Nigerian City, 1966 to 1986*. Portsmouth, NH: Heinemann.

Apter, Andrew. 1999. "IBB = 419: Nigerian Democracy and the Politics of Illusion." In *Civil Society and the Political Imagination in Africa: Critical Perspectives*, edited by John Comaroff and Jean Comaroff, 267–307. Chicago: University of Chicago Press.

———. 2005. *The Pan-African Nation: Oil and the Spectacle of Culture in Nigeria*. Chicago: University of Chicago Press.

Ashforth, Adam. 2002. "An Epidemic of Witchcraft: The Implications of AIDS for the Post-Apartheid State." *African Studies* 61 (1): 121–43.

———. 2005. *Witchcraft, Violence, and Democracy in South Africa*. Chicago: University of Chicago Press.

———. 2011. "AIDS, Religious Enthusiasm and Spiritual Insecurity in Africa." *Global Public Health* 6 (S2): S132–S147.

Barber, Karin. 1982. "Popular Reactions to the Petro-Naira." *Journal of Modern African Studies* 20 (3): 431–50.

Barnett, Tony, and Justin Parkhurst. 2005. "AIDS: Sex, Abstinence, and Behaviour Change." *Lancet* 5 (9): 590–93.

Bastian, Misty. 1993. "'Bloodhounds Who Have No Friends': Witchcraft and Locality in the Nigerian Popular Press." In *Modernity and Its Malcontents: Ritual and Power in Postcolonial Africa*, edited by Jean Comaroff and John Comaroff, 129–66. Chicago: University of Chicago Press.

Bayart, Jean-François. 1993. *The State in Africa: The Politics of the Belly*. London: Longman.

Becker, Felicitas, and P. Wenzel Geissler. 2007. "Searching for Pathways in a Landscape of Death: Religion and AIDS in East Africa," *Journal of Religion in Africa* 37: 1–15.

Berry, Sara. 1985. *Fathers Work for Their Sons: Accumulation, Mobility and Class Formation in an Extended Yoruba Community*. Berkeley: University of California Press.

———. 1989. "Social Institutions and Access to Resources." *Africa* 59: 41–55.

Biehl, Joao. 2005. *Vita: Life in a Zone of Social Abandonment*. Berkeley: University of California Press.

———. 2007. *Will to Live: AIDS Therapies and the Politics of Survival*. Princeton, NJ: Princeton University Press.

Bledsoe, Caroline, and Gilles Pison, eds. 1994. *Nuptuality in Sub-Saharan Africa: Contemporary Anthropological and Demographic Perspectives*. New York: Oxford University Press.

Bleek, Wolf. 1976. *Sexual Relationships and Birth Control in Ghana: A Case Study of a Rural Town*. Amsterdam: University of Amsterdam.

Bond, Virginia, Elaine Chase, and Peter Aggleton. 2002. "Stigma, HIV/AIDS, and the Prevention of Mother-to-Child Transmission in Zambia." *Evaluation and Program Planning* 25 (4): 347–56.

Bornstein, Erica. 2005. *The Spirit of Development: Protestant NGOs, Morality and Economics in Zimbabwe*. Stanford: Stanford University Press.

Bratton, Michael. 1989. "The Politics of Government-NGO Relations in Africa." *World Development* 17 (4): 569–87.

Brockerhoff, Martin, and Hongsook Eu. 1993. "Demographic and Socioeconomic Determinants of Female Rural to Urban Migration in Sub-Saharan Africa." *International Migration Review* 27 (3): 557–77.

Brown, Lisanne, Kate Macintyre, and Lea Trujillo. 2003. "Interventions to Reduce HIV/AIDS Stigma: What Have We Learned?" *AIDS Education and Prevention* 15 (1): 49–69.

Bunnell, Rebecca, John Paul Ekwaru, Peter Solberg, Nafuna Wamai, Winnie Bikaako-Kajura, Willy Were, Alex Coutinho, Cheryl Liechty, Elizabeth Madraa, George Rutherford, and Jonathan Mermin. 2006. "Changes in Sexual Behavior and Risk of HIV Transmission after Antiretroviral Therapy and Prevention Interventions in Rural Uganda." *AIDS* 20 (1): 85–92.

Caldwell, John, Pat Caldwell, and Pat Quiggin. 1989. "The Social Context of AIDS in Sub-Saharan Africa." *Population and Development Review* 15 (2): 185–234.

Campbell, Catherine. 1995. "Male Gender Roles and Sexuality: Implications for Women's AIDS Risk and Prevention." *Social Science & Medicine* 41: 191–210.

———. 2003. *Letting Them Die: Why HIV Prevention Programmes Fail*. Bloomington: International African Institute/Indiana University Press.

Campbell, Catherine, Carol Ann Foulis, Sbongile Maimane, and Zweni Sibiya. 2005. "'I Have an Evil Child in My House': Stigma and HIV/AIDS Management in a South African Community." *American Journal of Public Health* 95 (5): 808–15.

Campbell, Catherine, Morten Skovdal, and Andrew Gibbs. 2011. "Creating Social Spaces to Tackle AIDS-Related Stigma: Reviewing the Role of Church Groups in Sub-Saharan Africa" *AIDS and Behavior* 15: 1204–19.

Casanova, Jose. 2001. "Religion, the New Millennium, and Globalization," *Sociology of Religion* 62: 415–41.

Castro, Arachu, and Paul Farmer. 2005. "Understanding and Addressing AIDS-Related Stigma: From Anthropological Theory to Clinical Practice in Haiti." *American Journal of Public Health* 95 (1): 53–59.

Chukwuezi, Barth. 2001. "Through Thick and Thin: Igbo Rural-Urban Circularity, Identity and Investment." *Journal of Contemporary African Studies* 19 (1): 55–66.

Clark, Samuel, Mark Collinson, Kathleen Kahn, Kyle Drullinger, and Stephen Tolman.

2007. "Returning Home to Die: Circular Labour Migration and Mortality in South Africa." *Scandinavian Journal of Public Health* 35 (S69): 35–44.

Cliggett, Lisa. 2005. *Grains from Grass: Aging, Gender, and Famine in Rural Africa.* Ithaca: Cornell University Press.

Cohen, Jonathan, and Tony Tate. 2006. "The Less They Know, the Better: Abstinence-Only HIV/AIDS Programs in Uganda." *Reproductive Health Matters* 14 (28): 174–78.

Cole, Jennifer. 2004. "Fresh Contact in Tamatave, Madagascar: Sex, Money and Intergenerational Transformation," *American Ethnologist* 31 (4): 573–88.

———. 2010. *Sex and Salvation: Imagining the Future in Madagascar.* Chicago: University of Chicago Press.

Cole, Jennifer, and Deborah Durham. 2007. "Introduction: Age, Regeneration, and the Intimate Politics of Globalization." In *Generations and Globalization: Youth, Age, and Family in the New World Economy,* edited by Jennifer Cole and Deborah Durham, 1–28. Bloomington: Indiana University Press.

Cole, Jennifer, and Lynn M. Thomas, eds. 2009. *Love in Africa.* Chicago: University of Chicago Press.

Comaroff, Jean, and John Comaroff. 1997. *Of Revelation and Revolution, Vol. 2: The Dialectics of Modernity on a South African Frontier.* Chicago: University of Chicago Press.

———. 2002. "Second Comings: Neo-Protestant Ethics and Millennial Capitalism in South Africa and Elsewhere." In *2000 Years and Beyond: Faith, Identity and the Common Era,* edited by Paul Gifford, 106–26. London: Routledge.

Connell, Raewyn. 1995. *Masculinities.* Cambridge: Polity Press.

Cooper, Diane, Jane Harries, Landon Myer, Phyllis Orner, and Hillary Bracken. 2007. "'Life Is Still Going On': Reproductive Intentions among HIV-Positive Women and Men in South Africa." *Social Science & Medicine* 65 (2): 274–83.

Cornwall, Andrea. 2002. "Spending Power: Love, Money and the Reconfiguration of Gender Relations in Ado-Odo, Southwestern Nigeria." *American Ethnologist* 29 (4): 963–80.

Corten, André, and Ruth Marshall-Fratani, eds. 2001. *Between Babel and Pentecost: Transnational Pentecostalism in Africa and Latin America.* Bloomington: Indiana University Press.

Dahl, Bianca. 2009. "Left Behind? Orphaned Children, Humanitarian Aid, and the Politics of Kinship, Culture, and Caregiving during Botswana's AIDS Crisis." PhD diss., University of Chicago.

Daloz, Jean-Pascal. 2005. "Trust Your Patron, Not the Institutions." *Comparative Sociology* 4 (1/2): 155–72.

de Waal, Alex. 1997. *Famine Crimes: Politics and the Disaster Relief Industry in Africa.* Bloomington: Indiana University Press.

Dilger, Hansjörg. 2006. "The Power of AIDS: Kinship, Mobility and the Valuing of Social and Ritual Relationships in Tanzania." *African Journal of AIDS Research* 5 (2): 109–21.

———. 2007. "Healing the Wounds of Modernity: Salvation, Community, and Care in a Neo-Pentecostal Church in Dar Es Salaam, Tanzania." *Journal of Religion in Africa* 37: 59–83.

———. 2010. "Introduction: Morality, Hope and Grief: Towards an Ethnographic Perspective in HIV/AIDS Research." In *Morality, Hope and Grief: Anthropologies of AIDS in Africa,* edited by Hansjörg Dilger and Ute Luig, 1–18. New York: Berghahn Books.

Dilger, Hansjörg, and Ute Luig, eds. 2010. *Morality, Hope and Grief: Anthropologies of AIDS in Africa.* New York: Berghahn.

Dinan, Carmel. 1983. "Sugar Daddies and Gold-Diggers: White Collar Single Women in Accra." In *Female and Male in West Africa*, edited by Christine Oppong, 344–366. London: George, Allen and Unwin.

Epstein, Helen. 2007. *The Invisible Cure: Africa, the West, and the Fight against AIDS*. New York: Farrar, Straus and Giroux.

Evans-Pritchard, E. E. 1937. *Witchcraft, Oracles and Magic among the Azande*. Oxford: Clarendon Press.

Farmer, Paul. 1992. *AIDS and Accusation: Haiti and the Geography of Blame*. Berkeley: University of California Press.

———. 1999. *Infections and Inequalities: The Modern Plagues*. Berkeley: University of California Press.

Fassin, Didier. 2007. *When Bodies Remember: Experiences and Politics of AIDS in South Africa*. Berkeley: University of California Press.

Federal Ministry of Education. 2006. *Basic and Senior Secondary Education Statistics in Nigeria, 2004 and 2005*. Abuja, Nigeria.

Federal Ministry of Health. 2009. *National HIV/AIDS and Reproductive Health Survey*. Abuja, Nigeria.

Ferguson, James. 1990. *The Anti-politics Machine: "Development," Depoliticization, and Bureaucratic Power in Lesotho*. Cambridge: Cambridge University Press.

———. 2006. *Global Shadows: Africa in the Neoliberal World*. Durham: Duke University Press.

Fortes, Meyer. 1978. "Parenthood, Marriage and Fertility in West Africa." *Journal of Development Studies* 14 (4): 121–48.

Garner, Robert C. 2000. "Safe Sects? Dynamic Religion and AIDS in South Africa." *The Journal of Modern African Studies* 38 (1): 41–69.

Geissler, P. Wenzel, and Ruth Prince. 2010. *The Land Is Dying: Contingency, Creativity and Conflict in Western Kenya*. New York: Berghahn Books.

Geschiere, Peter. 1997. *The Modernity of Witchcraft: Politics and the Occult in Postcolonial Africa*. Charlottesville: University of Virginia Press.

———. 2009. *The Perils of Belonging: Autochthony, Citizenship, and Exclusion in Africa and Europe*. Chicago: University of Chicago Press.

Geschiere, Peter, and Josef Gugler. 1998. "The Urban-Rural Connection: Changing Issues of Belonging and Identification." *Africa* 68 (3): 309–19.

Guerts, Kathryn. 2002. *Culture and the Senses: Bodily Ways of Knowing in an African Community*. Berkeley: University of California Press.

Gifford, Paul. 1990. "Prosperity: A New and Foreign Element in African Christianity." *Religion* 20: 373–88.

———. 2004. *Ghana's New Christianity: Pentecostalism in a Globalizing Economy*. Bloomington: Indiana University Press, 2004.

Gore, Charles, and David Pratten. 2003. "The Politics of Plunder: The Rhetorics of Order and Disorder in Southern Nigeria." *African Affairs* 102 (407): 211–40.

Graf, William. 1988. *The Nigerian State: Political Economy, State Class and Political System in Post-colonial Era*. London: Heinemann.

Gray, Ronald H., David Serwadda, Godfrey Kigozi, Fred Nalugoda, and Maria J. Wawer. 2006. "Uganda's HIV Prevention Success: The Role of Sexual Behavior Change and the National Response. Commentary on Green *et al.* (2006)." *AIDS and Behavior* 10 (4): 347–50.

Green, Edward C. 2003. *Rethinking AIDS Prevention: Learning from Successes in Developing Countries*. Westport, CT: Praeger.

Gruskin, Sofia, Rebecca Firestone, Sarah MacCarthy, and Laura Ferguson. 2008. "HIV and Pregnancy Intentions: Do Services Adequately Respond to Women's Needs?" *American Journal of Public Health* 98 (10): 1746–50.

Gugler, Josef. 1991. "Life in a Dual System Revisited: Urban-Rural Ties in Enugu, Nigeria, 1961–87." *World Development* 19 (5): 399–409.

———. 2002. "The Son of a Hawk Does Not Remain Abroad: The Urban-Rural Connection in Africa." *African Studies Review* 45 (1): 21–41.

Gugler, Josef, and William Flanagan. 1978. *Urbanization and Social Change in West Africa.* Cambridge: Cambridge University Press.

Gugler, Josef, and Gudrun Ludwar-Ene. 1995. "Gender and Migration in Africa South of the Sahara." In *Migration Experiences in Africa*, edited by Jonathan Baker and Tade Aina, 257–68. Uppsala: Nordiska Afrikainstitutet.

Haller, Dieter, and Cris Shore, eds. 2005. *Corruption: Anthropological Perspectives.* London: Pluto.

Haram, Liv. 2010. " 'We Are Tired of Mourning!' The Economy of Death and Bereavement in the Time of AIDS." In *Morality, Hope and Grief: Anthropologies of AIDS in Africa*, edited by Hansjörg Dilger and Ute Luig, 219–39. New York: Berghahn Books.

Harneit-Sievers, Axel. 2006. *Constructions of Belonging: Igbo Communities and the Nigerian State in the Twentieth Century.* Rochester: University of Rochester Press.

Harrell-Bond, Barbara. 1975. *Modern Marriage in Sierra Leone: A Study of the Professional Group.* Paris: Mouton.

Haynes, Jonathan. 2007. "Nollywood in Lagos, Lagos in Nollywood Films." *Africa Today* 54 (2): 131–50.

Hilhorst, Dorothea. 2003. *The Real World of NGOs: Discourses, Diversity and Development.* London: Zed Books.

Hirsch, Jennifer. 2007. "Gender, Sexuality, and Antiretroviral Therapy: Using Social Science to Enhance Outcomes and Inform Secondary Prevention Strategies." *AIDS* 21 (S5): S21–S29.

Hirsch, Jennifer, Jennifer Higgins, Margaret Bentley, and Constance Nathanson. 2002. "The Social Constructions of Sexuality: Marital Infidelity and Sexually Transmitted Disease—HIV Risk in a Mexican Migrant Community." *American Journal of Public Health* 92 (8): 1227–37.

Hirsch, Jennifer, Sergio Meneses, Brenda Thompson, Mirka Negroni, Blanca Pelcastre, and Carlos del Rio. 2007. "The Inevitability of Infidelity: Sexual Reputation, Social Geographies, and Marital HIV Risk in Rural Mexico." *American Journal of Public Health* 97 (6): 986–96.

Hirsch, Jennifer, Holly Wardlow, Daniel Jordan Smith, Harriet Phinney, Shanti Parikh, and Constance Nathanson. 2009. *The Secret: Love, Marriage, and HIV.* Nashville: Vanderbilt University Press.

Homsy, Jaco, Rebecca Bunnell, David Moore, Rachel King, Samuel Malamba, Rose Nakityo, David Glidden, Jordan Tappero, and Jonathan Mermin. 2009. "Reproductive Intentions and Outcomes among Women on Antiretroviral Therapy in Rural Uganda: A Prospective Cohort Study." *PLoS One* 4 (1): e4149: 1–10.

Hosegood, Victoria, Nuala McGrath, Kobus Herbst, and Ian Timæus. 2004. "The Impact of Adult Mortality on Household Dissolution and Migration in Rural South Africa." *AIDS* 18: 1585–90.

Horton, Robin. 1967. "African Traditional Thought and Western Science." *Africa* 37 (2): 155–87.

————. 1993. *Patterns of Thought in Africa and the West: Essays on Magic, Religion and Science*. Cambridge: Cambridge University Press.

Hunter, Mark. 2002. "The Materiality of Everyday Sex: Thinking beyond 'Prostitution.'" *African Studies* 61 (1): 99–120.

————. 2005. "Cultural Politics and Masculinities: Multiple-Partners in Historical Perspective in KwaZulu-Natal." *Culture, Health & Sexuality* 7 (4): 389–403.

————. 2010. *Love in the Time of AIDS: Inequality, Gender, and Rights in South Africa*. Bloomington: Indiana University Press.

Igoe, James, and Tim Kelsall, eds. 2005. *Between a Rock and a Hard Place: African NGOs, Donors and the State*. Durham, NC: Carolina Academic Press.

Iliffe, John. 2006. *The African AIDS Epidemic: A History*. Oxford: James Currey.

Imo State Government. 1997. *Government White Paper on the Report of the Judicial Commission of Inquiry into the Disturbances of 24–25 September 1996 in Owerri*. Owerri, Nigeria: Office of the Secretary to the State Government.

Isiugo-Abanihe, Uche. 1994. "Extramarital Sexual Relations and Perceptions of HIV/AIDS in Nigeria." *Health Transition Review* 4: 111–25.

Janzen, John. 1978. *The Quest for Therapy: Medical Pluralism in Lower Zaire*. Berkeley: University of California Press.

Johnson-Hanks, Jennifer. 2006. *Uncertain Honor: Modern Motherhood in an African Crisis*. Chicago: University of Chicago Press.

Kaler, Amy, and Susan Watkins. 2001. "Disobedient Distributors: Street-Level Bureaucrats and Would-Be Patrons in Community-Based Family Planning Programs in Rural Kenya." *Studies in Family Planning* 32 (3): 254–69.

Kalichman, S. C., and L. C. Simbayi. 2003. "HIV Testing Attitudes, AIDS Stigma, and Voluntary HIV Counselling and Testing in a Black Township in Cape Town, South Africa." *Sexually Transmitted Infections* 79: 442–47.

Kamat, Sangeeta. 2004. "The Privatization of Public Interest: Theorizing NGO Discourse in the Neoliberal Era." *Review of International Political Economy* 11 (1): 155–76.

Karanja, Wambui. 1987. "'Outside Wives' and 'Inside Wives' in Nigeria: A Study of Changing Perceptions of Marriage." In *Transformations in African Marriage*, edited by David Parkin and David Nyamwaya, 247–61. Manchester: Manchester University Press.

Kasfir, Nelson. ed. 1998. *Civil Society and Democracy in Africa*. London: Frank Cass.

Kirk-Greene, Anthony. 1971. *Crisis and Conflict in Nigeria*. London: Oxford University Press.

Klaits, Fredrick. 2010. *Death in a Church of Life: Moral Passion during Botswana's Time of AIDS*. Berkeley: University of California Press.

Laher, Fatima, Catherine Todd, Mark Stibich, Rebecca Phofa, Xoliswa Behane, Lorato Mohapi, and Glenda Gray. 2009. "A Qualitative Assessment of Decisions Affecting Contraceptive Utilization and Fertility Intentions among HIV-Positive Women in Soweto, South Africa." *AIDS and Behavior* 13 (S1): 47–54.

Lambek, Michael. 2010. "Introduction." In *Ordinary Ethics: Anthropology, Language, and Action*, edited by Michael Lambek, 1–36. New: Fordham University Press.

Lambert, Michael. 2002. *Longing for Exile: Migration and the Making of a Translocal Community in Senegal, West Africa*. London: Heinemann.

Lawoyin, T. O., and Ulla M. Larsen. 2002. "Male Sexual Behavior during Wife's Pregnancy and Postpartum Abstinence Period in Oyo State, Nigeria." *Journal of Biosocial Science* 34 (1): 51–63.

Leclerc-Madlala, Suzanne. 1997. "Infect One, Infect All: Zulu Youth Response to the AIDS Epidemic in South Africa." *Medical Anthropology* 17 (4): 363–80.

———. 2003. "Transactional Sex and the Pursuit of Modernity." *Social Dynamics* 29 (2): 213–33.

Link, Bruce, and Jo Phelan. 2001. "Conceptualizing Stigma." *Annual Review of Sociology* 27: 363–85.

———. 2006. "Stigma and Its Public Health Implications." *Lancet* 367: 528–29.

Little, Kenneth, and Ann Price. 1973. "Some Trends in Modern Marriage among West Africans." In *Africa and Change*, edited by Colin Turnbull, 185–207. New York: Knopf.

Livingston, Julie. 2005. *Debility and the Moral Imagination in Botswana*. Bloomington: Indiana University Press.

Luke, Nancy. 2005. "Confronting the 'Sugar Daddy' Stereotype: Age and Economic Asymmetries and Risky Sexual Behavior in Urban Kenya." *International Family Planning Perspectives* 31 (1): 6–14.

Lurie, Mark, Paul Pronyk, Emily de Moor, Adele Heyer, Guy de Bruyn, Helen Struthers, James McIntyre, Glenda Gray, Edmore Marinda, Kerstin Klipstein-Grobusch, and Neil Martinson. 2008. "Sexual Behavior and Reproductive Health among HIV-Infected Patients in Urban and Rural South Africa." *Journal of Acquired Immune Deficiency Syndromes* 47 (4): 484–93.

Lurie, Mark, and Samantha Rosenthal. 2010. "Concurrent Partnerships as a Driver of the HIV Epidemic in Sub-Saharan Africa? The Evidence Is Limited." *AIDS and Behavior* 14 (1): 17–24.

Lurie, Mark, Brian Williams, Khangelania Zuma, David Mkaya-Mwamburi, Geoff Garnett, Michael Sweat, Joel Gittelsohn, and Salim Karim. 2003. "Who Infects Whom? HIV-1 Concordance and Discordance among Migrant and Non-migrant Couples in South Africa." *AIDS* 17 (15): 2245–52.

Maes, Kenneth. 2012. "Volunteerism or Labor Exploitation? Harnessing the Volunteer Spirit to Sustain AIDS Treatment Programs in Urban Ethiopia." *Human Organization* 71 (1): 54–64.

Makinwa-Adebusoye, Paulina. 1990. "Female Migration in Africa." In *Conference on the Role of Migration in African Development: Issues and Policies for the '90s, Vol. I: Commissioned Papers*, 198–211. Dakar: Union for African Population Studies.

Mann, Kristin. 1985. *Marrying Well: Marriage Status and Social Change among the Educated Elite in Colonial Lagos*. Cambridge: Cambridge University Press.

Marshall, Ruth. 1991. "Power in the Name of Jesus." *Review of African Political Economy* 52: 21–38.

———. 1993. " 'Power in the Name of Jesus': Social Transformation and Pentecostalism in Western Nigeria Revisited." In *Legitimacy and the State in Twentieth Century Africa*, edited by Terence Ranger and Olufemi Vaughan, 213–46. London: Macmillan.

———. 1995. " 'God Is Not a Democrat': Pentecostalism and Democratisation in Nigeria." In *The Christian Churches and the Democratisation of Africa*, edited by Paul Gifford, 239–60. New York: Brill.

———. 2009. *Political Spiritualities: The Pentecostal Revolution in Nigeria*. Chicago: University of Chicago Press.

Marshall-Fratani, Ruth. 1998. "Mediating the Global and the Local in Nigerian Pentecostalism." *Journal of Religion in Africa* 38 (3): 278–313.

Masquelier, Adeline, ed. 2005a. *Dirt, Undress, and Difference: Critical Perspectives on the Body's Surface*. Bloomington: Indiana University Press.

———. 2005b. "The Scorpion's Sting: Youth, Marriage and the Struggle for Social Maturity in Niger." *Journal of the Royal Anthropological Institute* 11 (1): 59–83.

Maxwell, David. 1998. "'Delivered from the Spirit of Poverty': Pentecostalism, Prosperity and Modernity in Zimbabwe." *Africa* 28 (3): 350–73.

Mberu, Blessing, and Michael White. 2011. "Internal Migration and Health: Premarital Sexual Initiation in Nigeria." *Social Science & Medicine* 72 (8): 1284–93.

McCall, John. 2002. "Madness, Money, and Movies: Watching a Nigerian Popular Video with the Guidance of a Native Doctor." *Africa Today* 49 (3): 79–94.

Meagher, Kate. 2006. "Social Capital, Social Liabilities, and Political Capital: Social Networks and Informal Manufacturing in Nigeria." *African Affairs* 105 (421): 553–82.

———. 2009. "The Informalization of Belonging: Igbo Informal Enterprise and National Cohesion from Below." *African Development* 34 (1): 31–46.

———. 2010. *Identity Economics: Social Networks and the Informal Economy in Nigeria*. Suffolk: James Currey.

Mercer, Claire. 2002. "NGOs, Civil Society and Democratization: A Critical Review of the Literature." *Progress in Development Studies* 2 (1): 5–22.

Merry, Sally Engle. 2006. *Human Rights and Gender Violence: Translating International Law into Local Justice*. Chicago: University of Chicago Press.

Meyer, Birgit. 1998a. "The Power of Money: Politics, Occult Forces, and Pentecostalism in Ghana." *African Studies Review* 41 (3): 15–37.

———. 1998b. "'Make a Complete Break with the Past': Memory and Post-colonial Modernity in Ghanaian Pentecostalist Discourse." *Journal of Religion in Africa* 28 (3): 316–49.

———. 1999. "Commodities and the Power of Prayer: Pentecostalists Attitudes toward Consumption in Contemporary Ghana." In *Globalization and Identity: Dialectics of Flow and Closure*, edited by Birgit Meyer and Peter Geschiere, 151–76. Oxford: Blackwell.

———. 2004. "Christianity in Africa: From African Independent to Pentecostal-Charismatic Churches" *Annual Review of Anthropology* 33: 447–74.

Meyer John. 2010. "World Society, Institutional Theories, and the Actor." *Annual Review Sociology* 36: 1–20.

Mitsunaga, T. M., A. M. Powell, N. J. Heard, and Ulla M. Larsen. 2005. "Extramarital Sex among Nigerian Men: Polygyny and Other Risk Factors." *Journal of Acquired Immune Deficiency Syndrome* 39 (4): 478–88.

Moore, Ami, and Joseph Oppong. 2007. "Sexual Risk Behavior among People Living with HIV/AIDS in Togo." *Social Science & Medicine* 64 (5): 1057–66.

Morrell, Robert, Elaine Unterhalter, Relebohile Moletsane, and Debbie Epstein. 2001. "Missing the Message: HIV/AIDS Interventions and Learners in South Africa." *Canadian Women's Studies* 21 (2): 90–95.

Mosse, David, ed. 2011. *Adventures in Aidland: The Anthropology of Professionals in International Development*. New York: Berghahn.

Mosse, David, and David Lewis, eds. 2005. *The Aid Effect: Giving and Governing in International Development*. London: Pluto Press.

Moyo, Dambisa. 2009. *Dead Aid: Why Aid Is Not Working and How There Is a Better Way for Africa*. New York: Farrar, Straus, and Giroux.

Mudimbe, V. Y. 1994. *The Idea of Africa*. Bloomington: Indiana University Press.

Myer, Landon, Chelsea Morroni, and Kevin Rebe. 2007. "Prevalence and Determinants of Fertility Intentions of HIV-Infected Women and Men Receiving Antiretroviral Therapy in South Africa." *AIDS Patient Care and STDs* 21 (4): 278–85.

National Agency for the Control of AIDS. 2010. *United Nations General Assembly Special Session (UNGASS) Country Progress Report: Nigeria*. Abuja, Nigeria: National Agency for the Control of AIDS.

National Intelligence Council. 2002. *The Next Wave of AIDS: Nigeria, Ethiopia, Russia, India, and China* (ICA 2002–04D). Washington, DC: National Intelligence Council.

Nichter, Mark, ed. 1992. *Anthropological Approaches to the Study of Ethnomedicine*. Amsterdam: Gordon and Breach Science Publishers.

Niehaus, Isak. 2007. "Death before Dying: Understanding AIDS Stigma in the South African Lowveld." *Journal of Southern African Studies* 33 (4): 845–60.

Nguyen, Vinh-Kim. 2010. *The Republic of Therapy: Triage and Sovereignty in West Africa's Time of AIDS*. Durham: Duke University Press.

Obadare, Ebenezer. 2005. "A Crisis of Trust: History, Politics, Religion and the Polio Controversy in Northern Nigeria." *Patterns of Prejudice* 39 (3): 265–84.

Obiechina, Emmanuel. 1973. *An African Popular Literature: A Study of Onitsha Market Pamphlets*. Cambridge: Cambridge University Press.

Ojikutu, Bisola, and Valerie Stone. 2005. "Women, Inequality, and the Burden of HIV." *New England Journal of Medicine* 352: 349–52.

Okonjo, Kamene. 1992. "Aspects of Continuity and Change in Mate-Selection among the Igbo West of the River Niger." *Journal of Comparative Family Studies* 13 (3): 339–60.

Oladele, Ososanya, and William Brieger. 1994. "Rural-Urban Mobility in Southwestern Nigeria: Implications for HIV/AIDS Transmission from Urban to Rural Communities." *Health Education Research* 9 (4): 507–18.

Orubuloye, I. O. 1997. "Sexual Networking, the Use of Condoms, and the Perception of STDs and HIV/AIDS Transmission among Migrant Sex Workers in Lagos, Nigeria." In *Sexual Cultures and Migration in the Era of AIDS: Anthropological and Demographic Perspectives*, edited by Gilbert Herdt, 216–24. Oxford: Clarendon Press.

Orubuloye, I. O., John Caldwell, and Pat Caldwell. 1991. "Sexual Networking in Ekiti District of Nigeria." *Studies in Family Planning* 22 (2): 61–73.

———. 1997. "The Cultural, Social and Attitudinal Context of Male Sexual Behavior in Urban South-West Nigeria." *Health Transition Review* 5: 1195–207.

Paden, John. 1973. *Religion and Political Culture in Kano*. Berkeley: University of California Press.

Padilla, Mark, Daniel Castellanos, Vincent Guilamo-Ramos, Armado Matiz Reyes, Leonardo Sanchez Marte, and Martha Arredondo Soriano. 2008. "Stigma, Social Inequality, and HIV Risk Disclosure among Dominican Male Sex Workers." *Social Science & Medicine* 67 (3): 380–88.

Parikh, Shanti. 2007. "The Political Economy of Marriage and HIV: The ABC Approach, 'Safe' Infidelity, and Managing Moral Risk in Uganda." *American Journal of Public Health* 97 (7): 1198–208.

Parker, Richard, and Peter Aggleton. 2003. "HIV and AIDS-related Stigma and Discrimination: A Conceptual Framework and Implications for Action." *Social Science & Medicine* 57 (1): 13–24.

Parsitau, Damaris. 2009. "Keep Holy Distance and Abstain till He Comes: Interrogating a Pentecostal Church's Engagements with HIV/AIDS and the Youth in Kenya." *Africa Today* 56 (1): 45–64.

Patton, Cindy. 1989. "The AIDS Industry: Construction of 'Victims,' 'Volunteers,' and 'Experts.' In *Taking Liberties: AIDS and Cultural Politics* edited by E. Porter and S. Watney. London: Serpents Tail.

Peel, Michael. 2011. *A Swamp Full of Dollars: Pipelines and Paramilitaries at Nigeria's Oil Frontier*. New York: I. B. Tauris.

Persson, Asha, and Wendy Richards. 2008. "Vulnerability, Gender and 'Proxy Negativity':

Women in Relationships with HIV-Positive Men in Australia." *Social Science & Medicine* 67 (5): 799–807.

Petryna, Adriana. 2002. *Life Exposed: Biological Citizens after Chernobyl*. Princeton, NJ: Princeton University Press.

———. 2009. *When Experiments Travel: Clinical Trials and the Global Search for Human Subjects*. Princeton, NJ: Princeton University Press.

Pfeiffer, James. 2002. "African Independent Churches in Mozambique: Healing the Afflictions of Inequality." *Medical Anthropology Quarterly* 16: 176–99.

———. 2004. "Condom Social Marketing, Pentecostalism, and Structural Adjustment in Mozambique: A Clash of AIDS Prevention Messages." *Medical Anthropology Quarterly* 18 (1): 77–103.

———. 2011. "Pentecostalism and AIDS Treatment in Mozambique: Creating New Approaches to HIV Prevention through Anti-retroviral Therapy." *Global Public Health* 6 (S2): S163–S173.

Phinney, Harriet. 2008. " 'Rice Is Essential but Tiresome; You Should Get Some Noodles': Doi Moi and the Political Economy of Men's Extramarital Sexual Relations and Marital HIV Risk in Hanoi, Vietnam." *American Journal of Public Health* 98 (4): 650–60.

Piot, Peter, Robert Greener, and Sarah Russell. 2007. "Squaring the Circle: AIDS, Poverty and Development." *PLoS Medicine* 4 (10): 1571–75.

Population Reference Bureau. 2006. *World Population Data Sheet*. Washington, DC: Population Reference Bureau.

Preston-Whyte, Eleanor, Christine Varga, Herman Oosthuizen, Rachel Roberts, and Frederick Blose. 2000. "Survival Sex and HIV/AIDS in an African City." In *Framing the Sexual Subject: The Politics of Gender, Sexuality, and Power*, edited by Richard Parker, Regina Maria Barbosa, and Peter Aggleton, 165–90. Berkeley: University of California Press.

Prince, Ruth, Philippe Denis, and Rijk van Dijk. 2009. "Introduction to Special Issue: Engaging Christianities: Negotiating HIV/AIDS, Health, and Social Relations in East and Southern Africa." *Africa Today* 56 (1): v–xviii.

Rankin, William, Sean Brennan, Ellen Schell, Jones Laviwa, and Sally Rankin. 2005. "The Stigma of Being HIV-Positive in Africa." *PLoS Medicine* 2 (8): e247.

Renne, Elisha. 2010. *The Politics of Polio in Northern Nigeria*. Bloomington: Indiana University Press.

Rhine, Kathryn. 2009. "Support Groups, Marriage, and the Management of Ambiguity among HIV-Positive Women in Northern Nigeria." *Anthropological Quarterly* 82 (2): 369–400.

Robbins, Joel. 2004. "The Globalization of Pentecostal Christianity." *Annual Review of Anthropology* 33: 117–43.

Rödlach, Alexander. 2006. *Witches, Westerners, and HIV: AIDS and Cultures of Blame in Africa*. Walnut Creek, CA: Left Coast Press.

Scheper-Hughes, Nancy. 1992. *Death without Weeping: The Violence of Everyday Life in Brazil*. Berkeley: University of California Press.

Schoepf, Brooke. 1992. "Women at Risk: Case Studies from Zaire." In *The Time of AIDS: Social Analysis, Theory, and Method*, edited by Gilbert H. Herdt and Shirley Lindenbaum, 259–86. Newbury Park, CA: Sage Publications.

Schuller, Mark. 2009. "Gluing Globalization: NGOs as Intermediaries in Haiti." *PoLAR: Political and Legal Anthropology Review* 31 (1): 84–104.

Seeley, Janet, Steven Russell, Kenneth Khana, Enoch Ezati, Rachel King, and Rebecca Bunnell. 2009. "Sex after ART: Sexual Partnerships Established by HIV-Infected Persons

Taking Anti-retroviral Therapy in Eastern Uganda." *Culture, Health & Sexuality* 11 (7): 703–16.

Setel, Philip. 1996. "AIDS as a Paradox of Manhood and Development in Kilimanjaro, Tanzania." *Social Science & Medicine* 43 (8): 1169–78.

———. 1999. *A Plague of Paradoxes: AIDS, Culture, and Demography in Northern Tanzania.* Chicago: University of Chicago Press.

Silverstein, Stella. 1984. "Igbo Kinship and Modern Entrepreneurial Organization: The Transportation and Spare Parts Business." *Studies in Third World Societies* 28: 191–209.

Simone, AbdouMaliq. 2011. "The Urbanity of Movement: Dynamic Frontiers in Contemporary Africa." *Journal of Planning Education and Research* 31 (4): 379–91.

Simone, AbdouMaliq, and Abdelghani Abouhani, eds. 2005. *Urban Africa: Changing Contours of Survival in the City.* London: Zed Books.

Simpson, Anthony. 2009. *Boys to Men in the Shadow of AIDS: Masculinities and HIV Risk in Zambia.* New York: Palgrave Macmillan.

Skovdal, Morten, Catherine Campbell, Claudius Madanhire, Zivai Mupamberiye, Constance Nyamukapa, and Simon Gregson. 2011. "Masculinity as a Barrier to Men's Use of HIV Services in Zimbabwe." *Globalization and Health* 7 (13): 1–14.

Smith, Daniel Jordan. 1999. "Having People: Fertility, Family, and Modernity in Igbo-Speaking Nigeria." PhD diss., Emory University.

———. 2001a. "Ritual Killing, '419' and Fast Wealth: Inequality and the Popular Imagination in Southeastern Nigeria." *American Ethnologist* 28 (4): 803–26.

———. 2001b. "Romance, Parenthood and Gender in a Modern African Society." *Ethnology* 40 (2): 129–51.

———. 2001c. "Kinship and Corruption in Contemporary Nigeria." *Ethnos* 66 (3): 344–64.

———. 2001d. "'The Arrow of God': Pentecostalism, Inequality and the Supernatural in South-Eastern Nigeria." *Africa* 71 (4): 587–613.

———. 2003a. "Imagining HIV/AIDS: Morality and Perceptions of Personal Risk in Nigeria." *Medical Anthropology* 22 (4): 343–72.

———. 2003b. "Patronage, Per Diems and 'The Workshop Mentality': The Practice of Family Planning Programs in Southeastern Nigeria." *World Development* 31 (4): 703–15.

———. 2004a. "Youth, Sin and Sex in Nigeria: Christianity and HIV-Related Beliefs and Behaviour among Rural-Urban Migrants." *Culture, Health & Sexuality* 6 (5): 425–37.

———. 2004b. "Premarital Sex, Procreation and HIV Risk in Nigeria." *Studies in Family Planning* 35 (4): 223–35.

———. 2004c. "Burials and Belonging in Nigeria: Rural-Urban Relations and Social Inequality in a Contemporary African Ritual." *American Anthropologist* 106 (3): 569–79.

———. 2005. "Legacies of Biafra: Marriage, 'Home People' and Human Reproduction among the Igbo of Nigeria." *Africa* 75 (1): 30–45.

———. 2007a. *A Culture of Corruption: Everyday Deception and Popular Discontent in Nigeria.* Princeton, NJ: Princeton University Press.

———. 2007b. "Modern Marriage, Men's Extramarital Sex, and HIV Risk in Nigeria." *American Journal of Public Health* 97 (6): 997–1005.

———. 2008. "Intimacy, Infidelity, and Masculinity in Southeastern Nigeria." In *Intimacies: Love and Sex across Cultures*, edited by William Jankowiak, 224–44. New York: Columbia University Press.

———. 2009. "Managing Men, Marriage and Modern Love: Women's Perspectives on

Intimacy and Male Infidelity in Southeastern Nigeria." In *Love in Africa*, edited by Jennifer Cole and Lynn M. Thomas, 157–80. Chicago: University of Chicago Press.

———. 2010. "Promiscuous Girls, Good Wives, and Cheating Husbands: Gender Inequality, Transitions to Marriage, and Infidelity in Southeastern Nigeria." *Anthropological Quarterly* 83 (1): 123–52.

Smith, Daniel Jordan, and Benjamin C. Mbakwem. 2007. "Life Projects and Therapeutic Itineraries: Marriage, Fertility, and Antiretroviral Therapy in Nigeria." *AIDS* 21 (S5): S37–S41.

———. 2010. "Antiretroviral Therapy and Reproductive Life Projects: Mitigating the Stigma of AIDS in Nigeria." *Social Science & Medicine* 71 (2): 345–52.

Smock, Audrey. 1971. *Ibo Politics: The Role of Ethnic Unions in Eastern Nigeria*. Cambridge: Harvard University Press.

Sontag, Susan. 1989. *AIDS and Its Metaphors*. New York: Farrar, Straus and Giroux.

Spronk, Rachel. 2012. *Ambiguous Pleasures: Sexuality and Middle Class Self-Perceptions in Nairobi*. New York: Berghahn Books.

Steinberg, Jonny. 2008. *Sizwe's Test: A Young Man's Journey through Africa's AIDS Epidemic*. New York: Simon and Schuster.

Susser, Ida, and Zena Stein. 2000. "Culture, Sexuality and Women's Agency in the Prevention of HIV/AIDS in Southern Africa." *American Journal of Public Health* 90 (7): 1042–48.

Swidler, Ann. 2006. "Syncretism and Subversion in AIDS Governance: How Locals Cope with Global Demands." *International Affairs* 82 (2): 269–84.

———. 2009. "The Dialectics of Patronage: Logics of Accountability at the African AIDS-NGO Interface." In *Globalization, Philanthropy, and Civil Society: Projecting Institutional Logics Abroad*, edited by David Hammack and Steven Heydemann, 192–220. Bloomington: Indiana University Press.

Swidler, Ann, and Susan Watkins. 2007. "Ties of Dependence: AIDS and Transactional Sex in Rural Malwai." *Studies in Family Planning* 38 (3): 147–62.

Szeftel, Morris. 2000. "Between Governance and Underdevelopment: Accumulation and Africa's 'Catastrophic Corruption.'" *Review of African Political Economy* 27 (84): 287–306.

Takyi, Baffour. 2003. "Religion and Women's Health in Ghana: Insights into HIV/AIDS Preventive and Protective Behavior." *Social Science & Medicine* 56: 1221–34.

Thomas, Felicity. 2007. "'Our Families Are Killing Us': HIV/AIDS, Witchcraft and Social Tensions in the Caprivi Region, Namibia." *Anthropology & Medicine* 14: 279–91.

Thomas, Felicity, Mary Haour-Knipe, and Peter Aggleton, eds. 2010. *Mobility, Sexuality and AIDS*. New York: Routledge.

Thornton, Alice, Frank Romanelli, and Jana Collins. 2004. "Reproduction Decision Making for Couples Affected by HIV: A Review of the Literature." *International AIDS Society* 12 (2): 61–66.

Thornton, Robert. 2008. *Unimagined Community: Sex, Networks, and AIDS in Uganda and South Africa*. Berkeley: University of California Press.

Ticktin, Miriam. 2011. *Casualties of Care: Immigration and the Politics of Humanitarianism in France*. Berkeley: University of California Press.

Trager, Lilian. 2001. *Yoruba Hometowns: Community, Identity and Development in Nigeria*. Boulder, CO: Lynne Rienner.

Treichler, Paula. 1999. *How to Have Theory in an Epidemic: Cultural Chronicles of AIDS*. Durham: Duke University Press.

Turner, Victor. 1967. *The Forest of Symbols: Aspects of Ndembu Ritual*. Ithaca: Cornell University Press.

———. 1968. *The Drums of Affliction: A Study of Religious Processes among the Ndembu of Zambia*. Oxford: Clarendon Press.

Uchendu, Victor. 1965. *The Igbo of Southeastern Nigeria*. Fort Worth, TX: Holt, Reinhart and Winston.

Ulin, Priscilla. 1992. "African Women and AIDS: Negotiating Behavior Change." *Social Science & Medicine* 34 (1): 63–73.

Wardlow, Holly. 2006. *Wayward Women: Sexuality and Agency in a New Guinea Society*. Berkeley: University of California Press.

———. 2007. "Men's Extramarital Sexuality in Rural Papua New Guinea." *American Journal of Public Health* 97 (6): 1006–14.

Watkins, Susan. 2004. "Navigating the AIDS Epidemic in Rural Malawi," *Population and Development Review* 30 (4): 673–705.

Watkins, Susan, Ann Swidler, and Thomas Hannan. 2012. "Outsourcing Social Transformation: Development NGOs as Organizations." *Annual Review of Sociology* 38: 285–315.

Watts, Michael. 2004. "Resource Curse: Governmentality, Oil, and Power in the Niger Delta, Nigeria." *Geopolitics* 9 (1): 50–80.

———. 2007. "Petro-Insurgency or Criminal Syndicate? Conflict and Violence in the Niger Delta." *Review of African Political Economy* 144: 637–60.

White, Luise. 1990. *The Comforts of Home: Prostitution in Colonial Nairobi*. Chicago: University of Chicago Press.

White, Michael, Blessing Mberu, and Mark Collinson. 2008. "African Urbanization: Recent Trends and Implications." In *The New Global Frontier: Urbanization, Poverty and Environment in the 21st Century*, edited by George Martine, Gordan McGranahan, Mark Montgomery, and Rogelio Fernandez-Castilla, 301–16. London: Earthscan.

Whyte, Susan Reynolds. 1997. *Questioning Misfortune: The Pragmatics of Uncertainty in Eastern Uganda*. Cambridge: Cambridge University Press.

———. 2005. "Going Home? Belonging and Burial in the Era of AIDS." *Africa* 75 (2): 154–72.

Whyte, Susan Reynolds, Sjaak van der Geest, and Anita Hardon. 2002. *Social Lives of Medicines*. Cambridge: Cambridge University Press.

Wojcicki, Janet. 2002a. "Commercial Sexwork or Ukuphanda? Sex-for-Money Exchange in Soweto and Hammankraal Area, South Africa." *Culture, Medicine and Psychiatry* 26: 339–70.

———. 2002b. "'She Drank His Money': Survival Sex and the Problem of Violence in Taverns in Gauteng Province, South Africa." *Medical Anthropology Quarterly* 16 (3): 267–93.

Wolpe, Howard. 1974. *Urban Politics in Nigeria: A Study of Port Harcourt*. Berkeley: University of California Press.

World Health Organization (WHO). 2007. "2.5 Million People in India Living with HIV, according to New Estimates." Accessed July 6, 2007. http//:www.who.int/mediacentre/news/releases/2007/pr37/en/.

Yamba, C. Bawa. 1997. "Cosmologies in Turmoil: Witchfinding and AIDS in Chiawa, Zambia." *Africa* 67 (2): 200–23.

Zelizer, Viviana. 2005. *The Purchase of Intimacy*. Princeton, NJ: Princeton University Press.